WordPress® SEO Success

Search Engine Optimization for Your WordPress Website or Blog

JACOB AULL

800 East 96th Street,
Indianapolis, Indiana 46240 USA

WordPress® SEO Success: Search Engine Optimization for Your WordPress Website or Blog

ISBN-13: 978-0-7897-5288-8
ISBN-10: 0-7897-5288-3

Library of Congress Control Number: 2014937423

Printed in the United States of America

First Printing May 2014

Trademarks

All terms mentioned in this book that are known to be trademarks or service marks have been appropriately capitalized. Que Publishing cannot attest to the accuracy of this information. Use of a term in this book should not be regarded as affecting the validity of any trademark or service mark. WordPress is trademarked by The WordPress Foundation.

Warning and Disclaimer

Every effort has been made to make this book as complete and as accurate as possible, but no warranty or fitness is implied. The information provided is on an "as is" basis. The author and the publisher shall have neither liability nor responsibility to any person or entity with respect to any loss or damages arising from the information contained in this book.

Special Sales

For information about buying this title in bulk quantities, or for special sales opportunities (which may include electronic versions; custom cover designs; and content particular to your business, training goals, marketing focus, or branding interests), please contact our corporate sales department at corpsales@pearsoned.com or (800) 382-3419.

For government sales inquiries, please contact governmentsales@pearsoned.com.

For questions about sales outside the U.S., please contact international@pearsoned.com.

Editor-in-Chief
Greg Wiegand

Executive Editor
Rick Kughen

Development Editor
William Abner

Technical Editor
Rebecca Lieb

Managing Editor
Sandra Schroeder

Project Editor
Seth Kerney

Copy Editor
Barbara Hacha

Indexer
Tim Wright

Proofreader
Jess DeGabriele

Publishing Coordinator
Kristen Watterson

Book Designer
Mark Shirar

Compositor
Bumpy Design

CONTENTS AT A GLANCE

TABLE OF CONTENTS

4   WordPress On-Page Architecture and Basic SEO Execution   81

11   Bringing It All Together—Testing, SEO, PPC, Social and Mobile, and Analytics   265

About the Author

Jacob Aull has been in the Internet marketing business since such a label existed. Drawing from his BFA in graphic design from the Savannah College of Art and Design in 1994, Jake began doing web design and branding in the late 1990s as a partner in his own creative agency. While transitioning deeper into online marketing strategies, research, and search engine optimization, Jake achieved an M.S. in Marketing from Georgia State University's Robinson College of Business in 2009. There he customized his degree program and executed an independent capstone thesis project on social media marketing. In late 2010, GSU RCB asked him to write and teach its first course on Social Media Marketing, which he continues today, bringing in real-world companies and projects for students.

He was an editor for Pearson-Prentice Hall's first *Social Media Marketing* textbook, and was the author for its accompanying instructor's manual. He has been published with articles and interviews in sources such as the *Atlanta Business Chronicle, OZ Magazine,* renown bloggers, GSU's *The Biz Magazine*, and Atlanta Business Radio X.

He was a cofounder and chair for the Atlanta Interactive Marketing Association Social Media SIG, speaking and bringing in prominent experts for Atlanta business community seminars. He has spoken in many associations and venues on social media marketing and search engine optimization. He is president of SCAD Alumni in Atlanta and is principal of Zen Fires Digital Marketing, providing SEO and digital marketing services to a variety of eCommerce and other clients.

Dedication

This book is dedicated to my marvelous, supportive wife and child!

Acknowledgments

This book is made possible by all the folks in my life who have said "why not?" along the way. My thanks to author Jim Kelly who helped me make sense out of this process. This book would be nothing without the Spirit, the inspiration. Great thanks to all my clients and anyone in the last five years who thought I had something worth offering! Sincere thanks to all my GSU students who keep me on my toes on the subject—I keep on keepin' on to give you something worthwhile every week! My thanks to the great WordPress meetups and WordCamp Atlanta! And my gratitude goes to Que Publishing, who looked at my proposal and said "why not?"

Gratitude to the best little coffee shop where I wrote this book, Rev. My great thanks and appreciation go to my parents and sisters and to all my teachers and the mentors who have led and inspired me along the way of life; in most cases, hopefully you know who you are. If not, let me buy you a book.

Another check off the bucket list!

We Want to Hear from You!

As the reader of this book, *you* are our most important critic and commentator. We value your opinion and want to know what we're doing right, what we could do better, what areas you'd like to see us publish in, and any other words of wisdom you're willing to pass our way.

We welcome your comments. You can email or write to let us know what you did or didn't like about this book—as well as what we can do to make our books better.

Please note that we cannot help you with technical problems related to the topic of this book.

When you write, please be sure to include this book's title and author as well as your name and email address. We will carefully review your comments and share them with the author and editors who worked on the book.

Email: feedback@quepublishing.com

Mail: Que Publishing
         ATTN: Reader Feedback
         800 East 96th Street
         Indianapolis, IN 46240 USA

Reader Services

Visit our website and register this book at quepublishing.com/register for convenient access to any updates, downloads, or errata that might be available for this book.

Introduction

This book is for:

- Beginners (WordPress.com, new bloggers, copywriters in WordPress)
- WordPress and SEO familiars (web designers/developers, SEO copywriters, SEMs)
- Advanced SEO (SEOs new to WordPress, WordPress SEOs wanting to learn more)

Why a Book?

Okay, I have a confession. I read books on digital marketing. I like them. Prior to writing this book, I wrote the *Instructor's Manual* for Tuten and Solomon's *Social Media Marketing* textbook. I raise the point not to gloat but to address a common question: When people know my field and my outlook on books, they ask, "Why a book? The field changes too fast!" A good point, but the major thing I find missing in the digital marketing industry is strategic outlook. There are a lot of questions and focus on technology changes and tactics, but very little strategy. This is what you can glean from books that is much harder to obtain from random blog posts. Books are holistic and strategic. They give the reader an overall approach instead of the fragmented thoughts of the business web today. So this has been my driving goal: to educate others on strategic outlook and planning for WordPress and search engine optimization success. That or try to come up with a decent joke to put in a big book on technology. One of the two.

SEO and the World Today

The amazing thing about the practice of search engine optimization (and search engine marketing, or SEM) is that it crosses so many boundaries. I come from a web design background (started in the late 1990s), so I always had familiarity with SEO and input the basics when building a website, even in the Web 1.0 days. However, I got heavy into SEO when studying social media and digital marketing in my M.S. program at Georgia State University. So I thought of these as marketing disciplines rather than something else. Going into bookstores, however, I would find SEM/PPC and social media in the marketing section (presumably because it is "advertising") but not SEO. SEO books would not be in the programming section, but in the graphic and web design section (beside books on Photoshop, Fireworks, and prominent web design firms and trends). This fascinates me because I thought of SEO as more the copywriter's role, or the social media marketer's role, or even the developer/programmer's role than the designer's. But, it did fit my own progression, so perhaps there was some alignment there.

Regardless, the fascinating thing about SEO is that I believe it applies to all aforementioned parties. How can a copywriter write good, organic web copy without knowing any SEO principles? How can a marketer plan online marketing strategies and campaigns without understanding the principles, role, and value of SEO? And how can a developer build a site without knowing how to execute SEO essentials in the code and server documents? Arguably, all these are the roles of a good SEO practitioner. But it is essential that the other parties grasp the value and process involved for best success. And with that, let's throw another role onto the table—the web project manager. How else can we know when to incorporate and ask questions of the SEO in the total web creation process?

Organic content strategy (and hence social media) plays heavily with SEO. It is the honey that attracts searchers, binds media, and fills the architecture. Because content crosses so many media, it makes sense. So think of it that way. Read this book, learn the value of SEO and how to execute it, and meet the web user goals you want met. Best success to you and your WordPress blog and/or website—the World Wide Web awaits!

1

What Is SEO and Do I Really Need It?

Chapter objectives and questions:

- Understand the role and value of search engine optimization (SEO) and content strategy.
- Understand search engine history, the "long tail," and modern application.
- Understand what WordPress is and how it begins to factor into SEO.
- Provide an overview of SEO in today's digital world.

A Day in Your Life...

So you wake up one morning, wonder what to wear, and decide to check the weather. You have a client meeting 40 miles away, so you check the weather app on your smartphone, input the location, and see what the temperature will be.

You aren't sure how casual or formal the office and personnel are, so you Google them to see their website. A photo comes up in the Images results on the Google SERP (or search engine results page; the listings from your search), and you click through to their WordPress website with more office photos and see that it looks formal. But what about your direct contact? How formal is she? You look her up in LinkedIn and finally determine that your brown sport coat is definitely required.

Okay, now what color shirt would look the best? You search Google Images for "brown sport coat outfits" and see some possibilities you like for combining blue shirts with brown coats. Then you click through to a WordPress eCommerce site with a blog on fashion and search for related opinion posts and comments.

Next, you pull up your map app on your iPhone to identify the best route to take. What about coffee en route? You look in Yelp to see locations and reviews—you don't want a place that will take too long. You find one and click through to the shop's mobile website (a progressive WordPress mobile site) to ensure you'll recognize the photo from the street.

You hit the road, find and pull into the coffee shop drive-through, and place your order. It looks like a nice place—you'll have to come back. You search for them in Foursquare, "check in," and save their profile in your "To-Do List." You click through, "Like" it, and hashtag post about it in Facebook so that others might search and find it there.

As you drive longer, you ask Siri (the voice-driven info service on the iPhone) to locate the office on your map. You arrive early (thanks to the route you searched), park, and sit in the car, pull out your tablet, and decide to take care of a couple things before your meeting.

So the world of search is always with us. When we're online, we're searching.

A (Brief) History of SEO

In the early years of search engines—as with their predecessors, computer programming commands—the search engines couldn't understand or accurately cater to the syntaxes of common phraseology, statements, and questions. To achieve the search engine results we wanted, we had to learn to think, and talk, like the search engines—with keywords and query strings. Ironically, as time progressed, several things happened:

- We spent more and more time online (and more time in search engines).
- We learned how to think more like search engines (and also to filter out ad results and fruitless directory/landing page results).
- We went from using myriad search engines with scattered results to identifying a favorite search engine (and speaking its language; for example, AskJeeves, which today is Ask.com).
- Simultaneously, the search engine(s) grew wise to human phraseology and contextual keyword search. Suddenly, a word was not merely a literal word from a dictionary, but search results were affected by the surrounding words.

- Google hit the scene and became king.
- MSN attempted to compete with Google using a new search engine also planted on Yahoo!—Bing.
- The search engines grew with semantic interpretation of keywords, integrating search history, social media content data, and web user interest to affect search results.
- And Google was king.

Google is still king. It keeps releasing notable updates, and YouTube (also part of Google) is considered the world's second largest search engine. Google's other search properties include Google Blog Search, Google Images, Google Books, and so on.

Bing, although small in use compared to Google, keeps trying. (At the time of writing this book, Google is at 67% and Bing is at 29% of web search engine usage; see http://searchenginewatch.com/article/2289560/Googles-Search-Market-Share-Shoots-Back-to-67.) But Yahoo! (which still represents 11% of web search engine usage while utilizing Bing as its current search engine) has many legacy search content sites and directories that haven't completely died yet. Yahoo! Finance, Yahoo! Sports, and Yahoo! Local are just a few. For obvious reasons, Bing is the default search engine and common home page for Microsoft hardware and Internet Explorer; consequently, it acquires use that way. It will be interesting to see what Yahoo! does going forward with its efforts in publicity. Many big-name search engines that were popular prior to Google have withered to almost nothing. RIP AltaVista, Lycos, and Netscape.

What's the Long Tail—and Just How Long Is It?

We can't talk about SEO and its history without chatting about the "long tail." So bear with me while I explain this critical attribute to search marketing strategy.

In the 1890s, a little-known company called Sears and Roebuck started mailing catalogs—first of watches and jewelry, then of general merchandise. It revolutionized business. The company was able to offer a broad variety of items to people all over the country. What someone in Maine didn't want out of the catalog, someone in San Francisco might buy. And because their products didn't involve multiple shipments, multiple warehouses, and price markups along the way, the Sears catalog could sell products—whether general or niche—at cheaper prices than other stores across America.

From this, an ongoing industry of catalog direct-mail marketing was born. Direct-mail marketing approaches, target segments, and statistical analyses birthed email marketing strategies, list buying, and frequency measurement. Catalogs had been able to reach niche buyers with niche products because the only costs were those of including the specific products in the overall catalog. Email had the capability to reach audiences through an additional channel and was a low-cost alternative to direct mail. The statistical segmentation of direct mail, and then email, could efficiently market to audience micro segments.

Because I'm sure the majority of my readers love knowing about the history of statistical calculation, here's more on that: Email marketing inherited direct-marketing segment testing approaches, where certain materials would be sent to one segment "A," with an alteration in materials sent to other segment "B" (and additional, multiple segments if desired). In email marketing, recipients could be directed to a web landing page (which could also be slightly differentiated per segment). This "A/B" or "multivariate" testing continues today in search marketing. Whether in PPC advertising, or even in SEO, such testing strategies can be very revealing.

I just want to know why no one buys those bright red long johns anymore. Those always look so sweet in old westerns.

In 2004, Christopher Anderson, Editor-in-Chief for *WIRED Magazine*, wrote an article there about his "long-tail theory" for business in the digital age (www. wired.com/wired/archive/12.10/tail.html). He then wrote a book about the same and revolutionized digital marketing and SEO. The premise shows the traditional restrictions of costs, assets, locations, and markets for brick-and-mortar businesses that always hindered them from going after the extreme niche customer. Anderson went on to show how not only were most of those barriers removed for eCommerce retailers, but the digital realm (search engines and social media) allowed for low-cost marketing, connecting niche product content with consumers all over the world. Not only could modern businesses connect to previously untapped niche customers anywhere, but by doing so they extended their product life cycle— they could achieve new sales for products beyond their mass markets. This is the "infinite niche"—the idea that there is always one more customer out there worth tapping.

The idea, the moniker—everything about "long-tail" jelled with search engine optimization. Extreme niche keywords could be applied to search marketing. Why should search marketers fight for broad, competitive terms such as "shoes" when they could target their positioning, and see more successful results, from keyword searches such as "black leather wedge heel shoes for women." It also follows that someone searching for the latter, and finding related products on a website, is much closer to purchase than someone merely searching for "shoes."

So why not micro target accordingly?

Traditional Business Versus The Digital Long Tail

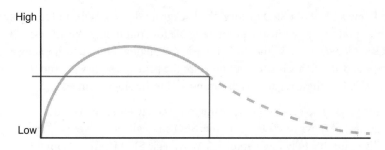

▌= Traditional brand or product revenue cycle moving to
▌"the long tail" continuing niche awareness and profitability online (dotted).

▌= The high expenses levels of traditional or brick-and mortar business
▌and consequent marketing limitations.

Figure 1.1   The long tail of twenty-first century business.

Today we face a brick-and-mortar business world continuing to collapse when faced with competition and reduced costs of eCommerce, greater variety of products (long tail), and the shifting sands of the economy (see Figure 1.1). U.S. eCommerce spending has gone from $122 billion in 2007 to $186 billion a year (at the time of this writing; see http://marketingland.com/first-time-retail-e-commerce-spending-surpasses-50-billion-second-quarter-in-a-row-43071). We have arrived at a thought-provoking time in retail called "showrooming," which means that traditional brick-and-mortar stores are used by consumers to see, touch, and feel a specific product on the shelves. Only then do they go online to make the purchase for a cheaper price. All these issues should be considered in SEO strategy, particularly for consumer goods.

The market forces in this mix include the following:

- Weakened traditional economy
- Growth in Internet use (for work and leisure)
- Fewer brick-and-mortar stores available
- Increased retail competitiveness
- More and more comfort in consumer online purchasing, security, and credit card transactions
- More and more comfort between consumers and search engines
- Consumer behavior driven more by premeditated purchases thanks to personal spending concerns, competitive pricing, ease of online research, and social ratings and recommendations from friends and other consumers.

Fifteen "WordPress SEO Success" Principles

So we know a bit about SEO history, the background of the web, and long johns. Let's put it into focus with something tangible for conducting WordPress SEO, the real deal. People complain that SEO is always changing. From a technology and tactical standpoint, this is true. But here are the principles I have found to be timeless in SEO. Use these regardless of timing and technology changes:

1. Identifying objectives and focusing on strategy more than tactics is critical! Always be clear what your SEO strategic objectives are (we'll dive into this fully in Chapter 3, "A Strategic SEO Upfront Content Approach"), such as

    *   Corporate brand awareness

    *   Service expert content leadership

    *   Sales/lead-generation

    *   Testing/research

    *   Social/reputation management

2. The rising tide floats all boats—That applies to your web architecture, digital footprint, SEO plans, social media use, and blogging. The more you do, the more content you have. The more you optimize, the more the whole network and its rankings benefit.

3. SEO is complex enough—Don't make it more so, such as with

    *   The latest whiz-bang, untested technology.

    *   Multiple keywords targeted (right now, search engines prefer one unique, primary keyword for each page of content).

    *   Premium tools with big promises (yet with data little better than the free Google Analytics). There are definitely some good tools out there that can offer analytics, such as social posting and click-through analytics and relationships to your website. If you want this data, more than Google Analytics, by all means buy it. But most people don't maximize the use of their Google Analytics accounts.

    *   Don't buy bunches of URLs or build crazy cross-linking scenarios for yourself; all those redirects can actually hurt you. And you don't want to divide your rich content and link juice. Keep it simple. (Read more on link juice and network architecture in Chapter 4, "WordPress On-Page Architecture and Basic SEO Execution.")

    *   Keep it free; like social media, the best content is free.

- Got automation? When in doubt, don't automate. It's natural to think automation is better than nothing (automated content/ articles/spinning, automated social media pushes, and so on). But often search engines penalize automation. And don't set default/ repeat content for SEO elements such as meta descriptions—search engines don't like it.

- Don't do mass submissions—the promise of every sketchy (black- and gray-hat) firm—for example, "We'll submit your bookmarks and posts to over a thousand channels." Most of the time, this is spam, and the channels to which they are submitted are irrelevant or worse—black hat. (More is described on the unfortunate prac- tices of tricky black-hat SEOs later in this chapter.)

4. Search engines value "the little guy." The real, sincere SMEs (subject- matter experts), continually blogging and generating fresh, honest, original web and social content—these are the ones that search engines will reward—certainly not the SEO black- or gray-hat.

5. There are no guarantees in SEO, and "Number One" takes time.

   - The search engines see and accredit you over time.

   - You can do everything right and still it will take time to get to the top. (Remember, it's best to be the genuine, honest expert content- creator).

   - Sometimes blacklisting, IP-sharing, poor reputation, or other under- the-radar elements can keep you from good SEO results.

   - You can't meet all ideal SEO expectations.

   - SEO is about compromise. That's okay. Breathe easy.

   - In fact, we'll even give you the major sources of compromise in digi- tal marketing and SEO (Chapter 3).

6. Social media and reputation management (monitoring brand mentions in social media, reviews, and on SERP) are critical.

7. Start with niche keyword SEO and progress to broad results and success—from long-tail to head or short-tail.

8. Content is king. It's a digital marketing cliché, but it's true. Search engines love good, unique, but relevant content. The more such con- tent, the better (not exceeding page word-count maximums or page- load times), but don't duplicate content!

9. Traditional keyword metatags don't matter. However, you can make the argument that they work for rich snippets/microdata. Tools such as Yoast and All-in-One SEO offer options for this. (More on this later.)

10. Write for your readers, not for search engines if, for no other reason, you'll get better rankings from having more readers that are reading more of your content.

11. Google (and other engines) can tell you what you need to know.

    • They provide recommendations for keywords and SEO (thanks to many tools discussed throughout this book, such as AdWords Keyword Planner and Webmaster Tools, which can draw from general consumer search records as well as your own website crawl data).

    • They even complete your search terms, showing you what they expect based on the majority of searches. (Go ahead—try searching for the word "subservient chi..." and see how far you get before it lists the viral web classic "subservient chicken.")

12. SEO is independent, but must work in concert with other digital marketing efforts. SEO is not PPC. For starters, it's not paid, hence the term "earned media" (Your online social engagement efforts "earn" customer responses, shares, follows, and the like.) But they can work together, such as with copywriting or UI (for more on this see Chapter 3).

13. Canonicalization is critical—You don't want search engines perceiving duplicate web pages, which is what canonical errors are; and most of the time you don't even know this is happening.

    • This is especially true with WordPress; fortunately, there are WordPress plug-ins that will execute canonicalization commands.

    • However, you have to know what/where they are; this book shows you how.

14. WordPress evolves.

    • You have to monitor and update the theme, plug-ins, and so on.

    • Too many plug-ins means too many conflicts.

    • The advantage of WordPress is that so many items are built for it.

    • The disadvantage of WordPress is that so many items are built for it.

- Plug-ins, themes, versions—all can conflict with each other.

- When in doubt, go back to keeping SEO simple.

15. Last one: Believe it or not, you have the power to make the search engines your friends or enemies. So follow the principles and instructions here and make them your BFFs!

What Makes WordPress WordPress?

Open source software is one of the defining divisions between the old world of Web 1.0 and that of Web 2.0. Just as web programmers started building websites in the 1990s completely from scratch, in the 2000s they shared code and practices to produce standards and collaborative platforms. Programmers with a passion would collectively contribute, from across the world, to a free, common platform—completely "open" to those involved. Hence "open source."

WordPress just recently celebrated its tenth anniversary, and the WordPress.org resources celebrated this with various documentation of their developers and history (to read more on that you can visit http://wordpress.org/about/history/chapter3.pdf). For WordPress, just as with many open source solutions, multiple developers across the world had ideas and passion for building something new. To share and develop across a common body of foundational code for WordPress (called b2, just like in bingo), developers had to "fork" it. They had to take it, duplicate strands, test, and split it some more. Hence, "forking." (Yeah—I said "forking." Settle down.) Working with the common body of code and in PHP language (in contrast to other languages such as .NET or JAVA) the programmers were able to integrate templatization functionality and the ease of working with plug-ins and widgets in a MySQL database structure and content management system (CMS) user interface.

Although the WordPress PHP code is complex in background, even HTML developers can find it easily compatible to their own in case they ever need to edit code. Other common programming systems for open source, CMS-based websites include Joomla, Drupal, and Blogger. Of these, the biggest is WordPress, at over 20% usage and growing. (Of all websites, the next largest is Joomla, with 3.2% at the time of this writing; http://w3techs.com/technologies/history_overview/content_management/all.) A CMS allows for us humble lay persons to edit and add content on a website without having to learn complex programming or lots of 1s and 0s. You log in to your CMS, enter the backend editing software user interface, pull up the page you want to add/edit—and voila! Type away. I always tell clients that before we create their WordPress website, they should open a free blog account on WordPress.com and just play around to get the feel for it. You can even block it from search engines or require password access if you want. By doing this, you get comfortable and alleviate any fears of making mistakes. The backend CMS is almost the same as that of a more robust WordPress website, meaning you're ready to edit content on your new site! So what are you forking afraid of? Just do it already!

Content Strategies and Keyword Search

Think that SEO is a purely technical process? That web programming is equitable to rocket science? And that you need to memorize several technology blogs to get it? Afraid you'll have to stop sleeping just to find the time to keep up? Here's the good news: Google favors the little guy—remember, from our principles? That's right; the ongoing search engine strategy is to weed out the tricksters of the trade, the professionals who look for the technological back doors and purchased content to conduct SEO. Instead, Google is continuously looking for ways to reward the actual bloggers and writers of original, fresh, industry-relevant and expert content. Do the necessary research and work on this level, and you're already going in the right direction. (See more on content strategies in Chapter 3.)

What Drives the Search Results You Receive?

This should be a very simple question, but it's not. Part of the reason is that search engines won't list all the factors and their weights because they don't want to be taken advantage of by SEOs (again, Google favors the little guy). Regardless, SEO gurus and software firms (and me) spend a lot of time researching and writing about how you can improve your rankings with the search engines. Note that these factors do change somewhat, particularly as Google releases its updates (in the past, such as Panda and Penguin—I'll bet the next one is Paparazzi or something).

Search engines drive search results via their algorithms. Their algorithms are ongoing technological interpretations of searches, content—everything the search engine can use to make sense out of the web—and they use that to best serve relevant results to searchers. This is a simple answer. But what all is judged by these algorithms, and what are their weighting factors? These are the answers Google doesn't easily let out of the bag.

Years ago, a team of university Internet science researchers produced a study analyzing search engines as beehives. The concept still works today. As searchers, we have the chance to choose between, and take in, the information results communicated from the search engines—like information returned to the hive from the countless bees who have researched surrounding fields. The more bees who have foraged the same area means more communication within the hive about that specific area. The fields beyond where few have gone means less information communicated within the hive. Similarly, search engines value and serve content both based on how many people are interested in that specific area of content (demonstrated by keywords searched) and how many have visited the specific sites within that field. So if you're interested in a specific area of information, the search engine results you'll receive will be ranked by a specific site's available information and how many other visitor "bees" have already been there and stayed, socially shared, or responded to said info. And here we get into the quality of the content, in part gauged by those visitor activities, in part by "bounces" versus visitors' length of time on a site.

In other words, if web searchers land and stay upon a site for a while, they are displaying a quality of content, an evaluation, whereas those who land on a site and immediately "bounce" back to the search engine represent a poor quality of content on the site's behalf and a poor resulting search engine ranking. These elements all factor into the probabilities of a site being communicated in listings by the search engines. And like Internet trends, more and more bees will trend by visiting one site en masse now and another one later.

 Note

Want to Learn More?

Interested in more on this study "Web search engine working as a bee hive?" See it at http://citeseerx.ist.psu.edu/viewdoc/summary?doi=10.1.1.161.4991.

As an SEO myself, I have my favorite go-to expert info sources on the web, such as SEOMoz, Google's own info resources, Danny Sullivan/Search Engine Land, and so on. You should know that browser history also affects search results. In other words, the more I visit those sources online, the more I will be served such sources in my similar Google searches (when using the same browser without dumping browser history). This much we know. What's interesting is that even with all this, when I search my same browser for various keyword strings similar to "how do search results get served to me," the results strangely include everything from "serving in the military" to "best restaurant dishes served." But nothing (at least not on the SERP page 1) pertaining to my specific queries (note that there's nothing in my recent browser history pages visited pertaining to the military nor serving restaurant dishes). I tried at least four different questions to get my requested answer. No luck. I say all this to demonstrate it as the kind of search experience encountered 10 years ago. It's just peculiar now. Google is basically saying, "Hey, I don't know exactly what you mean, so I'm giving you these results instead." This is similar to what it does when you input misspellings; it tries to correct them for you. Yes, Google is like your mother. Or your spouse.

Regardless, know that browser history does typically skew your search results. Given my profession, if I search the word "media," Google should serve me more results on "social media" than the news media, television, or the paparazzi. So as SEOs, whenever we want to test search engine crawls of keywords or sites neutrally, we should empty our total browser history (see Figure 1.2 for clearing browsing history in Google Chrome). Be sure that you are also dumping your cookies (or toss your cookies—really, it's whichever you prefer), because cookies do hamper search engine spiders and consequently alter results (same with session IDs, which are session-temporary cookies).

Figure 1.2   Clearing browser data.

In addition, when you're seeking neutral search engine results, log out of your Google, Yahoo!/MSN, email, and social media accounts. You probably don't even realize that much of the time you are already logged in to your search engine account, and it is remembering the keywords you've searched there as well as your own web and blog content. Regardless of the computer or browser, your account history is embedded.

 Tip

Search Tricks

There are tricks a searcher can use to filter the kinds of search results she wants. For example, searching keyword phrases utilizing the words "OR," "AND," or "NOT." And if a user searches phrases directly with full "quotes," the primary search results are pages comprising that specific phrase, with all words, in that order. So if you search specifically for "Four score and seven years ago," you will get results with that famous speech specifically. What you should not get are speeches by Miley Cyrus or Justin Bieber. Want more? Using a tilde (~) to precede your Google search keywords will include synonyms to that keyword's results in your SERP. It's helpful if you aren't absolutely certain of the specific word you're looking for to search.

Over the years in SEO, we talk about contextual search versus semantic or latent semantic content and indexing. In those grand old days of the startup web, a keyword was just a keyword. Search results included just that keyword. Google, in continual advancement, started analyzing our keywords based on the overall context of the total keyword phrase searched, and likewise for the copy it indexed. Google was attempting to interpret the meaning of the keywords.

Today, with semantic analysis, Google associates synonyms, as well as searchers' own orientations, to serve specific semantic content results for matches. Theoretically, it's possible for a searcher to receive results including only synonyms of his keyword phrase, without his keywords in the content at all. For me, this is what makes my own search dilemma at the start of this section so fascinating. Google should have known, given my keyword phrases and search history, that I didn't care about "serving in the military" or "serving the best restaurant dishes." Typically, it knows. But, no worries, it's just semantics.

All these factors go into the search engine's analysis of the searcher, for the targeted results served. But the search engine also examines the quality of the websites being served in the results. For example, if a web user is searching for "bees and flower pollination" there may be a website with half its content about this theme. But if the other half of content is completely unrelated, perhaps about the sport of curling in Quebec, Canada, then there is confusion and lesser quality, and consequently poorer rank for the site (on either content theme). I can't tell you how many unrelated websites I've come across where half the content is about Canadian curling. It's a bloody epidemic.

Yet another example of poor quality of content on a site would be bounce rate. If the vast majority of web searchers land on a site but "bounce" back to the SERP in under 30 seconds, this is another indication of poor web content quality (or a misrepresented content theme). Assessing factors like these, the search engines assign "trust" and "authority" scores to websites, and again, the higher they are, the better the rank and search results.

Attributes of Search Engine Results Listings

Most web users—93%, in fact—begin their web sessions with a search engine. (Wow, that's a lot!) So it's pretty clear that the search engine results page (SERP) is where the rubber meets the road. Do your optimized results appear there? How high, and how many of the following items were included to aid the optimized listing? Figure 1.3 shows an example of a SERP.

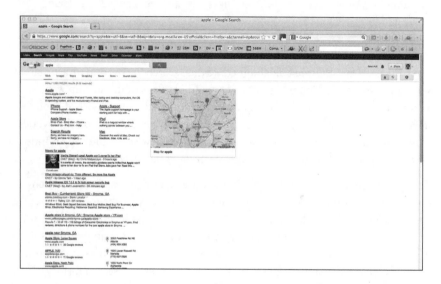

Figure 1.3   The Search Engine Results Page.

- **Cached page:** I consider cached page results to be one of the more temporal aspects of the SERP (see Figure 1.4). Five to seven years ago, Google served and emphasized results on the SERP with the option of clicking through on a listing to its "indexed page version." This would bring up an older version of the specific web page or blog post result, showing highlighted instances of your specific keywords. Today such results are far less relevant, but still accessible (via clicking the arrow below the primary listing link). For one, website content is continuously updated—especially blogs (hint: think about this for your own WordPress blog) and indexed pages are always at least a couple of days old. However, due to semantic content and results, as previously discussed, a highly relevant web page or blog post result may use synonyms rather than your specific keywords.

Figure 1.4   A Google Cache Page.

- **Editorial results:** For certain educational or informational keyword searches, Google will serve primarily editorial results, meaning news and educational content rather than corporate or product promotional content. Why? Because, for whatever reason, Google interprets the keyword phrase this way. This is part of the reason that the best top-level domains (TLDs) are .edu. It is also a reason why you might want relationships with .edus for SEO—and ideally, inbound links! See more on inbound links further in this chapter).

- **Sitelinks:** So you've searched for something such as a specific university or hospital. It comes up number one in Google, and below its link and description you see additional subpage links of the site listed below in organized columns. For example, refer to the "Apple" listing in Figure 1.3. These are sitelinks. If you can achieve them, you want them. At the time of this writing Google chooses whether or not to serve them with your listing, but the better optimized your site is, the older it is, and the more traffic your pages receive, the more likely you are to achieve sitelinks.

- **Local/reviews channels/maps:** You've seen these: you search for a restaurant, or a plumber, and immediately a list of "pins" appears beside a small preview of Google Maps (refer to the Apple Store locations shown in Figure 1.3). Not only do these pins visually jump out at you, but they are "local" to the area you are searching, or the area *from which* you are searching. And they have stars—reviews or ratings. This type of vertical-results content holds a lot of weight and is a phenomenon of the web today. Read more on vertical results in Chapter 3.

- **Ads:** PPC, SEM, CPA (pay-per-click, search engine marketing, cost-per-action)—all these are different acronyms that surround the mystique of paid ads. On the search engine results page, these typically appear on the top and/or to the right (see Figure 1.5). Here's the question: When you search in Google and see both these and traditional organic listings, which do you click? There's an entire chapter in this lovely book devoted to PPC (Chapter 10, "PPC and Advertising"). You can enjoy more on paid ads there!

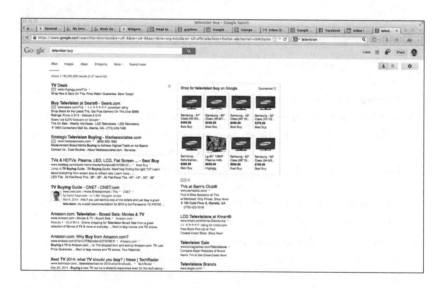

Figure 1.5 Ads appearing at the top and right side of the Google SERP.

- **Authorship:** In your Google accounts, such as your Google+ account, you can flesh out your whole profile, add your photo, bio, and so on. This is huge for WordPress because when you sync your WordPress blog with your Google accounts, and assign yourself as the author of your site blog posts, this information shows up in the Google SERP. And now this rich data will boost you in Google rankings as well (see Figure 1.6).

Note

Who Gets the Most Click Throughs?

There are many different stats which can be interpreted differently on the effectiveness of organic or SEO search results versus advertising click throughs. To answer this question for yourself, look at the industry you work in and data supporting its effectiveness in digital marketing. Resources such as PewInternet.org and niche industry associations are good places to seek such data.

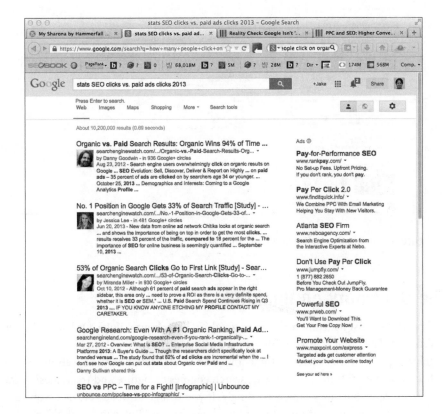

Figure 1.6   Organic Author information on the Google SERP listings.

- **Rich snippets:** Rich snippets are a broad term signifying organic search results with more data, reviews, or content options than Google's typical description for the web page in the SERP. (See Figure 1.3 for ratings in rich snippets. We'll get more into this in Chapter 3, but you can also visit www.schema.org.)

- **Images and video results:** The usual media search channels include YouTube, Google Images, and Flickr. But even in the standard SERP, images or videos can appear among the regular text listings, thanks to good SEO practice. Google can extract these images from your website (WordPress or otherwise) and video from YouTube. Google is not alone with all of this. Bing is a master imitator. Bing also shows images and other rich snippets in its SERP (see Figure 1.7).

Figure 1.7   The Bing SERP and Rich Snippets.

The Backstory on Backlinks

One of the most instrumental aids to good SEO is inbound links. Or backlinks. Or referrals. The point is, if you can get people linking to your website, it's a beautiful thing. When web users see these links and click through to your website, it becomes referral traffic. Either way, search engines recognize and track these links and increase your site's rank accordingly. If you're a great writer/blogger, you can entice others to share or repost your blog links. This is "link bait," and it's the ideal of SEO content and links. But you can plant inbound links to your website by leaving comments in others' blogs, forums, and social groups. Just don't blatantly self-promote yourself and your site. Social media is more about conversation and sharing helpful content than advertising copy. As in real life, how you present yourself in social media makes a big impact.

It is, however, quite acceptable to mention your latest blog post on your own social channels. And you should always list your website in web directories and digital location-based channels. These are all examples of inbound links. Use them to your advantage.

It may be tempting to share links (two-way) with other organizations. Some SEOs say this is better than nothing, but realize that Google will know and won't give you much credit for reciprocal links. Rather than two-way links, you want one-way inbound links. An option is to try to get your associations and advertising channels to give you one-way organic inbound links to your site. I always recommend clients get their suppliers, manufacturers, vendors, and so on to place one-way links to their websites.

In fact, this topic drives some SEOs to set up a complex, gray-hat network of linking between sites, to appear to achieve valuable one-way links between their disparate clients. This may look good on paper, but realize that Google spiders, follows, and indexes all these links. These kinds of patterns and SEO "tricks" are what Google is devoted to penalizing as its algorithms grow sophisticated over time.

SEO Ethics and the Hats We Wear

Remember the old Westerns where the good guy dressed in white, the bad guy in black, and Clint Eastwood wore whatever he wanted? Actually, this has nothing to do with Clint Eastwood, but today, white-hat SEOs are purely organic, playing everything by the book. Gray-hat SEOs might try to bend the rules a little here or there. But black-hat SEO comprises the tricks some SEOs use to try to fool the search engines. Black hat often achieves immediate boosts in results, but then gets penalized by search engines. Or sometimes you'll see significant hills and valleys in analytics—periods of success followed by periods of great drop. Google is continuously rewarding individual content contributors and penalizing SEO tricksters. Either way, do organic content honestly, by the book, writing web content about topics on which you're an expert. Now if you just like black top hats, that's okay— like in old, grand Hollywood musicals, Ginger Rogers and Fred Astaire or something. Dang, that boy looked good in a black top hat.

I'll give you an example. Black-hat SEO would be spammed content: comments and blog posts spammed across unrelated channels. If you've ever blogged, you've seen these spam comments or blog posts; they make no sense, and they are full of misspellings, poor grammar, and so on (see Figure 1.8). Or it could possibly be directly copying and optimizing competitors' content and brand names without permission.

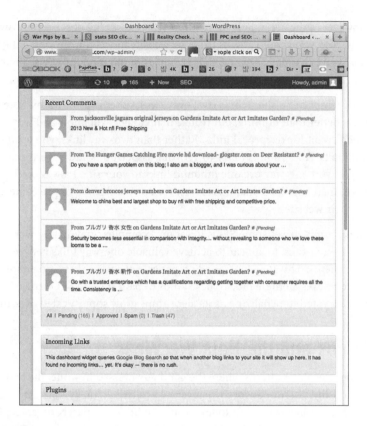

Figure 1.8   Flagged Spam Comments in the WordPress Dashboard.

Here's an example of gray-hat SEO. Many SEO vendors will sign clients and, instead of optimizing the client's website, they'll create a web landing page or a new microsite or directory listings for the client on their own server and domain name. They charge the client monthly for these services. They mention this to the client upfront, and will achieve some SEO results for the client (hence it's not pure black hat). But the client still does not have an optimized website, and if they ever want to stop paying the vendor because they are not achieving new sales or they want to try different marketing tactics, the client is left with zero SEO. So these SEO vendors own their clients down to their red long johns. The clients lose any value they had achieved. Had they just optimized their website correctly, upfront, they could have gotten better SEO results anyway, because Google prefers larger, content-rich websites and prefers them as the primary domain for the owner. The search engines have certainly moved more value in this direction over the years, and I believe the industry will continue to advance in this direction, making that third-party microsite practice more black hat.

2

The Search Engines, WordPress, and SEO Tools

Chapter objectives and questions:

- Get a deeper understanding of the search engines themselves and affiliated technologies.
- Learn about the junction of the world of WordPress with the legacy of SEO.
- Does WordPress make SEO easier? How and why is WordPress SEO different?
- An introduction to the power and technologies of WordPress and its SEO affiliations: WordPress and the technologies of search.
- You may (or may not) have seen these tools already in WordPress. What are they really? How do they help?

What's the Word on WordPress?

WordPress is many wonderful things. If you're reading this book, chances are you already know a thing or two about the power of WordPress. WordPress is blogging and social networking, it's the foundation for forums, it's a website format, it's a foundation for RSS fed content, and so on. Whatever the format, WordPress sites are flexible for importing existing content—whether from other WordPress blogs, Blogger, Tumblr, or other media. I often tell clients to start getting familiar with

WordPress and its content-editing controls by opening a free blog on WordPress.com. It has the momentum, the user base, the technology plug-ins—everything that you need to get started. But enough about abstracts. Specifically, what is WordPress? We'll explore the following:

- **Cloud-based blogging software:** WordPress (and other blogging software) was "in the cloud" before that was a buzzword! It means that the files, login, and content all reside over the Internet and can be accessed anytime, anywhere from any computer. This applies whether you have a free blog on WordPress.com or a fully built and customized website from a WordPress.org theme.

- **An open-source technology format:** Open-source technology means it's not closed up behind firewall or proprietary code. It's open; anyone at any time can crack open the code, play with it, and come up something new to add on to the WordPress foundation. For example, new SEO plug-ins—yes, you could generate your own SEO plug-in and offer it among the others! What are you waiting for? You can do that right now!

- **A collaborative, commenting, and sharing online community (or foundation of communities):** WordPress is a format on which online communities can be built, and WordPress.org is its own such community and forum. There are also countless real-world physical meet-ups for WordPress builders and users, representing the WordPress community at large.

- **A free CMS (content management system) platform for individual website- and blog-content input and editing:** The miracle of Web 2.0 websites and blogs is the ease of allowing users to add and edit their own content via CMS without requiring a web developer or knowing code. Hello WordPress!

- **A suite of countless free (and paid), customizable website and blog templates.** You don't have to start from ground zero or reinvent the wheel! Someone may have already designed and built a website theme that you like. WordPress makes this easy by allowing designers to upload new themes, and enabling you to search across thousands to download and install.

- **A resource for countless free (and paid) website and blog add-ons, plug-ins, widgets, tools, enhancements, and the like, for everything from SEO to eCommerce to appointment booking.** Themes are one thing, plug-ins are quite another! Search for and add on the capabilities to do just about anything with your WordPress site with these components.

- **A specific technology format for distinguishing specific web- and blog-site designers and developers, as in, "I'm a WordPress website SEO."** Enough said. You wanna join the club?

- **A resource for Q&A forums on all the preceding topics.** The WordPress Codex is its expansive online library of info, resources, and forums for any/all WordPress-related questions! See http://codex.wordpress.org.

- **And all this comes with a free Ginsu knife set if you act now!** Actually, this last one is wrong—it doesn't come with any knife sets, unless someone with a particular WordPress website offers them!

Is WordPress Better (or Easier) for SEO?

With technological advancement, anything is possible. But when deep programming functionality is the goal, SEO flexibility is often a sacrifice. In other words, hard-core programmers build web technologies to meet programming goals, not SEO ones. So be wary of specific web-hosting platforms, CMS packages, and pre-existing sites. WordPress is not only unusually SEO-friendly, it often makes SEO execution easier than other platforms, including traditional HTML sites!

Traditionally, good SEO has meant "needs to get into the code" of HTML or other language websites. So many SEOs have to know a bit of code, and many developers know a bit of SEO.

There are many (non-WordPress) CMS packages and website-hosting formats that have included SEO tools and inputs to make it easier for their customers' SEO attempts. These cover everything from complex eCommerce vendors such as PrestaShop, to free build-your-own website server tools, such as on GoDaddy.com (by the way, I have had clients with websites in both and I have manually implemented and achieved solid SEO results). But these "cheat programs" are often incomplete, inefficient, and can even harm SEO.

For example, often there are offers to promote one's website to thousands of search engines, directories, and listings. This is spam, plain and simple. Or the web hosts themselves will offer to do SEO coding. I don't trust these options without knowing everything behind the scenes. And when possible, I try to get into the backend code to do my own SEO implementations. All this can end up being a lot of hassle and potentially more work than just manual implementation SEO on a traditional HTML site.

WordPress, however, has proven SEO-expert-approved plug-ins that which require only form field inputs to drive the SEO execution. And the WordPress format is clean for spiders to crawl. For example, you've doubtless visited websites with "messy" filenames and extensions, even as simple as www.example.com/index.asp (for home page). WordPress smartly keeps all URLs as www.example.com (for home page) and www.example.com/next-page/. All this intelligence saves you a lot of coding and communicating directly with the search engines.

But at the end of the day, do these plug-ins help get you the search engine results you need? Yes they do. So you can breathe easy now, and read on.

SEO Approaches for Starting Your Business

Suppose you're just getting your business started; you don't even have a name yet or primary product or service. What good is SEO this early in the game? Actually, a lot. In this sense, online search = demand. I like to tell clients that good SEO keyword research can help them identify their best location or product/service just by analyzing what people are searching for online. In other words, let other people tell you what your business should be based on what they want. For my thinking, this is invaluable to any industry, but especially to eCommerce.

Here's how to do it:

- Start by writing a list of all of your interests and skill sets; for example, baking cupcakes, dessert retail, pastry decor, food photography, and so on.
- Take the list and start running keyword research through tools such as Google Keyword Planner or a spy tool such as www.KeywordSpy.com. Just Input your keywords in the appropriate field and click Enter or Search to see your data results.

   For more specifics, see the "Google Keyword Research in 10 Steps" sidebar.

 Note

What's a Spy Tool?

Search marketing "spy tools" are so called because they allow us to spy on competitors for SEO health, primary keywords, and search advertising activity. Some of these tools are SpyFu.com, KeywordSpy.com, and iSpionage.com.

GOOGLE KEYWORD RESEARCH IN 10 STEPS

Good keyword research is critical to all aspects of SEO and can produce search volume, sites, and advertisers using the keywords and new keyword recommendations. Here's how to do it with a search marketer's best friend—Google's AdWords Keyword Planner. Instructions at the time of this writing: Be aware that Google does change its tools, locations, and processes more often than KeywordSpy.com or other spy tools. And Bing of course offers similar resources at http://www.bing.com/toolbox/keywords):

1. Go to http://adwords.google.com/keywordplanner.

2. Log in with your Gmail account or create a new account.

3. First-timers are asked to set a time zone and currency. Don't worry! AdWords is Google's advertising platform for PPC and other media, but you don't have to pay to do keyword research and get ideas (see Figure 2.1). For more on AdWords campaigns, see Chapter 10, "PPC and Advertising."

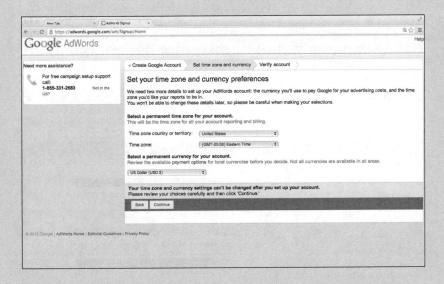

Figure 2.1   Google AdWords Keyword Planner Setup.

4. Follow the steps as it asks you to sign in and verify your new AdWords account (see Figure 2.2).

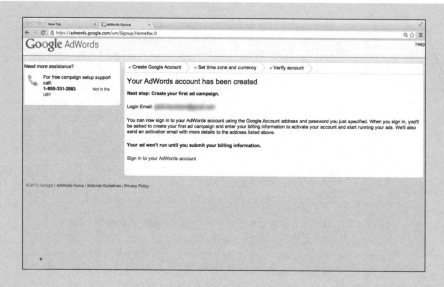

Figure 2.2   Google AdWords verification.

5. An AdWords Welcome page opens, and you want to select **Keyword Planner** from the Tools and Analysis drop-down menu (see Figure 2.3).

Figure 2.3   Google AdWords Welcome page.

6. On the Keyword Planner page, you'll see the option Search for New Keyword and Ad Group Ideas, which is the option you want for keyword research (see Figure 2.4).

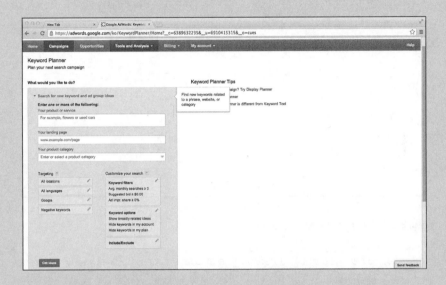

Figure 2.4   The Search for New Keyword and Ad Group Ideas option.

7. Input as many or as few of the available fields for the info you want (the products, services, or keywords you want to research at minimum).

8. After entering to get results, select the **Keyword Ideas** tab to get those keyword recommendations (see Figure 2.5).

9. Be sure to capture the data so it's most useful to you. The data download files are M.S. Excel-compatible. Screenshots are another option if you just want quick, visible reference in the current format.

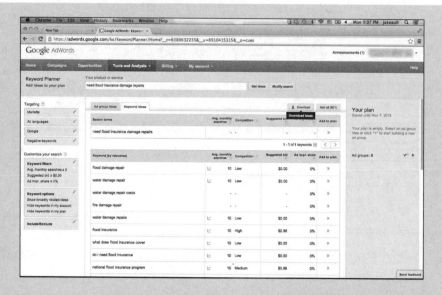

Figure 2.5   Select the Keyword Ideas tab.

10. There you go! You can do this as many times, with as many different keywords, locations, and so on as you like! Cross-reference your data, plan future PPC campaigns, discuss it at parties—get wild!

- These tools will not only identify how many people are searching for the service online, but will also identify how heavy the competition is.
- Ideally, you find the perfect match for yourself across the quadrants, as shown in Figure 2.6.

Your Skill and Experience	Your Interest
Adequate Search Volume for a New Business	Low Competition

Figure 2.6   Try to find a match across all the quadrants.

- Unfortunately, measured search volume can only go so deep. SEO tools have floors; they can provide reliable data based on only so much web traffic for a keyword, location, or website. In other words, if you want to know how many people are searching for food-sculpting and decor in Kalamazoo, MI, don't expect to have accurate data. However, Google Keyword Planner will make recommendations to you on keywords for small locations.

- But a key player we're diving into here is "Location." Large metro areas have more differentiated services (for the sake of competition and size of audience). For example, Los Angeles can afford to have shops exclusively devoted to food sculpting services. Kalamazoo may not. When no one else around you does what you do on a broad level, that is your differentiation (not bad as long as you also have enough demand).

- So in Kalamazoo, food sculptors may just be "bakers." And we can assess competition merely by searching for "bakers, Kalamazoo, MI" in our search engines and location-based directories such as Yelp, MerchantCircle, Foursquare, CitySearch, and so on.

Either way, this is a method of identifying demand (search volume) and/or competition. After you define your primary business offerings, then comes the fun part of putting it all together (including, oh yeah, your website), and all the strategic planning that we cover in the next chapter!

 Tip

Give It to Me Easy

Want to know the easiest first step to getting your website or blog indexed by search engines? Open an account on the search engine and submit the site to be indexed. Yup, it's that easy. Of course, there's a lot more to do it right, but that's the first step.

Keep in mind that although this chapter introduces the brilliance of WordPress technologies and the tools to make it work best with SEO, you don't want to begin executing any SEO without strategic planning and understanding the existing web properties you and your competitors proliferate, all of which is conveniently discussed in Chapter 3, "A Strategic SEO Upfront Content Approach."

Integrating SEO During Test-Site Build

The ideal for SEO practice in general is to start working on the site as it's being developed and written. This way, you can strategically plan, get approval, and integrate your content and SEO all while building the site. Of course you can still optimize a website after build, but you might as well post the optimized content on your site right the first time, rather than going back and changing everything in the interests of SEO after completed build and publish. This can also be a good way to see how your headlines and optimized content would appear before actually going live.

Also, when you're working with a beta (not live) site, you can test out the various plug-ins to ensure there are no conflicts. Often you don't even know there's a plug-in conflict until something bizarre and unrelated to SEO doesn't work on your site, such as font size or image placement. Many WordPress developers like to use the stripped-down generic themes to start to test for technology conflicts. Among themes with cluttered code and complex, unstable functionality, Genesis and WooThemes have a good reputation for their sturdiness and support. Regardless, be sure to check Discourage Search Engines from Indexing Your Site from the WordPress Dashboard Settings in the Reading section. However, realize that even with this checked, I have had Google index my test site.

With a live site that needs to be maintained and enhanced, it is a very delicate situation to add more plug-ins. In fact, for a live site I would recommend doing smaller SEO items manually (such as search engine submissions, XML sitemaps, search engine analytics, accounts, setups, and so on. Read more on this in Chapter 4, "WordPress On-Page Architecture and Basic SEO Execution," and Chapter 5, "Real-World Blogging").

Installing Temporary WordPress Sites

Another alternative for SEO content planning and review, if the site is already built, is to set up an extra copy of the existing website on a temporary location, such as on a hidden subfolder of the original site or even your own site. For a small, uncomplicated WordPress site, this can easily be done by following these steps:

1. Log in to the WordPress Dashboard.

2. Click the Tools menu, and then select **Export Content** (see Figure 2.7).

Figure 2.7   WordPress content export.

3. Choose All.

4. Download it somewhere—to a Dropbox account, a server, a shared cloud account, your hard drive, and the like.

5. Install your new website location or subfolder as a new WordPress site via your hosting server tools. This varies by hosting server, but hosts such as BlueHost or GoDaddy allow one-click installs to set up a new WordPress-platform site wherever you want. Don't worry about the theme or all the images right now; this is about retaining the copy you will be affecting for SEO.

6. Log in to your new WordPress site and go to the Tools menu and Import your previously downloaded WordPress content file.

7. To import, select WordPress, and you will be asked to Install the WordPress Importer (see Figure 2.8).

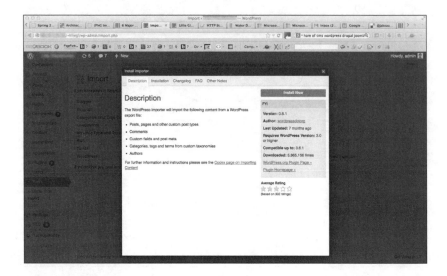

Figure 2.8   WordPress Importer.

8. Go ahead and Install and Follow the Directions as shown in Figure 2.9 to import your content.

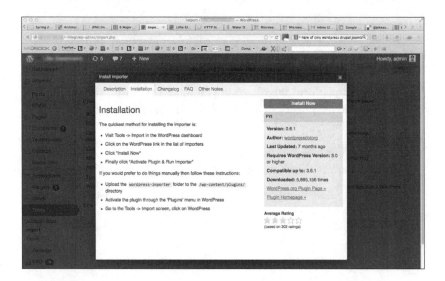

Figure 2.9   WordPress Importer Install.

9. For your SEO package, you can now go to the Plugins menu and select Add New (see Figure 2.10).

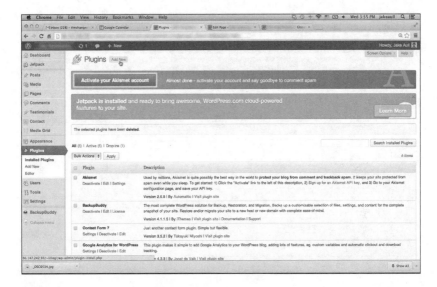

Figure 2.10   Adding New WordPress Plugins.

10.   Here you can Search for the Yoast WordPress SEO plug-in or an alternative (see Figure 2.11).

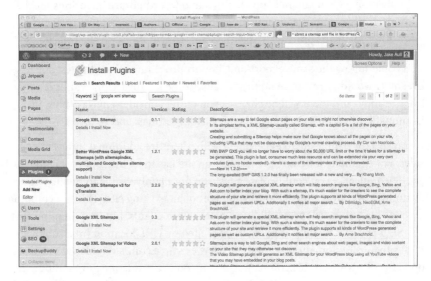

Figure 2.11   WordPress Plugin Search Results.

11.   Be sure to select the exact plug-in you want from the results—the results may show you competitors' or "light" versions of the plug-in. Then click Install and Activate the plug-in and reference any additional directions from the plug-in for use (see Figure 2.12).

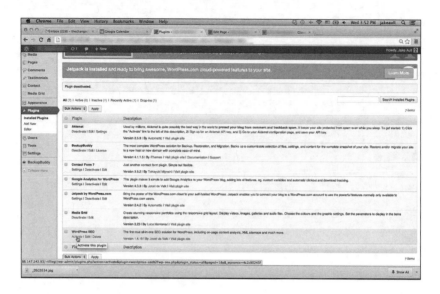

Figure 2.12 WordPress Plugin Activation.

12. Now you can play with the SEO plug-in settings and effects within your new WordPress site installation without worry of affecting the original, live site. When you're happy with your keyword phrase inclusions for the site's pages or posts, document them to get approval from your client. After they are approved, make these implementations on the live site.

You could follow the same export-and-import procedures from the test site to go live, but I wouldn't recommend this because someone invariably will have revised live site copy, and there will be changes you didn't consider anyway (plug-in incompatibilities, image settings, theme custom settings, and so on).

If you strictly want a site to experiment with, there are additional things to consider. For example, for true SEO results, the site has to be live and visible to crawlers. Theoretically, you could create a test site not plainly visible to public visitors by doing a WordPress install on a subfolder of an existing site. This is a common practice for web developers building a beta site for clients, but keep in mind that any SEO experimentation is going to be stinted by URL location (in a subfolder rather than root domain; for example, www.example.com/subfolder/about-us as opposed to www.example.com/about-us). If you're conducting SEO setups and experimentation from a test site, the change in page-level URLs after the site goes live will confuse both the SEO plug-ins as well as (more detrimentally) the search engines themselves; that is, search engines won't know if the correct URL is www.example.com/subfolder/about-us or www.example.com/about-us. There are ways to redirect the search engines after going live, such as with 301 redirects (commands to tell the search engines that a previously indexed page has moved to a new

URL, as we will discuss throughout this book), but this level of SEO confusion is not good upfront strategy unless completely necessary.

However, there are some things you can do to try to prepare your SEO prior to full website launch. Specifically, these will be heavily affected by a good SEO strategy, keyword research, and SEO page-level plans (covered in Chapter 3). For example your keyword inclusion for website pages and blog posts can be planned and written into headlines, copy, tags, and so on, all while the site is being built.

 Tip

The WordPress Codex

Be sure to take advantage of the wealth of knowledge available in the WordPress Codex—the wiki behind all things WordPress—for technology descriptions, instructions, and troubleshooting. See for yourself; get familiar with the WordPress.org tools and information, tutorials, forums, and FAQs regarding its technology and how-tos at http://codex.wordpress.org, and search for "SEO plugins" via http://wordpress.org/plugins/search.php?q=SEO. As you can see, there are a few options to choose from. As I'll repeat throughout this book, be careful—plug-ins can cause conflicts (see Figure 2.13).

Figure 2.13 WordPress Codex.

Choosing Plug-ins for Customized WordPress Websites and Blogs

On one level, WordPress is like other free online blog offerings, such as TypePad, Google's Blogger, or Tumblr. But WordPress is an open source web-building format like Drupal or Joomla. Drupal and Joomla both have communities of developers, themes, and plug-ins. But they do not have as many users or contributors as WordPress. These open source developers and contributors are who make WordPress continue to grow in popularity for both users and developers.

 Tip

Balance These Issues in Your Website and SEO Planning

- How much SEO time and activity you want to invest in the site.

- How many and which plug-ins and functionality you will already have within your site (even if it's a new site, certain SEO functionality comes with the theme, or with your add-ons, such as art gallery plug-ins).

- How much you know about, and how comfortable you are performing manual SEO and technology operations (such as setting up Google Analytics and Webmaster Tools, which are easy enough to do manually without needing to install a superfluous plug-in. This is discussed in depth in Chapters 4 and 5.)

- You will have to balance your upfront research and reviews regarding any technology issues and the results (refer to Figure 2.12).

Now that we know a little something about WordPress, how does it mesh with the world of SEO? That whole foundation of existence for WordPress—the realm of open-source programmers creating, testing, and offering technological solutions under this common umbrella—has existed not only for the foundation of WordPress itself, but it continues to grow for WordPress themes and plug-ins. Basically, there's always someone building the next plug-in and SEO integrations for WordPress. As you'll continue to see in this book, this can have chaotic results, but it can also play the role technology is meant to perform—to make complex jobs easier and successful for those who use it. So are there technology offerings for SEO compatible with WordPress? Yes, more than a thousand. And some of them are worth using. Let's dive into some options for trying out WordPress for your scenario.

1. First off, are you just playing around? Or are you cautiously proceeding with a live site and seeking one specific function? Keep your objective clearly in mind. You don't want a bad plug-in (or series of plug-in experiments) to crash a live site.

2. Search for the specific functionality you want. If there are more than a thousand SEO plug-ins, you may not want to endlessly install different plug-ins for their own sake, unless you're truly in no-consequences experimentation mode with a test site.

3. Look at the star ratings and reviews. If the plug-in is rated less than four out of five stars, it might not be worth the time. Do the reviews say anything about conflicts?

4. How new/old is the plug-in? If it's new and untested, can you afford to be the guinea pig?

5. How frequently has it been updated? Plug-ins should be updated to avoid conflicts just as WordPress itself is continuously updated.

6. Check your existing plug-ins for specific functionality before adding another plug-in to do the same job. For example, your broader SEO plug-in may have sitemap.xml or noFollow options. Check these before adding another plug-in and losing track of which plug-in is the primary driver. (If that terminology doesn't make sense yet, don't worry—by the end of the book you'll be a walking SEO dictionary, providing great conversation topics for the next party mixer you attend). You don't want a situation where one plug-in is saying one thing for the search engines, another plug-in is saying something different, and you don't know which one is the primary, or worse—you don't know which one the search engines are seeing. Also be aware that some themes automatically come with their own SEO tools. Be careful. These are not going to be as good as those I discuss next. At worst the theme's SEO tools will conflict; at best they'll cause confusion as to which fields you should use within the WordPress backend for SEO. Issues like this cause some WordPress developers to do their building from the more stripped-down themes such as Twenty-Ten or Genesis.

7. Are you seeking a plug-in for something that you could easily do without? If you can afford to experiment, then very well, but if you have a live site, can you afford a plug-in conflict? For example, don't add another plug-in just to tie your Google Webmaster Tools to your Google Analytics if you don't have to; this can be simple enough to do with your Google account. Or don't install a plug-in exclusively for SEO page titles. You have other ways to execute these.

8. When installing new plug-ins, do them one at a time, and keep a log of what was installed when. This becomes even more important when more than one person is working on the site backend at a time (for example, a developer and an SEO).

9. Proof the site for quality assurance (QA) after installing the plug-in to ensure nothing has been negatively affected. Be sure to do cross-browser troubleshooting across all major browsers and versions to ensure the site looks and operates correctly in all environments. This is another scenario that can reveal plug-in conflicts.

Now is the point in this book where we start discussing deeper, specific WordPress technologies: SEO tools! This is in no way a comprehensive list; these are just some I am familiar with. Some of these I have not used extensively, some I have. There are plenty of other plug-ins that other SEOs may have used and loved, in which case you can use your abilities to research in WordPress.org per the methods previously mentioned. Keep in mind that all these plug-ins are used in actual built and customized WordPress websites and blogs, in contrast to the free blogs available at WordPress.com. However, there are still SEO enhancements for that, which will be covered later in this book. So there's my disclaimer. Here follows an intro to some WordPress SEO plug-ins and their functions.

Essential SEO Technologies, Tools, and Plug-ins for WordPress Sites

Here are some of the more popular plug-ins for WordPress, with a description of what they do, how they compare, and which ones you need. Again, you must be careful that plug-ins do not cause conflicts with each other, with your theme, or with WordPress updates. Make certain your plug-in is continuously updated over time with WordPress versions.

- **Akismet:** The good news is that the world is on WordPress. The bad news is that so are hackers and spammers. Use antispam plug-ins such as Akismet to help you stand strong against hacks and crashes.

- **JetPack:** If you thought WordPress plug-ins and functionality were a world unto themselves and superseded anything from the free WordPress.com software, think again! JetPack pulls in helpful attributes from WordPress.com, such as WordPress analytics. Sure, Google Analytics is better and more comprehensive, but if you're addicted to the filtered, at-a-glance data from WordPress.com, these are helpful features of a plug-in. Another example is allowing WordPress.com same-user logins. JetPack offers a number of these features, requiring only login and connection to a WordPress.com account.

- **Google Sitemap Generator or Google XML sitemaps:** A sitemap. xml file is a necessary file that captures the structure and pages of your website and communicates these to the search engines when submitted. XML stands for Extreme Markup Language, a modern equivalent of old HTML website file formats. Often the sitemap file can be gathered and crawled by the search engines without your knowledge—for example, as part of other plug-ins or software accounts. When optimizing a new website, you want to be sure to submit a correct sitemap file. After you set it up and point the search engines to it, Google can regularly crawl it. There are several methods, as well as WordPress plug-ins, to allow for generating and submitting sitemap.xml files for your site, but prior to installing a new plug-in, ensure the regular SEO plug-in you use doesn't already include sitemap submission, as Yoast does, for example. (We'll get into the hands-on mechanics of these implementations in Chapters 4 and 5.)

 Caution

Playing the Name Game

There are so many WordPress plug-ins, even of the same functionality, ˙ that the names can be very similar. Be sure you know which one you are researching and using before you install it. For example, there are both a Google XML Sitemaps plug-in (plural) and a Google XML Sitemap plug-in (singular). I personally have had good luck with the former plug-in and bad luck with the singular version.

- **Google Analytics/Google Webmaster Tools:** Make your search engine happy. Google loves Google (and Bing loves Microsoft and Yahoo!). Integrate and sync its various channels—for example, Google+, YouTube, Google Analytics, and so on.

 Tip

Google+, Local, and Maps

You may think like many others that "no one's on Google+. What's the point?" Well, Google's on Google+, and it does boost search rankings accordingly. What's more, Google's location-based profiles for businesses (formerly GooglePlaces) are now part of the Google+ business pages. Meaning that when you search for "plumbers," and you get the results with pins, reviews, and the Google map, those individual listings are

Google+Local profiles. And website Contact Us pages can achieve Google benefit by displaying their Google+Local maps within the website. Note that for many of these Google tools, there are independent plug-ins for WordPress, but first check if your primary SEO plug-in (such as All-in-One SEO or Yoast) already allows for such syncing and integrations. Remember the WordPress SEO Success Principles: you don't want anymore plug-ins than you absolutely have to have! See more on Google+ in Google SERP rankings: http://moz.com/blog/google-plus-correlations.

- **RSS Feed/Twitter Feed and other widgets and plug-ins for feeding social content are not big SEO enhancements, but very advisable nonetheless.** They are great on your site or blog for the following:
  - Showing current, social dynamism by using the tool and showing fresh content.
  - Additional, relevant content your website wouldn't otherwise have. So if your site is short on content, you may consider piping in an industry trade pub or partner content.
  - Piping in your own social channel content to demonstrate your social activity and to promote your use of that channel.
  - Showing your online reviews and/or how many people are "talking about you."
- **Social Sharing Widgets:** Major plug-ins for social sharing include AddToAny, ShareThis, Sociable, and SocialShare. Incorporating these (or at least some of these) social functions is critical to your site and SEO in the modern context! (See Chapter 8, "Social Media Connectivity," on social media for details about plug-in importance and use!)
- **Backup Buddy:** Backup Buddy allows you to migrate a completed WordPress site from one server or location to another.

SEO Comprehensive Management Plug-ins for WordPress

Table 2.1 shows an analysis of major features of the big three comprehensive SEO plug-ins for built and customized WordPress websites and blogs (from WordPress. org in contrast to the free blogs from WordPress.com). This table is based on the primary features these tools promote, and my own use. There may be options to achieve some of the features that I have not easily found in use, and which the tools don't advertise. If you don't understand all these features, no worries. *The fundamentals are those in bold italic.* Now here's the big question: What happens if you don't use all these features? All-in-One claims that even if you only install it and never touch it, that the plug-in still achieves you some optimization. There are many options to tell WordPress to put default content in for SEO effects. For example, a post's headline defaults to become the URL slug and browser page title as well. That is certainly better than nothing. (Be sure to use your keywords in your headlines!) What you don't want are defaults that duplicate content from page to page, such as duplicate browser page titles. In Chapter 4, I've included a Basic SEO Checklist; you should refer to that for implementing SEO fundamentals on any site, even free WordPress.com blogs.

 Note

All Greek to You?

Don't know what half of these terms are? Don't worry! This chapter is just an overview of tools and features; We get into hands-on explanation and instruction on these in Chapters 4 and 5. You have the rest of the book (and the glossary in the back) to understand it all.

Table 2.1   SEO Plug-in Comparison (for Out-of-the-Box, Non-Premium Versions)

SEO Plug-in Features	All-in-One SEO	Yoast WordPress SEO	SEO Ultimate
Google Analytics	*Yes*	*Yes*	*No*
Webmaster Tools	*Yes*	*Yes*	*No*
Sitemap XML submissions	*Yes*	*Yes*	*No*
Keyword recommendations for pages	*Yes*	*Yes*	*No*
Good interface usability	*Yes*	*Yes*	*No*
Beginner-friendly, ease-of-use	*Yes*	*No*	*No*
Page titles and slugs	*Yes*	*Yes*	*Yes*
Meta descriptions	*Yes*	*Yes*	*Yes*
Canonicalization	*Yes*	*Yes*	*Yes*
Blog category/archives/tags indexing, singular URLs and nonduplication	*Yes*	*Yes*	*Yes*
On-page SEO recommendations	No	Yes	No
Image alt tags	Yes	Yes	No
Page NoFollow/noIndex	Yes	Yes	Yes
AutoTags	No	No	Yes

SEO Plug-in Features	All-in-One SEO	Yoast WordPress SEO	SEO Ultimate
Microdata/micro tags/rich snippets	No	Yes	Yes
Author ID	Yes	Yes	Yes
Breadcrumbs	No	Yes	No
Anchor and link analysis	Yes	Yes	Yes
Remove blog category bases	No	Yes	Yes
Snippet previews	Yes	Yes	No
Plays nicely with others	Yes	Yes	No
eCommerce integration	Yes	No	No
Duplicate content control and analysis	Yes	No	No
301 redirects	No	Yes	No
404 page analysis	No	No	Yes
.htaccess & robots.txt editor	No	Yes	No
ADDITIONAL CLAIMS	"ONLY plugin to provide SEO Integration for WP e-Commerce sites"	"WordPress SEO is the most complete WordPress SEO plugin that exists today for WordPress.org users."	"This all-in-one SEO plugin gives you control over title tags, noindex, meta tags, Open Graph, slugs, canonical, autolinks, 404 errors, rich snippets"
MORE INFO:	http://wordpress.org/plugins/all-in-one-seo-pack/	https://yoast.com/wordpress/plugins/seo/	http://wordpress.org/plugins/seo-ultimate/

The three SEO plug-ins in this table are not the only ones. They are just the most popular, with the best reviews. Platinum SEO and SEO Pressor are two less-used others. So be wary, do your research, and carefully pick your best plug-ins, making sure they don't cause conflicts. Some WordPress themes also automatically come with their own SEO tools. Be careful. They are not going to be as good or comprehensive as All-in-One SEO or Yoast WordPress SEO. At worst, the theme's SEO tools will conflict; at best, they'll cause confusion as to which fields you should use within the WordPress backend for SEO. It's these types of reasons causing WordPress developers to run to the more stripped-down themes, such as WordPress theme Twenty-Ten or Genesis themes. Stripped-down WordPress themes: good. You, however, stripping down to build WordPress sites: not so good.

3

A Strategic SEO Upfront Content Approach

Chapter objectives and questions:

- How do we start the SEO and content strategy?
- What are the best SEO content objectives, plans, and guides?
- How do I pick the best keywords?
- How do I captain this ship and manage the sails (the WordPress SEO tools)?

It is instrumental to form strategic plans to drive the web build and SEO process. Each of these steps is explored in depth in this chapter:

1. Conduct digital audits.

2. Write the digital strategy brief.

3. Conduct the keyword research.

4. Plan network architecture.

5. Sitemapping.

6. Assess content and keywords.

7. Write SEO page forms.

Step 1: Conduct Digital Audits

Your blog or website does not exist in a vacuum. This is an important driver for doing an audit of your digital footprint. Even if you didn't have a website before, if your name has existed, chances are you have a digital footprint. So often companies don't realize that their presence can already be found on so many existing directories, social sites, and blogs. Location-based business directories such as whitepages.com pull business license registrations and include the business info in their listings for consumer convenience. Social sites can also contain information about you and your company history by trading info with other databases. Years ago, Plaxo.net attempted to be a networking site with calendaring but never gained a huge following. Today it still retains valuable information. All these digital assets can contribute to SEO benefits, such as inbound links and social reputation.

 Tip

Researching Digital Footprints

Regardless of how heavy a digital footprint you think you do or do not have, it's invaluable to research the channels of your industry. Specifically,

- Traditional industry and services' competitors' websites
- Keyword and content competitors in the SERP
- Industry experts and bloggers
- Trade publications
- Third-party landing pages, web promotional pages, and microsites
- Industry online advertising and listings
- PR and article resources
- Social reputations (social profiles, additional inbound links, local directories and reviews)
- Overall SEO data and observations about the preceding items

You might think you already know these characters, but you'll be surprised, particularly by keyword and content competitors. These are sites that are already coming up top-of-the-list for the keyword search results that you want! Often these can be sites that you don't consider to be true competitors at all, such as directories or content resources such as Wikipedia or About.com. Either way, you must be aware that they are beating you at the keyword and content game.

If Wikipedia is winning, what is their content about? Is it of interest to your audience? You might want to be writing content like that on your own site, especially if Wikipedia's version of your brand name presents a nocturnal marsupial in New Guinea that sucks entire chickens down through hollow tree limbs to feast on their blood—sweet! Your guiding digital audits can help you in all respects. These digital audits can guide you to define your new site's competitive positioning. Do you want to fit or break the mold of your overall industry? Now's your chance to achieve your brand messaging differentiation.

What Should You Check These Sites For?

You'll want to refer to a checklist for your audit, so try using the list that follows. All this will give you great, valuable data for an audit report. But be careful with the time investment; if you're an SEO conducting this work for a client, be sure the budget will cover the checklist. If not, balance the most important SEO activities for the buck (or for the bang!).

What to Research on Sites

- **Canonicalization:** Canonicalization is a big word that sounds important, and it is. Since the beginning of the web, we have identified website URLs as either http://example.com or http://www.example.com/. These are subtle differences to you and me, but very, very important differences to search engines. If an SEO hasn't done her job to tell the search engines correctly, the engines see both examples as two different websites. They don't know which to serve in results, and they don't know how to rank them as one. You'll start accumulating inbound links for both URLs (read more about this in the "Inbound Links" bullet item), and eventually giant meteors hit us as the sky is falling! Don't let this happen to you. We'll get more into how to fix canonicalization errors in Chapter 4, "WordPress On-Page Architecture and Basic SEO Execution," and Chapter 5, "Real-World Blogging," but for now you should understand what they are. If your competitor has them, that's an easy win for you right there! The web analysis tools you use for your digital audits can reveal if canonicalization errors exist.

- **Social and keyword monitoring (reputation management):** Important research to do, for both your own brand and competitors', is social reputation monitoring. Where do brand names appear online? What are people saying about them? In which social and local channels do they appear, and where don't they? (See the tools for social and keyword monitoring in the "Tools to Use for Your Audit" section.)

- **Rank and authority:** The search engines and analytics tools examine the websites for SEO quality and use their algorithms to assign rank and authority scores to these sites. Basically, the higher the better. Read more on this in Chapter 7, "Analytics for WordPress."

- **Search engine traffic:** Yes, you can see what kind of web traffic your competitors have been getting! This assumes that their site is search-engine friendly and has been achieving good, regular visitors. Remember that the data from these analysis and spy tools is not as reliable as Google Analytics. But some data is better than no data!

- **Primary keywords:** What are the most relevant keywords for the sites in question? This is great info to have. But what do you do with this info after discovery? First, in most cases you do want to focus your own website SEO for short-tail keywords—you know, lone keywords such as "pie," "shoes," or "software." These are the most competitive, but you still want to integrate them into your site and have content devoted to them (chances are, you will anyway, by default). But this is also your opportunity to differentiate your "sweet spot" and chase after those keywords. The total process of online industry audits, as well as a client strategic marketing interview, can all funnel toward this knowledge. I once had a law firm client who, when they hired me, started by saying they served anyone and everyone and wanted their SEO to reflect that. By the end of the marketing interview, we identified that that wasn't their sweet spot, those weren't good clients for them, and that didn't present their best services. So we targeted the work at which they excelled and optimized for long-tail keyword phrases, such as "surety contract litigation Atlanta." They were now differentiated and branded. They could promote their expertise on their website and get discovered for those specific keywords more often than their competitors.

- **Inbound links:** Inbound links are also called backlinks. If they send you web traffic, they are referrals. But they are links, located on web properties outside of your website, which are directed back to your site. Conversely, outbound links are the links you have on your site to send traffic elsewhere. These backlink web properties are critical to assess for several reasons:

  - The more of them you have, the higher rank you achieve in the search engines.

- You want to know who's giving you "props" (and if it's only your own social sites).
- It's best if the links are all from various sites. However, they may all be from one referral domain. Either way, you want to know (and if it's the latter, set a strategy to achieve the former).
- Are you, in turn, providing reciprocal links (that is, two-way links; one-way links are best)?
- Who has the link juice, the higher authority score? Are you the gainer or the loser in the equation?

Google Analytics and Webmaster Tools provide some indications of your own inbound links, but other tools exist whose sole purpose is this reporting; they will provide this info whether the site is yours or a competitor's. MajesticSEO, Blekko, and OpenSiteExplorer—all featured sites within the SEO Book Toolbar—will conveniently report backlinks for the site in question. Not only is this info good for gauging competitive SEO, it also reveals good sources for industry, competitive content, and content quality. Remember, third-party content sources, such as industry directories or trade pubs, can be huge and beneficial to your own SEO.

You can see Google Analytics only for your own site's data. But often website owners have no idea if or where they have such accounts. I hear the story once a month—they had their website built three years ago, they've lost touch with the designer, they don't have emails or paperwork on special accounts' access, and they don't even know if the website ever had Google Analytics turned on. Fortunately, this is an easy assessment for you to make.

 Tip

Finding Google Analytics

Want to know if a site already has Google Analytics set up? A good way to start is to view the home page source code in your browser (such as Google Chrome, see Figure 3.1), pull up the website in question, and through the web developer options, view the source code or developer tools. On viewing the code, do a simple search for "Google." Does it reveal Google Analytics code or not?

Figure 3.1   Google Chrome Web Developer Tools source code.

If the code is there for your own site, you should do everything in your power to obtain access to that account. Try logging in to Analytics.Google.com with the company's existing Gmail account. Don't know the password? Ask Google for a temporary password. Still no go? Try hunting down the web designer; search in LinkedIn, Facebook, wherever. Check all old email accounts, ask the previous digital marketer. You can start from scratch with new code if you absolutely need to, but you will not have any previous data shown if you do. All this goes for Bing as well, but the truth is, not many web developers or SEOs care to go that deep for the much smaller Bing, especially because Google Analytics will already show the quantity of Bing referrals to the site. Enjoy your quest for the holy data!

 Note

Exploring Website Code

I know it's scary, but there are a number of reasons that it's worthwhile to examine the code of a website:

- You can identify the platform in some cases (for example, if it is PHP/WordPress, traditional HTML, and so on).

- You can see if it has some SEO sophistication already built in, such as Google Analytics and Webmaster Tools code.

- You can identify the types of linking structures—are there noFollows or noIndex operators there?

- Google Chrome has great tools for viewing the page source in browsers. It will highlight which areas and style sheets apply to each other and potential errors in the site. It will preview the site in one pane and the code in another, and show the code and its corresponding visual sections. It's a beautiful thing.

The Tools to Use for Your Audit

- **SEO Book Tools:** SEOBook.com is a great, free, SEO industry resource of information and technology (see Figure 3.2). You'll find a number of great tools there, offering some data that even WordPress analytics and the coveted Google Analytics don't easily provide. However, remember that all different tools and different algorithmic data need a baseline in common. The best way to operate on this with these tools is in competitive measure. To say it more specifically, SEO Book Tools and spy tools (discussed later) are great for understanding competitive strengths and weaknesses in the digital space. Using the same tool to compare an inbound link's quantity and quality across your competitors and your own website is worthy research. Using a common tool to measure web traffic or search referrals, across major competitors, gives you a common benchmark and worthy data. The further we get away from apples and apples, however, makes it more difficult to justify. I believe that some data is better than no data, so dive into these tools and have fun! Just don't forget to click all the "?"s and "i"s within the tools and algorithms to understand exactly what they're measuring for you.

- **How to do it?** First, you should already have the Firefox browser installed. If not, find Firefox via your existing web browser; download, install, and run Firefox. Then go to http://tools.seobook.com/ seo-toolbar/ and download and install the SEO Book Toolbar (see the toolbar within Firefox and some of its tools in Figure 3.2). You will instantly notice the plethora of analytics tools right there on the top of your browser. Try them out and see what they do. Some of them, such as Quantcast, OpenSiteExplorer, Blekko, and MajesticSEO, have already been discussed.

- **Spy Tools:** Spy tools allow you to "spy" on any sites on the web. Examine their primary keyword drivers, their PPC ads, web traffic, ranking, and so on. These are typically freemium tools (meaning they provide both free and advanced paid levels). Revisit the Note on these in Chapter 2, "The Search Engines, WordPress, and SEO Tools," for more info.

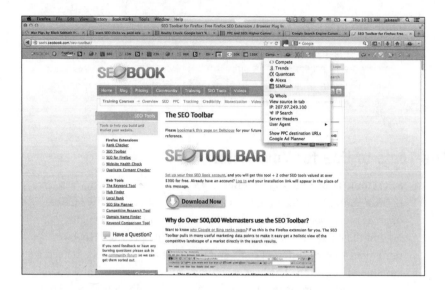

Figure 3.2   SEO Book Tools and the SEO Book Toolbar for Firefox.

- **SocialMention.com:** Input any brand name or keyword to discover where mentions occur. In the words of SocialMention, "From across the universe...." (See more on SocialMention.com results and analytics in Chapter 7 and Chapter 8, "Social Media Connectivity.") This is similar to Google Alerts. You can set up your Google Alerts to email you whenever and wherever specific brand name or keyword mentions occur.

- **HootSuite:** Technically it is a social dashboard, and I will go into more depth in Chapter 8 on integrating social functionality with WordPress. But for our purposes here, it is a social dashboard useful for monitoring your brand name and keywords for Twitter and Facebook (and others). You set up an account (it can be the free version) in HootSuite and sync with your Twitter and Facebook accounts. HootSuite then gives you the option to set up "streams," cascades, like your social walls, to view preferred content. By setting up streams to search for your various words, such as brand names, you can see all this data in one resource. So if you're mentioned in the social space, you can find it, judge the SEO value, and determine if there's an opportunity to reach out and request an inbound link to your site, if it's not already there.

What Should a Good Competitive Audit Look Like?

Here's the type of research the data might reveal:

- A site achieves 30,000 searches for the brand name per month.
- The most common brand services industry keyword searches receive 35,000 a month at most.
- The site's search engine traffic continually trends up.
- Unique visitors (first-time visitors to the website) trend down.
- The observations that you as an SEO might make here are that the brand has become a household name and when people want facial tissues they search the brand name Kleenex. Because of this occurrence, the majority of website visitors already know the name and have previously visited the site. All this is good, but there must be fringe keywords for services that can align SEO for this site.
- The digital audit should present these observations, data, and recommendations accordingly.

Step 2: Write Your Strategy Brief

A good digital audit is instrumental in driving your SEO strategy brief. But there is other input that must be taken into account as well. For my SEO client contracts I discuss all the following issues with them and then issue the final document of my notes back to them before proceeding to the next step: keyword research.

- **Objective:** Is your primary objective to achieve more sales leads from the site? Or perhaps to spread brand awareness? Be careful here, because what the SEO might presume for a primary objective can be very different from expectations from the information architect or others. (This, along with the need for compromise, is discussed in the "Compromises in Digital Planning" section.)
- **Marketing plan and pieces:** Do you have an existing marketing or digital plan to work with? What kinds of existing media and pieces has the company tried? What examples do you have to reference for branding, messaging, and the like?
- **Drivers/Problems:** Why are these your objectives? What are the market drivers in the mix? What business or industry problems occur to drive these objectives?

- **Target audience and search behavior:** You want to identify your primary audience for your website keywords and copy. One of the things discussed later is that you may have different objectives for your SEO than for the rest of your digital marketing. Likewise, you may want to target a different audience than your typical customer. Your existing customers have most likely already visited your site, know how and where to find what they want, and how to contact you.

  So it is very common for websites to target prospects and new visitors. There's more on this discussed throughout this chapter, but it's something to focus your website strategy. To aid you in this process, you can also research the demographics of a specific website's visitors with tools like Quantcast and GoogleTrends, and overall analysis of web and social users with resources like Pew Internet Research.

  Important questions to ask yourself here include these: What do you think the target's search approach is for your services? At what point of the process do you think prospects search? What is their role with social media relative to your industry?

- **Positioning and messaging:** What is your brand positioning and your brand voice? Should you take a more niche, differentiated positioning for your online representation and your online messaging? Do you need more differentiation online versus competitors?

- **Any additional selling points:** Spell out your services as benefits for the customer. What are the deliverables, sought by customers, which your company provides? Why would customers want them from you?

- **Integrated marketing communications (IMC), ad campaigns, and the like:** What other marketing materials does your SEO integrate with? Is it part of an ad campaign, or is it overall corporate branding? Will there also be SEM/PPC advertising?

- **Web strategy:** You have your primary objective; what's your web strategy? Will you focus heavily on location-based SEO? PPC advertising to support the SEO? Google Images or YouTube video?

- **Starting, preliminary, suggested keywords, or terminology:** The client or project approver usually has some good input on industry phrases, customer phrases, and potential keywords. These are instrumental to starting the keyword research phase (along with the digital audit).

- **Future, ongoing SEO, and social media:** What are you planning for implementation between this new site-build SEO and ongoing post-build SEO efforts? After the foundation of your web content and keyword integration is complete, blogging and social media are great for ongoing SEO success. A critical component to social media (and organic search content overall) is to know your resources; don't commit to time or content you won't be able to achieve. Identify and plan accordingly.

Your digital strategy brief is your guide, and it's crucial. Refer to it constantly throughout your website and SEO process. It is the leading hand that guides your next steps and your SEO page plans. Even so, don't forget to get the necessary approvals, and don't forget about the necessary compromises. Compromises? We don't need no stinking compromises! Actually, yes, we do.

Compromises in Digital Planning

Some areas of digital marketing may have to be compromised in spite of SEO; you can't meet all aspects of perfect SEO upfront. There are other contributors to digital marketing that must be consulted in the planning and generation processes. From these parties and compromises, the website objectives and digital strategy brief can be formed. The parties, personnel, and roles that may have to be consulted and accommodated prior to website SEO execution can include the following:

- **Branding:** Brand messaging may be very different from optimal SEO messaging, and often the branding goals may be very different from the SEO goals. For example, you may want your SEO to serve a new target audience in contrast to traditional brand positioning to customers and your market at large. Or you may want SEO for a product promotion goal in contrast to SEO for overall corporate brand awareness.

  Whatever your relationship with branding, I always recommend using keyword research (for both keyword/consumer demand, as well as competition) as part of the branding process. This is why I say great branding and brand positioning are uniquely tied to consumer search. What do the people want? What do they search for? And what are competitors NOT providing? Search can reveal all; that is, keyword research can show the actual products/services customers are searching for and the actual language they use to describe them. So why not be "the what" that people are searching for?

- **Target audience:** Every market's target audience is different and behaves differently in social media. For example, someone in a financial forum asking questions about investments is going to have a different approach and phraseology than one commenting on a blog about sci-fi animated films. Take the same principle and apply it to search—not only the terminology, but the casualness of approach will differentiate target audiences and search behavior. The better you know your audience, the better you'll know the content to serve them—and the strings of words they'll enter into search engines.

- **Image/design:** Search engines love relevant and unique content—the more the better. This can be in conflict if your company is striving for a simplified content, graphic-heavy web look (especially if it's Adobe Flash, which spiders really can't crawl!).

- **User interface and web usability:** Although many will argue that what is good for usability is good for the search engines, there can still be road blocks here. A good information architect's (IA) focus is to serve the web user more than the search engines.

- **Copywriting:** A good copywriter will often find issues with specific keyword phrases and an SEO's attempt to force them in copy and headlines. But like the IA, his/her best interest is in serving the web user. So a compromise is often necessary between these roles and SEO. However, a good copywriter can also be the SEO's best friend; both should work together for aspects such as the strategy and value of link-baiting and writing for semantic content indexing. (Don't worry, we'll dive into this in Chapter 6, "In-Depth Hands-On SEO Execution.")

- **A/B or multivariate testing:** Testing is yet an alternative, different goal for digital marketing. The effects for this type of optimization are quite different. Testing requires a clear, controlled environment. Often, such search marketing testing requires subtle differences between isolated, singular web landing pages, such as for campaigns. You can have one campaign directed to one landing page or microsite and another directed to the alternative. There's a lot of fun stuff to get into when we discuss such testing. So if you want to skip ahead and dive in, you'll find more in Chapter 7.

- **Sales lead-generation and copy-behind forms:** Sales departments will often prefer websites to act as lead-generation (as discussed elsewhere in this book). This is all good and fine, but lead-generation typically requires incentivized content behind a lead-generation form (customer info-capture, see Figure 3.3). Any content behind a form cannot be crawled, so it becomes an SEO barrier. Again, valid SEO compromises must take place. Who was that politician who said that the middle of the road was only for road kill? I'm not sure how successful he would have been as a digital marketer.

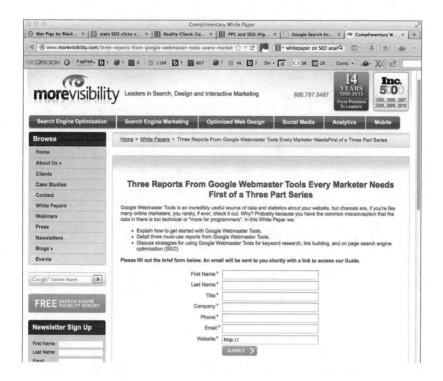

Figure 3.3   Customer incentive lead-generation form.

- **Programmers root for best, fast, cleanest web development:** Iterative compromises are required between technology developments. The best tools for the programmer are often not what are best for SEO. Deep-web IT security measures may daunt crawlers. Although IT may want more content behind a login form, for SEO it is best the other way. Hard-core programmers are also often not fans of WordPress—they prefer other tools for CMS (content management system; platform allowing for easy user content editing) within their platforms. This allows them more customization and integrations. Programmers may want to use more iFrames and .js/jQuery functionality, piping in certain content and linking out to other servers or third-party services—more items acting as robot stumbling blocks. IP address, dynamic URLs, and server hosting issues can also be contested between IT programmers and SEOs. After all IA issues are on the table and agreements or compromises have been met, it is best to document a timeline of SEO, site changes, and analytics. In other words, the two will often be working down separate paths, with the SEO optimizing and the programmer building and testing. Without good communication (as is usually the case), multiple problems ensue. Hence, a timeline (see Figure 3.4) of events must be set up, documented, and followed for easy troubleshooting when there are problems. (Trust me, there are always problems in a build.)

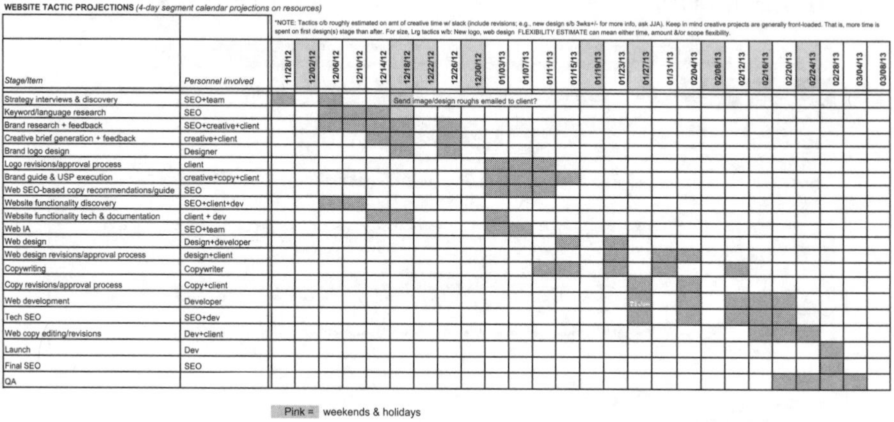

WEBSITE TACTIC PROJECTIONS *(4-day segment calendar projections on resources)*

NOTE: Tactics c/b roughly estimated on amt of creative time w/ slack (include revisions; e.g., new design w/b 3wks+/- for more info, ask JJA). Keep in mind creative projects are generally front-loaded. That is, more time is spent on first design(s) stage than after. For size, Lrg tactics w/b: New logo, web design. FLEXIBILITY ESTIMATE can mean either time, amount &/or scope flexibility.

Stage/Item	Personnel involved
Strategy interviews & discovery	SEO+team
Keyword/language research	SEO
Brand research + feedback	SEO+creative+client
Creative brief generation + feedback	creative+client
Brand logo design	Designer
Logo revisions/approval process	client
Brand guide & USP execution	creative+copy+client
Web SEO-based copy recommendations/guide	SEO
Website functionality discovery	SEO+client+dev
Website functionality tech & documentation	client + dev
Web IA	SEO+team
Web design	Design+developer
Web design revisions/approval process	design+client
Copywriting	Copywriter
Copy revisions/approval process	Copy+client
Web development	Developer
Tech SEO	SEO+dev
Web copy editing/revisions	Dev+client
Launch	Dev
Final SEO	SEO
QA	

(Date columns: 11/28/12, 12/02/12, 12/06/12, 12/10/12, 12/14/12, 12/18/12, 12/22/12, 12/26/12, 12/30/12, 01/03/13, 01/07/13, 01/11/13, 01/15/13, 01/19/13, 01/23/13, 01/27/13, 01/31/13, 02/04/13, 02/08/13, 02/12/13, 02/16/13, 02/20/13, 02/24/13, 02/28/13, 03/04/13, 03/08/13)

Annotation in Strategy row: Send image/design roughs emailed to client?

Pink = weekends & holidays

Figure 3.4 A detailed timeline is crucial when trying to avoid communication issues.

Finally, there will always be some kind of compromise between the SEO and the client for unexpected reasons. (It's okay. It's not politics, just SEO.)

THE NATURE OF SEO AND SOCIAL MEDIA FOR WEBSITE MESSAGING AND POSITIONING

First, organic search, like social media, is about pull, rather than push, marketing. The point is to pull in customers, in contrast to "pushing" TV or web ads directly on them. Organic search is based on what people are actually looking for—the honey that draws them in. This is why it works. This is also a great demonstration of the value of inbound links. You can advertise all day long, but if you have organically pollinated links across the Web (or "the net," as we used to call it), again, you're pulling consumers in by interest rather than shouting at them.

So organic content needs to consider the topics at hand and how best to serve the reader. In marketing communications, we identify utilitarian versus hedonic consumer behavior, research, and product interest. Essentially, utilitarian approaches comprise researching factual "needs" such as costs, efficiency, and power features of appliances, for example. Whereas hedonic approaches involve emotional or impulsive desires—the color of a jet ski, its speed, décor, and so on. Content strategy should identify serving one, the other, or both types of consumers and products.

Taking these concepts one step further, it follows that there would be user approaches to keyword search also based on hedonic and utilitarian desires. This includes not only the keyword phrases input, but also the channels searched. For example, location-based search channels would most likely be utilitarian; that is, Yelp, YP.com, and Google Maps, whereas channels such as StumbleUpon or Pinterest would likely receive hedonic web users and searches.

Creative types, such as web designers, who need to search metaphors can be the extreme end of hedonic searches. A web designer might search for web icons to use on a project—metaphoric imagery or icons for copy about product benefits for the user, or a nonprofit's requests for reader donations. Stock art online catalogs are growing more and more accustomed to serving such searches.

Search engines have to evolve, just as they have from their beginning when algorithms attempted to understand how people searched. Over time, we learned how to predict effectively the way search engines thought (which became a two-way street as the technology did likewise). It is fair to say that theoretically this becomes an ongoing, back and forth evolution—a cross-pollination. Perhaps more future examples become the examples of entire books and libraries online, in which content can have, for example, more emotional poetic themes versus strictly technical manuals of steps and instructions.

Step 3: Identify and Research Your Keywords

To begin with, there are some commonly understood terms in keyword search. For example, in eCommerce, the difference is understood between searches entering "free" in their search terms versus "buy." Similarly, the search term "info" indicates desire for information over purchase. You should also consider optimizing for your keywords' synonyms, mistypes, and keyword stemming (verb tenses). I like to use Google's Keyword Planner, but I also like to use spy tools to identify best keywords and competitors' sites. Again, Keyword Spy and the SEOBook Toolbar are also great for providing tools for keyword analysis and recommendations.

How to do it? Keyword research is one of the easier (but extremely important) aspects of SEO. Start by gathering the keyword and terminology suggestions from the client or approver, and likewise the keywords discovered by your digital audits. Run these back through keyword research tools and get recommendations by search volume, just as we did in Chapter 2. The goal? Identify what are the most relevant keywords with the most search volume.

Keep in mind that Google tools are great. Google is the expert and knows its own data better than anyone, but valuable tools such as Google Trends show "indexed" results rather than true search volume (see Figure 3.5). This means that Google will take the gamut of the results and distribute them from 1 to 100. So the top results shown are the top results (100), and likewise are the least. So all data is "indexed" or benchmarked. This is great for comparison, but not so good for hard volume numbers. Still, Google Trends conveniently shows not only the value of current searches for a keyword, but whether this is increasing or decreasing over time. Suddenly, that high-volume keyword phrase may not matter if it drops too low within the year. Google Trends also identifies the top geographic locations searching for specific keywords, which is also valuable to know. So suppose the top location searching for "white toilet seats" is Kalamazoo, MI. Wow—let's do some local SEO targeting for our business there! Regardless, if a location SEO strategy is essential for the project at hand, and if desired locations don't align with Google's list, I like to add a location name onto primary keyword phrases for the client. If we're targeting Chattanooga, TN, and the keyword phrase is "buy gray metal sutures," then it becomes "buy gray metal sutures Chattanooga."

Figure 3.5 Google Trends research.

Note

Demographics Research

Google Trends is not the only tool to report geographic or other demographics data for search and websites. For more on these tools, as well as analytics indexing, see Chapter 7.

From all this data and background, the optimizer can list recommendations on top keywords for the client or approver and get their John Hancock before creating SEO page plans. Do you think John Hancock was thinking about SEO when he signed the Declaration of Independence? His signature is easy to find!

Step 4: Plan Network Architecture

Now that you've identified your digital footprint, you need to clean it up. One of the more obscure issues in SEO is that of shared IP addresses. Larger corporations often have their own dedicated server web hosting. And particularly if they have been buying up smaller companies, they represent multiple web properties. The larger corporation can host them together on the same server for reasons of IT security and convenience. The larger of these sites are presumably not WordPress because complex, large corporate sites must be integrated with a number of large technologies such as Customer Resource Management (CRM) databases for sales data or Enterprise Resource Planning (ERP) systems with customer login accounts and finances. Smaller company websites or blogs (I would say less than 150 pages), however, may very well be WordPress. Regardless, an SEO might be tempted to set up inbound linking strategies and multiple content posting opportunities among the various sites.

You may have the same idea for setting up industry directories and multiple blogs for SEO effects on your own smaller-scale hosting service for, let's say, a small eCommerce site or multiple clients within the same industry you serve.

First, too many websites are like honeycombs where there are valuable pages full of honey but a lot of sections that have no value. Don't force your site structures to be so imbalanced. Don't spread all your link juice around your own field. In other words, do not devalue your own outbound links by passing their value to others of your same sites. Bigger than the loss of link juice within your own network, rumor has it that Google ignores (or possibly might penalize) heavy linking and content sharing within the same IP address. That's right—search engines look at IP addresses. So those 20 URLs you bought and have shared on the same GoDaddy server? Google knows—it always knows!

That is also why I recommend to clients that they spend the extra web hosting dollars to get a dedicated IP address (not necessarily a dedicated server, just a singular IP address for their domain/s). You don't want Google affiliating you with porn sites or directory/advertising scam sites that might be housed on the shared IP hosting offered by your web server.

So you've said your mea culpa, placed your most important content building on one primary domain to preserve link juice, identified any questionable outbound links and made notes for "noFollows," and so on. You still have those 50 other domains you purchased. What to do?

 Caution

Cloaked Domains and Redirects

At one time I had a client set up "cloaked domains," in which, regardless of the domain name you typed in, you would see the same website content on the specific URL at hand. Good idea, right? If you said "Yeah, perfect idea, sign me up, let's do it right now!" then you need to reread the previous chapters and smack your wrist with your iPhone. This perpetuates not only a canonicalization problem, but also an inbound link problem and even a branding problem. Solve it, solve it now, and set up your 301 redirects and traditional domain forwarding on the server side. Still, if you have 50 or even 20 domains being forwarded to the same URL, it looks a little fishy. I have a friend SEO who says never to do anything that porn sites might do. Good tip.

So now we know not to architect or encourage elaborate linking networks or build content across multiple sites and blogs that could be forged to enhance our one major site. But what if our digital audit reveals multiple past blogs, online articles, social profiles, and the like (assuming we can still access the content and profiles within)? List those and draw a diagram if you can to help keep your web resources in check (see Figure 3.6). However, if you have found old sites with blog content, that may be exported and imported into your new, primary WordPress site (if it makes sense to do so).

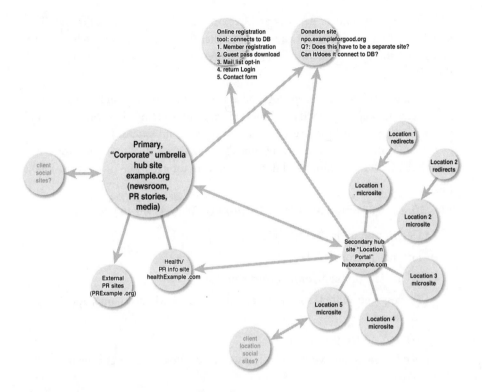

Figure 3.6   Planning network architecture.

 Tip

Repurposing Old Web Content

While old digital content may be out there, old blogs may not have the best content for our new orientation, and old social networks (such as Plaxo or Myspace) aren't really going anywhere worthy of continual posting or directing traffic to. (Big hint here: Don't direct new traffic to those old sites.) And that's fine. There's still some SEO value there for inbound links. And those old social sites can still come up in Google. Remember Flickr—the original Pinterest? Back in the days of the cavemen? That still comes up in the Google SERP, as well as Yahoo!. Just ensure those old sites have your current business info there, and link to your site. In fact, you could even provide a link to a subpage of your site that you specifically would like to see accumulate more traffic and better search engine rankings, such as your resources page or a page of your videos.

These are the elements of network architecture; identify them, think through them, and use them to your best SEO advantage rather then merely let old web resources sit without thought. Remember, they still represent your reputation out there on the Web.

After you have identified all appropriate assets of your own digital footprint, you need to identify specifically if and how you want them changed. So often these old web properties will list incorrect official company/brand names, URLs, and contact info (location directories are a prime example—we'll dive more into these in Chapters 7 and 8). I recommend filling out a form for each web property to follow up on.

Identification of Brand Mentions' Third-Party Web Assets to Change

- Description of the web channel.
- List the URL or mobile app.
- What's the problem, or incorrect copy?
- Do you control it? If so, list the account access URL, username, and password.
- Who to contact?
- Is it better to remove the mention/web asset altogether, or change it? Why?
- What do you want to change it to?
- Ideally when would you like it changed?
- Date of contact.
- What transpired?
- Backup plan if nothing can be changed.

Step 5: Sitemapping

In SEO we talk a lot about the word "sitemap." In most SEO contexts, however, we mean the sitemap.xml file that needs to be submitted to the search engines on a regular basis to aid the robots in crawling the site after it's built. We'll discuss this in Chapter 4. In this case, we're discussing the information architecture aspect of sitemapping. The IA act of designing the sitemap involves identifying web goals, existing content, web properties, and web traffic (and, hopefully, SEO and keyword input) to achieve a completed website according to objectives.

What is IA and where/when does it apply? As we've mentioned, IA stands for information architecture—the process of strategically identifying how your site can best be constructed with navigation, third-party tools, and so on. Early on in the process, I start discussions with clients about a new website with a standard, basic sitemap layout in Excel—although Microsoft's Visio is a more common IA and UI package for these purposes, and PowerPoint is another poor man's alternative. We discuss, and the client takes and adapts for further discussion. After the client approves page count, basic layout, and architecture, we proceed to web design and/ or if necessary, wireframes. For large clients and websites, this can be an elaborate, time-consuming process and even involve professional IA personnel. But for small business WordPress websites, this should be included as part of the price and standard web design process.

What makes the SEO unique here is that a good optimizer can direct the website architecture for easy crawlability. And a website should not be architected without SEO in mind. Why design and build a website that the spiders can't crawl? For example, it may be tempting to build a website with deeper and deeper pages, getting further into more detail about a specific topic. In fact, theoretically this idea sounds good for SEO as well—why not dive fully into your niche content? The problem is, all these deeper layers can inhibit spiders. Some SEOs will argue that if cleanly architected and linked, these deeper pages are very valid for SEO. Maybe so, but the closer to the surface of your domain, the quicker the crawlers can find it. What we're discussing here is a shallow architecture. For most WordPress websites (which have fewer pages than large corporate Fortune 1000 sites) this can be the best approach.

Another SEO opportunity in the sitemap design is to assign SEO-friendly menu page labels. This has to be a delicate maneuver, because the longer the menu labels, the more it can visually break the menu (especially when web visitors zoom in on their browser). So the web developer will want menu labels as short as possible (and rightfully so), while for the SEO, the more keywords integrated, the better. Again, there must be compromise. Regardless of the top menu, the SEO should have his way on the footer menu. Strategic footer menus are great for SEO, and I recommend fleshing those out with full keywords in the pages' listings (even if they don't exist on the top menu). Often you will see gray-hat SEOs abuse the footer with links such as these:

SmallTown lawyer | MainStreet pain attorney | BigCity attorney

Not only are these much heavier SEO tricks and less for usability (and don't fit the top menu at all), but they also often link off the site to SEO landing pages. These are the kinds of things search engines are cracking down on.

Here's an example of the Excel spreadsheet I consult with clients on. In this case it is very keyword friendly (see Figure 3.7).

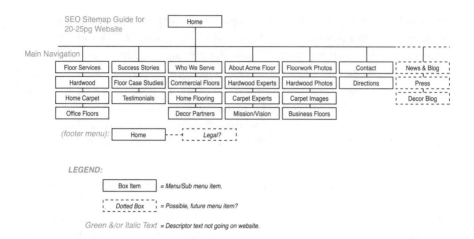

Figure 3.7   Simple Microsoft Excel drawn sitemap.

For either scenario, you're still finding the balance of page-level URL length. You want to maximize the keywords in URLs for SEO, but at the same time the URL can't have an unlimited length (even in the age of URL shorteners). You'll assign the page-level URLs in SEO page form, but a good guide is not to exceed 115 characters, and also not to use "stop" words in your URL, such as "the," "of," "and," "to," "with," and the like. Remember not to duplicate your keywords, or do keyword-stuffing, within a page URL. And longer URLs can dilute a specific keyword. However you go, you definitely don't want dynamic URLs (a rarity in WordPress) or default WordPress permalinks. For more on URL length, here is a great post: http://moz.com/blog/should-i-change-my-urls-for-seo.

Although shallow sites are a good SEO goal, you still want the site's content, on a page-to-deeper-page basis, to venture from light, intro, and marketing "fluff" copy on surface pages to in-depth content on the deepest page. For example, I always highly recommend that a site should have sectional landing pages or navigational pages. These are intro pages to a section and listings of its page contents and URLs. Although the links are already accessible via the menu, these navigational pages provide good bytes of info for those unsure of where they're going—and they've become a web standard. So if your site has a section on "zoo reptiles," that sectional intro page, accessible as the top-level navigation item, can tell you about the pages within it on snakes versus lizards versus turtles (good things to know!).

Set sitemap/customer journey goals: If you're redoing your website, chances are you also need to redo your sitemap. Navigation trends change. For example, it used to be popular for jump menus to allow users to select their preference of what type of content to visit next (outside of the menu navigation). And breadcrumbs are not used nearly as much these days as they once were. Remember? That list at the top of your page showing you started at Home, then went to About, then went to Foot Corns Services, to Foot Corns Induction and down the yellow-brick road to Oz, and all of that was how you got to where you are now? From a web usability standpoint, if you already have good menu navigation (and for larger sites, both top-level navigation and section-level side navigation), a detailed footer menu, as well as a call-to-action or list of relevant links within your current page content— well, how many menu navigation options do you need? Is your site that confusing? And what about the added consumption of real estate? Some SEOs feel that bread-crumbs are another good opportunity for valuable anchor text.

Personally, I place emphasis on the aforementioned anchor text locations that you already have and have strategic control over. Additional links might dilute the more strategic anchor text, such as in your page text calls-to-action. At times you may need to consider such elements because of other SEO barriers. Perhaps you have a corporate site founded on an ERP, or an IT-heavy hosting platform template that is SEO prohibitive. In these cases, you need all the help you can get. So if, for example, you are not able to rename dynamic URLs, such as http://www.example.com/7=fekl?12#$J90n, but are able to use breadcrumbs, that might help your overall SEO.

Regardless, a goal for your new sitemap should be clean, simple navigation (and shallow navigation is a good SEO goal as discussed). But gauge your other IA and web marketing goals to help drive your new sitemap along with your SEO goals. Do you want to get visitors to the shopping cart more easily? Does the nav not do justice to the library of content resources customers are asking for?

A common IA upfront approach is to survey; customers, company representatives, or those completely unfamiliar with your site can all have valuable input. From this research you can glean priorities of content and functionality. But this is also the time to do your keyword research. Do the survey results suggest keywords and desirable web content in line with the keyword phrases being searched online? If not, why do you think there's a difference?

The last thing I'll say on this point is to serve your target audience. Your existing customers and staff know what they expect from your website, but this should be very different from that of a prospect visiting your site for the first time. Past visi-tors will know what they want from your site, where (roughly) to find it, where to find your contact info, and so on. Unique visitors (first-time visitors to your site) will not. So how can you attract them, incentivize them, and move them through your site to achieve the objective? Let your website plan identify and prioritize these aspects.

A common web marketing motif is the funnel; I like to discuss the digital market-ing funnel with clients and how it applies to their website. Namely, your website goal is the bottom of the funnel. The primary start, when Google users search and see your listing and click through to the home page, is the top or mouth of the funnel. From there, what is the optimal journey to filter visitors down to the spout or goal? What was the typical journey on your previous site? How can it be better? Keep in mind that this is also how to think like Google Analytics, which provides a funnel as part of its reports (which we'll dive into in Chapter 7), showing the most common paths web users took and how they aligned with your desired paths to the goal.

Don't look at those lost along the way as failures. Your website needs to serve those as well, and if it's any good, it already does. This is why I discuss having light, marketing intro copy to sectional entry pages, and deep industry copy deeper into the site. You will have web visitors who are not yet ready to purchase or call you; they have to think about it. Maybe they're new to your industry or the sales cycle and they need to learn more on their way up. Maybe they're reviewing info information from a number of different vendors to rate and compare before purchase. How are you serving these prospects? Do you have the web content to give them now and keep them coming back later? You always want to keep your funnel full, hence serve prospects at all levels. Take this conceptual figure to heart and into content and page planning for your new site (see Figure 3.8).

Website Funnel for Customer Journey

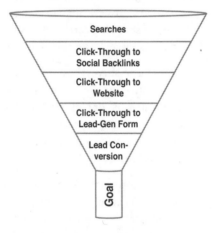

Figure 3.8 The Customer journey and website goals.

After you have objectives nailed down, it's time to get into the nitty-gritty of the sitemap design itself and all its fun issues. One issue with redoing your sitemap and site content is that typically the page-level URLs change as well. Again, this is a good thing; you have probably altered SEO keywords since your last website build. Your new page-level URLs should reflect these new keyword phrases, and you should have all this in your updated SEO strategic planning. You just have to ensure that you have set up the new pages and their URLs with 301-redirects from your old website's indexed pages. 3-oh-what-what-whats? Relax. We'll get into implementing 301 redirects in Chapter 4.

The point here is that you want to be very clear about what existing pages you have coming up in Google for what keywords and what reader content. You'll want to know where to direct search engine bots, and your web visitors, to go instead. All this should be represented in your new sitemap documentation and SEO page forms. But before we get too far ahead of ourselves, let's identify what exactly this site you're creating is supposed to achieve.

Suppose you're a small business in B-to-B (business-to-business, in contrast to retail business-to-consumer) and you want your website to facilitate lead generation. How can a website serve you leads? By capturing web visitor contact info for follow-up or by inciting customers to contact you. One way to incentivize info capture is to offer industry-specific, valuable content that requires login registration. So if a business sells high-end display monitors, it might have a video demo on the future of 3D monitor technology for business or a whitepaper on rating and comparing func-tionality of monitors for video conferencing (which could require registration/login to view). A real customer would find this information valuable enough to provide contact information in order to access.

As smart as this lead-capture approach is, however, it doesn't help SEO. Spiders can't crawl to the other side of lead-generation forms, leaving valuable content out of the SEO and SERP spectrum. From an SEO perspective, you want your best, most demanded content optimized. But again this shows the balancing act of SEO when presented with alternative web roles, goals, and personnel.

Identifying the Different Roles of Web and Blogsites

Although the web has advanced tremendously since the 1990s, it's still worth ref-erencing the basic web channel approaches from back then to identify the primary, driving purpose of your website features. Then, in the world of Web 1.0, it was fairly clear what type of website you were visiting by its functionality. The con-tent was very often awful and confusing; navigation was all over the place; design (if there was any design at all) was "experimental"; and the brand name may not be mentioned anywhere close to the top, but the functionality would make itself known. It had to. Programmers then didn't have all the quick and easy resources to integrate every type of functionality under the sun. Page load times were a big issue—the Internet ran on slow, noisy modems, monitors were set to low resolu-tion limiting display to 600x400 pixels, and browser frames were large and clunky, consuming more real estate than today. The costs of programming, inexperienced programmers, the incompatibilities of web languages and browsers, and the limitations of HTML web frames all directed the primary focal functionality of sites. Sound like your own private circle of hell? Believe it or not in some ways the limitations were advantageous, in that they elicited clear paths of web purpose and use.

So what were those identifiable site functions? Let's see what we can come up with:

- **Directories:** If you were visiting a directory, you knew it. It was a listing full of company names, URLs, and maybe email addresses and phone numbers for these, with brief company bios (if you were lucky). There also may have been banner ads.

- **Brochureware:** A corporate website was typically what we called "brochureware"—marketing fluff copy about the company, bios, and contact info. Often with a "mandatory" 1990s Flash intro. Essentially, it was brochure copy converted into a website, hence "brochureware."

- **Ad campaign landing pages:** These were basically single pages on the backend of a domain that achieved hits from banner ads, redirects, or even magazine ads.

- **Black-hat SEO pages:** These pages could have a variety of forms, but would often be full of meaningless jibber-jabber content and advertising (and metatags, and more metatags!). They would perform their SEO tricks to capture search hits from the various search engines to prove advertising value. Because such sites ruled search results, two things happened:

  - Valid directories became more important and would receive more traffic for people to find what they were looking for. Some of these even survive today. Yahoo! still has many legacy directories (local, sports, and so on).

  - Google was birthed out of the chaos to reward valid content for better search results and the age when metatags ruled search was dead.

- **Online news and magazine sites:** These sites were either large, pushing the envelope and attempting to solve the profit game (such as *The Wall Street Journal*, which continues the fight to this day) or were merely online articles displaying banner ads.

- **Content Aggregator Portals:** For lack of a better term, even then there were content aggregator sites which, like RSS feeds today, would pull in a variety of content options (images and/or text displayed across different frames) for the viewer to choose among for a deep dive. Today we can see such choose-your-content options displayed in paper.li, visual sites such as Pinterest and Tumblr, and as mentioned, RSS readers.

- **eCommerce:** This was constantly being re-approached (in fact, an entire bubble was blown and burst). But out of this Amazon survived and continually contributed to the advent of social media (such as with its innovative consumer reviews, ratings, and recommendations engines). The majority of America's side startup eCommerce sites didn't fare so well.

- **Login Portals:** Bigger corporations could have login "portals" where members could login to stores of niche industry information, specific data, or applications.

- **Encyclopedias and dictionaries:** These were, as expected, lists of searchable content listings. Even back then the legendary *Encyclopedia Britannica* began its attempts to achieve revenue online. But Wikipedia also was created from this web content model and, as a nonprofit, content-collaborative, Web 2.0 "wiki," it killed other encyclopedias as an industry. One of the ancient Web 1.0 golden oldies, still full of frames and all is NetLingo.com, which I reference to this day.

- **Forums:** The predecessor to social media was the forum. Clunky, unattractive, text threads going in all directions—but they were great for social engagement, consumer content, prosumer (consumer turned producer) expert advice from the groundswell and pure hobby fun discussions. They remain extremely relevant today. People are still very active in forums, with similar online behavior. They show up in search results because they tend to be focused on a specific niche topic or industry, are full of content and various contributors, and achieve a lot of return visits and activity. Don't knock them as antiquated. There are forum plug-ins for WordPress sites and are worth considering if helpful to your audience, such as a tech support forum.

Ironically, today's website channels are not so clear-cut. Although we can physically walk into a book store, coffee shop, or grocery store and immediately know the difference among all three, today's websites are full of myriad functionality and user content options. If asked, "What is social media?" we may immediately cite social networking software such as Facebook or Twitter. But the truth is almost every website out there today is social media. Incorporating social sharing, social follow, blogs, RSS feeds, ratings, reviews, and commenting, the state of Web 2.0 is the era of web-wide social media. Is a blog a blog or a magazine? Is a website primarily a website or a blog? And guess what: WordPress is driving this crazy train. It easily integrates all of these and more into sites. These functionality options are all available even for the simplest blog sites via the free WordPress.com. So, go nuts! If you're reading this book, you're already halfway there.

Refer back to my breakdown on these in Chapter 1, "What Is SEO and Do I Really Need It?"; even today, such examination can be good consideration to identify the major functional purpose of your site to serve your audience. Even with a free blogsite on wordpress.com you can strategically architect this way, with website, content aggregation, and social functionality (see Figure 3.9).

Figure 3.9   Free WordPress.com site with content tabs and social functionality.

After you've identified that the major purpose here is, for example, eCommerce sales, the navigation must be set up to conduct web visitors to your eCommerce goals for the site. If you want your site to maximize long-term customer retention sales, the site should accommodate this with customer program information or redemption vouchers. It doesn't always work out that there is alignment between SEO, IA, and the web marketing goals, but via linking, all three areas might find unity. How about that—what does that make this? Tri-partisan?

SEO Value and Authority-Based Architecture

When you have a sitemap near completion, you want to identify your linking strategy. Links have the most value when inbound from other websites. However, even within your own site, there is some value on which to capitalize. I recommend setting up a link wheel with calls-to-action going from (example) page: "home/bathroom-decor/ceramic-tile," to page: "home/kitchen-decor/tile-backboard," and from there to page: "home/outdoor-decor/barbeque-counter." Part of the reason for this is to input anchor text. Anchor links have text within the link itself (in contrast to just a spelled-out URL, or instead of saying "click here" you want to say "See our great bathroom decor ceramic tiles!"). This text can be valuable in SEO for the recipient page.

It is also valuable for the distribution of page-authority link juice. Just as the SEO analysis and SEO Book Tools assign authority scores to websites and specific web pages, you want to consider these valuation approaches within your own website linking.

I look at SEO architecture as a house of cards. The more cards you have in the mix is like the most pages of a website. You can set up the house of cards as a wide, endless structure that's only two levels tall. But your table to hold this house can be only so wide (like a website top-level menu can be only so wide). How equitable is weight-distribution at only two levels? The pyramid can't physically be too vertical and narrow; three cards can't be stacked on only three cards. So balance your weight and cards, a.k.a. web pages, optimally.

You should also be conscious of authority, yet another weight-balance issue. You can't have too many links on a page (regardless of website structure) because the spiders will be confused and devalue the page or links. The strongest, most crawl-friendly web page (like the home page) should be a good conduit for passing link juice (SEO page authority) to the next level of pages. But in most cases you don't just want to direct the web visitor primarily back to the home page (with a call-to-action, and so on). Why not? Let me count the ways:

- That's typically the page that comes up before all others in the search engine results page (SERP).
- Your web visitor probably visited there first.
- The home page is typically light, marketing intro copy that won't likely get your visitor closer to the goal.
- If the web visitor wanted to start the journey over, finding the home page is usually obvious. In other words, visitors already know how to get home—they just may not know how to find exactly what they're looking for.

- So give credit, link juice, to the pages of your site that may not achieve all the general web traffic, yet still contain valuable content.
- You want a call-to-action (CTA).

 Tip

Composing the Call-to-Action

You always want good CTAs—on website pages, blog posts, social media, you name it—to keep offering the visitor more, and a place to go, closer to the web marketing and site goal. This is also a great place to integrate links with anchor text. For example:

"And that's not all! Like it? See more on accounting for dog groomers here!" or:

"Now that you know all about them, expose yourself to purchasing and shipping options for cold metal sutures!"

So for your on-page linking, how can you accommodate these, while addressing similar page interest and relevance for the reader? How to keep the crawlers in order and passing authority, without having too many links on the page? There's no perfect answer here; you just have to look at your house of cards.

Fortunately, WordPress has great vehicles for testing all this. Don't over test and constantly change your primary navigation, because it will confuse both crawlers and web visitors. But keep in mind that with WordPress you have categories, tags, archiving—all additional navigational options for your blog. And you can build your primary nav to integrate menu items easily for a specific category on-the-fly (for any blog posts you label with that category name; for example, under your top level Success Stories label, you could feature your content category Hardwood Replacements). Or you can link from one content page to a specific archive of blog posts by time period, common tag, or whatever.

Although these are interesting possibilities for testing visitor click throughs, don't forget the canonicalization and "noFollow" issues inherent here (as discussed in this chapter). The last thing I will say here is very important. If you suspect specific user-content interest, or if your testing reveals this, it is far better to structure such content yourself in the site with actual navigation and linking. If you architect the site purposefully, directing to specific, individual pages and blog posts based on related interest (for example, with calls-to-action at the bottom of a page or post's content), it will make sense to the spiders. You will also thereby fully allow the spiders to crawl the links and content (instead of going through automated, noFollow URLs).

How to sum up simply? After you know what the people want, and the spiders want, give it to them directly, within a clear structure, like a sturdy pyramid of cards.

Step 6: Assessing Content and Keyword Relationships

What To Do and What Not To Do for Web Content

Ask the right questions upfront: Can you produce enough good content for search engines and your audience on your WordPress site? If the company has existed for a while, you can find and repurpose old content—brochures, articles, white-papers, and ads, for example. Such content can be placed in the news/PR or even blog section and displayed with old dates to demonstrate history and longevity for the company and help SEO with content that can be indexed. If the content is not already electronic text, it can be scanned and run through optical character recognition (OCR) software to convert to electronic text. Going through old PR, awards, and news article research can even excite the client, rather like going through old family albums. Memories or laughter can be sparked by the discovery process. You don't have to clutter the site with this—just organize useful content and optimize it for full search engine potential.

You also might have the idea to share content or blogging with others. That's a good idea, but be careful—there are good SEO ways to do this and bad ways. We'll dive deeper into this in Chapter 5. However, there are still big "no-nos" for content topics where search engines are concerned. The following is a paraphrased blog post from a group discussion on regularly debated content types in regard to search engine blocks. This is a good debate topic (try it at your next alumni event or Friday happy hour!), but realize that such content is dicey for search engines. It's best to stay away from these topics in your own blogging if you can:

- Viruses and malware.
- Leaked personal ID info (such as credit card numbers).
- Porn.
- Violent images (note that some people find this more debatable, and some sites are focused on this, such as news sites or activist sites).
- Hate content (some also find this in some cases pertinent; for example, to research hate messaging and groups).
- Hacking instructions.
- Bomb-making instructions.

- Pro-eating disorder sites (sites that teach people to enact anorexia or other disorders; some consider this helpful for research by parents or doctors).

- Satanism and Wiccanism (there seems to be a case for freedom of expression or religion for this type of content).

- Necrophilia (some feel this still has bearing for research as cultural phenomenon).

- Content farms (remember that this is bad for SEO, but the smart ones are hard to identify as such; gray hat is hard to nail down).

- Blackhat SEO boards—This might be helpful to research the spam tactics you should shield yourself against.

 Note

Want to Learn More?

For more, see the full discussion post: http://www.brafton.com/news/matt-cutts-on-search-content-standards-sessf.

Associating Best Keywords to Web Pages or Blog Posts

After doing keyword research, I like to write a simple plan to associate each primary keyword with a specific web page or blog post on the existing site (assuming this is a rebuild rather than a new site with no content). After I've read over the existing site's content, I take my client-approved keyword list and attach one primary keyword each. The list looks something like this:

Keyword-to-Page List

- **Primary keyword phrase:** 'Custom crystal awards'
  For which web page: "Art Gallery"
  URL = *example.com/glassblowing/glass-art-gallery*
- **Primary keyword phrase:** 'Glass custom trophies'
  For which blog post: "Studio Tours"
  URL = *example.com/custom-glass-blog/glassblowers-studio-tours*
- **Primary keyword phrase:** 'Corporate awards trophies'

  For which web page: "Testimonials"
  URL = *example.com/glasswork-testimonials*

Step 7: Writing the SEO Page Forms

You've made it to the end of the chapter—we're down to the final strategic step before implementation! After you've identified your primary keywords (and in the case of existing website content, what keywords you want to plant within which web pages), you want to produce what I call an SEO page form for each new web page/blog post and its new primary keyword. This is a great thought practice. It's more work than it looks like, and once it is completed you have the primary needs identified to execute for SEO on your new site.

As discussed in Chapter 2, some of the WordPress plug-ins for SEO, such as Yoast, are so advanced that they provide many of the recommendations for these fields for you. So here's my advice: If you're optimizing your own site and you have the authority to make these decisions, this SEO page form can be a more fluid process. You can work between the form and the plug-in's recommendations to execute your on-page optimization (just be sure to dot your "t"s and cross your eyes). But it's still helpful to have this tangible checklist outside of the website plug-ins to reference and document.

If you are performing SEO for a client or superior, you should fill out all SEO page forms and get sign-offs of approval before executing. Because after you're "live," there can be huge implications. Suppose the company's legal team has required a brand name to be buried, changed, or removed from public view (on the page you're optimizing). Or suppose the company is suddenly removing the very service for which you're optimizing verbiage. In many business scenarios, communication problems occur on a regular basis. Try the best you can to prepare for those, for you and your colleagues. Some of the items on this form may not make sense yet; that's okay, you have the rest of this book to learn. So look over the form, use it or abuse it, and complete your SEO strategy so you can get on with the rest of the book and the fun part—doing the work itself! (How's that for a CTA?)

The SEO Page Form Example

SEO Page Form for Individual Web Content Page or Blog Post

To be used for individual website pages, blog posts or other social media posts. Note: Please reference or fill this form out with all applicable info, and get approval, before publishing important web content online.

ITEM	VISIBLE WEB PROPERTIES (To be filled in below):
Existing Web Page or Post URL or Description (web location):	Current URL = http://example.com/blog/current-page-text
Content Headline; H1 (should contain major keywords):	Internal Corporate Communications Video Production
Content Subhead; H2 (Use keywords if sensible):	If you're seeking help on producing your internal corporate video, start here.
Links (list any links to be in the post, & their descriptions. NOTE: always use keywords, never use "click here" when putting links in copy):	"Read more on our internal communications video productions" URL = http://example.com/next-page-link
Primary and Secondary Keywords for Tags (major keywords and/or locations to be programmed into tags on this page in the code)?	PAGE PRIMARY KEYWORD: Internal communications video productions company Atlanta SAME PAGE SECONDARY KEYWORD: Georgia production video company
Blog Post Categories (preferably 1 or 2 categories to a post referencing keywords)?	Communications Videos
Blog Post Tags (blog content tags should also reference keywords)?	Communications, video production, Atlanta video

SEO EFFECTS	BELOW FOR PAGE CODE
Primary Image/Vid (if applicable, list image filename & title/ description & alt tag to use):	• Filename: internal-communications-video-acme.jpg • Alt tag: "Internal communications video productions"
Secondary Images/ Vids (if applicable, list image filename & title/ description & alt tag to use):	• Filename: atlanta-video-communications-aaa.jpg • Alt tag: "Atlanta video communications"
More Images/Vids (if applicable, list image filename & title/ description & alt tag to use):	
Web Page or Post SEO URL (web location):	New URL = http://example.com/blog-communicate/internal-communications-videos
Browser Page Title (in the code; should contain major keywords):	Internal Corporate Communications Video Production
Content Meta Description (what is the text on this page or post about? This will be the hidden meta description in code. Use one primary keyword.):	Internal communications video productions company Roswell, GA.; Event Video is a production video company to create your business videos.
Microdata, Rich Snippets, and Auto Tags (This will be the hidden in code. Opportunities to use more keywords per page.):	Auto tags: "communications," "videos" Show 4.5* reviews rich snippets
Notes/Other:	

The following is an example version of an internal document you could use to start the video production process:

INTERNAL CORPORATE COMMUNICATIONS VIDEO PRODUCTION

If you're seeking help on producing your internal corporate video, start here.

We recognize that internal communications video is one of many compelling tactics to help companies engage employees. We help our clients determine how and when to successfully use video production for communications strategies.

Our customers use video for business-critical information worldwide. Our video production solutions are an alternative to out-of-office meetings and trade shows. Office-based staff can access internal communications videos online and as needed when their schedules allow.

Ready to discuss your internal communications video production? Let's go! (*insert links to "Contact" page*).

Signature: _____

4

WordPress On-Page Architecture and Basic SEO Execution

Chapter objectives and questions:

- WordPress.com versus WordPress.org
- On-Page Architecture
- WordPress.com Blogging and Social Media Emphasis
- The Importance of Linking
- Big-Picture Progression of SEO Goals and Achievements
- Technical Aspects and SEO Controls in WordPress.com
- WordPress Analytics
- WordPress.com Resources

WordPress.com, WordPress.org—Which Way Do I Go?

Still a little confused as to the differences between WordPress.com free blogs, WordPress.org, and WordPress-platform custom websites? No problem—let's break it down again: WordPress.com is a free and easy tool for creating your own quick blog, much like Google's Blogger or Tumblr. If you've always wanted to start blogging as a hobby, WordPress.com is a great place to start (creating a blog on its own domain; for example, http://yourblog.wordpress.com). WordPress without the ".com" on the whole is actually a web format, a structure for creating sites of various orientations, and a content management system (as we discussed in Chapter 1, "What Is SEO and Do I Really Need It?" and Chapter 2, "The Search Engines, WordPress, and SEO Tools"). WordPress.org is an endless array of support resources, including themes and plug-ins for customized WordPress websites on custom URLs. Note that there is no "official" support for WordPress.com (as with so many modern open-source CMSs). But some of the support content available on WordPress.org can also be available for WordPress.com blog issues. So you can start by creating a free WordPress.com blog, get comfortable with the usability, controls, posting, and edits, then build a customized WordPress site from a broader availability of more editable themes, and then integrate the content from your original WordPress.com blog as we demonstrated in Chapter 2 on WordPress tools and technologies.

Both WordPress.com themes and WordPress.org themes for customized WordPress sites are similarly available for researching, choosing, and integrating for your blog (depending on which format you are using). In either scenario, you can try out different themes and preview how they look with your content. The major difference occurs in the WordPress.org theme customization for your own site. In these cases the sky is the limit—you can have full cascading style sheets (CSS) editing options, add on any plug-ins you want (although some may be incompatible) and open up your site for additional functionality, such as eCommerce or forum. This chapter specifically focuses on the more simplified scenarios for WordPress.com blogs while prepping you for latter chapters on SEO plug-ins and hands-on implementation for customized WordPress sites.

WordPress On-Page Architecture

In Chapter 3, "A Strategic SEO Upfront Content Approach," we discussed website architecture and strategy, but how your page or blog is wire-framed (planned for structure on a page level) and designed for visitors is also important. Again, you want to balance issues such as style and usability against SEO. This section is instrumental not only for planning the appearance of your WordPress.com blog, but for more advanced WordPress customized sites as well.

SEO and Low Value Pages

An important thing to consider while planning your WordPress blog architecture is the pages and their value for SEO. SEO works best on relevant, meaty content pages and blog posts. Likewise, as discussed in Chapter 3 on strategy, certain pages and menu items are standard, expected within the web lexicon of today. With that comes a burden of typically lesser-value pages for SEO. This is not absolute law, but realize that these pages are probably not going to be your content-deep SEO heavy-hitters:

- Contact page.

  Except with local SEO strategy if you integrate NAP, Google Maps, and some text, we'll dive more into this in Chapter 9, "Going Mobile and Local."

- About Us page.

- Directory pages.

  Sectional intro or landing pages. They usually have sub page links but not much text. But, as discussed in Chapter 3, they have an important position in the sitemap between the high-visit home page and the deeper real content pages.

WordPress On-Page Architecture Planning

If you are going to be blogging regularly, you want to use your WordPress.com theme options and widgets for the purpose of best usability. The default is to show your latest blog posts on the home page, but that's not a requirement. In fact, you don't have to show blog posts on your home page at all. You can structure the home page like an actual "page" and have the blog buried. But I don't advise this for a WordPress.com blog because presumably people will visit your blog to *read* your blog. Blog post teasers, however, are a smart way to utilize the home page— showing intro, sample text of various posts on your home page so that readers can choose to start reading what most interests them. All this points to options to consider in your on-page architecture, such as the following:

- **General length of posts.**
- **How many posts to show on the page:** WordPress gives you options as to how many posts to show on your home or blog page. So plan and decide; you don't want endless scrolling on your site, but you also want to show a wealth of content options for the reader.
- **Length of teaser text to display:** WordPress also allows you to control this. When showing multiple posts' teaser content, how much do you want to display?
- **Social share and commenting display:** These options are part of what make blogs, and WordPress, so great. We dive into this topic in depth in Chapter 5, "Real-World Blogging," and Chapter 8, "Social Media Connectivity."
- **Edit your blog name and tagline:** You've seen these. What's the name you want top front and center (the "Site Title") for your blog? Will you show your logo, and so on?

Note

Editing the Site Title

It's easy to forget—the default area for editing the WordPress title and tagline, from the side admin menu, is in **Settings** and **General** (as shown in Figure 4.1).

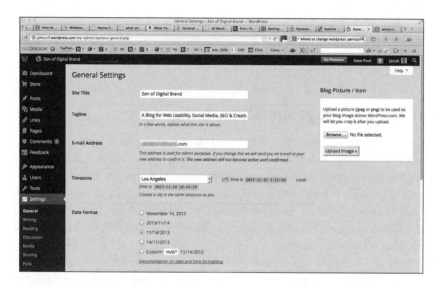

Figure 4.1   WordPress General Settings.

- **Which and how many navigational access widget options to show on the page:** In other words: Categories, Tag cloud, Archives, Top posts, Footer (and primary) menu, and so on. We dive into these questions in this chapter and Chapters 5 and 6 on blogging.
- **RSS feeds of blogs and/or social media:** Did you know that you can feed non-native content into your WordPress blog or site? For example, other blogs and your Twitter or other social feeds. We'll get into this more in this chapter and throughout this book.

 Tip

Choosing a WordPress.com Theme

When you go to choose your WordPress.com theme (or any WordPress theme, for that matter) you have endless choices available; you're swimming in a sea of perpetuity. If you have any thoughts going in about style, on-page elements, industry look-and-feel expectations, and the like, you should write those down and refer to them as you peruse. If you start with a theme but don't like it, you can always change it later. Nonetheless, it's always good to start with some vague notions in mind.

Here are some other considerations you want to be aware of as you make your choices:

- Logo display (some WordPress.com themes allow personal logo upload and display in a top logo area).
- Header graphic customization (if you want that).
- Theme color changes.
- Multiple locations for sidebar and/or footer (if desired).
- Graphic theme style to match your content and brand. (Is it more of a news site? Recipes? Travel blog?)

Social Sharing Options

It's critical to remember the difference between social share and social follow. My clients always put a great amount of focus and value on social follow. Social follow is what most people think of—those social icons displayed on your website or blog that allow web users to click through and follow, like, or connect to your social media profiles. Social share, on the other hand, gives your readers the opportunity to share or bookmark your blog or website content on their own social accounts.

If you definitely want social follow options on your site, that's fine—but realize it can be more harmful than helpful if you have no content on those sites. If people click through to follow you on Twitter or Like you on Facebook, and you have no consistent content there, it leaves them with a bad impression, a perception of unprofessionalism. So be careful what you publicize and where you invite people to collaborate with you. Social media is collaborative discussion. If you're not "talking" there, why would they join you? Because of this, I have occasionally counseled clients to list only one channel for social follow. LinkedIn is a good one (at least for business-to-business orientations), because organizations often have a profile there. (And guess what—if you don't think you have a profile there, you'd better check that!) Regardless, LinkedIn has traditionally been more static, with a basic About company description and contact info. There's much, much more you can (and should) do with your corporate LinkedIn profile (such as the new "Showcase"), but that basic info is very common.

For example, now LinkedIn allows for companies to make ongoing Updates on their company profiles, but for years it was merely a static profile. So it's convenient to allow people to follow your business there, even if you can't update it every week. Therefore, if you have to have only LinkedIn as your channel for website visitors to "follow," it's still acceptable to do this, and it is better than nothing.

What's so good about "social share?" By empowering (and encouraging) web and blog visitors to "share" your content, you still have a social media presence, but you're arming your fans to do the social media marketing for you! Social share allows them to easily promote your content on their *own* social media accounts, whichever they may be (so your business profile shows up in their personal Facebook updates, LinkedIn posts, or tweets).

But spreading the word and promoting yourself in the social space is only part of your reward. Guess what else you are getting for these social share widgets? SEO! That's right! You get SEO benefits—namely, inbound links from others, and consequently higher rankings.

Social Follow Options

Still not feeling 100% on the differences between social share and social follow? Well, you have social media profiles. And so does ACME the business. If you like ACME's latest blog post, you can share that on your own Facebook or Twitter page by clicking the Share icons from the blog post. Still with me? That's social "share."

But on their blog, ACME social marketers also ask you to "follow us on Twitter," and provide a link to their Twitter page. When you click to follow them, this is what you are doing—following their own Twitter, LinkedIn, Facebook, or Google+ page so that the company's posts will now appear on your own wall. Got it?

RSS Feeds of Social Content

RSS is one of the defining technologies of Web 2.0. In fact, it is so ubiquitous that much of the time you don't even realize when you're seeing or using it. What content feeds are RSS and what aren't? The ubiquity of modern web technologies makes it a difficult question to answer. For the user, the question may be irrelevant.

Any guess on what RSS stands for? "Really simple syndication." So if you thought it would have some hi-tech Tron-esque definition, think again. But what is it? For starters, it's that orange icon you see on websites (see Figure 4.2). That looks like ripples or waves in the corner. Or a non-colored rainbow.

Figure 4.2   RSS icon.

When you visit a blog or news site and click that icon, its purpose is to "feed" ongoing content into your RSS Reader. Google Reader used to be very popular, but Google took it down. Others include FeedBurner, Feedler, and more. But RSS technology can be used to pipe in various web and social content onto websites, blogs, or other social channels. It's content curation. In this case, we're discussing piping content into an RSS display widget (or iframe) on your WordPress site. How to do this? Simply log in to your WordPress dashboard and select the left-side menu options for **Appearance** and then **Widgets**. There you'll see your widgets for your sidebar. One of the options is RSS, and it works just as I've described here. You drag the RSS widget over to your sidebar and select what content to feed in. Keep in mind that there will be no search engine benefits or penalties associated with this. Search engines recognize RSS feeds as merely displaying preexisting content from an original source somewhere else. In fact, for customized WordPress.org theme sites, you could use a plug-in to be an entire web page on your site, displaying an RSS feed of outside content. For example, you could drive in your customer reviews, from your Google+ business/local page or Yelp page, to be your Testimonials page on your site. And you should have a testimonials page. (Reviews and RSS are discussed in Chapters 5 and 6 on blogging and Chapter 9 on mobile and local SEO).

The content could be anything from your Twitter feed to an industry trade pub to a blog. Here's what this content should represent:

- It should be attractive to your web viewers; it should draw them in and give them something they want.
- It should be relevant to your website content for the overall usability experience.
- It can be of great benefit if your site is very short on content. You can feed in an industry publication or blogger you know and help both of you.
- If you have a good blog, Twitter, or Facebook feed, you can highlight them while simultaneously driving followers to these.
- You might want to show the reviews you've received from customers in channels like Yelp or Google+. This way, there'd be no question of

authenticity (as some business owners might be tempted to write their own "customer reviews" to post on their own website).

- If you have upcoming seminars or other events, you can feed those in from a calendar.

For all these, remember that an RSS feed takes up important real estate on the page and will draw visual attention, especially if it's a dynamically changing Twitter or Facebook feed. So don't clutter your page or divide viewers' attention or drive them away from your primary goal or call-to-action.

Be careful with this: You don't want to send your web visitors out to other blogs instead of retaining them on your site. It is a good feature, however, for displaying additional relevant content to your web visitors if you have none.

Out-of-the-Box Blog Social Commenting by Users

"Out of the box" merely means noncustomized software; software (or in this case, a WordPress.com or WordPress.org theme) with strictly its default attributes. Don't forget that one of the truly social features of WordPress for engagement is the plain old simple commenting functionality. Yup—just the default options for readers to comment on WordPress blog posts. Social commenting and social ratings are defining characteristics of social media, and they're so commonplace today we don't even think about them. But these social commenting features allow readers to create their own WordPress profiles and make them visible while commenting on your (and others') WordPress blogs.

This is instrumental in the hub-and-spoke models we discussed in Chapters 3 and 8. This allows you to find other blogs, forums, and social groups where social users discuss your area of expertise. There you use your full profile to represent your identity and your own blog (and other social links). When you engage with your audience where they are already talking, give them the information they seek, and talk with them on their level, they will follow you back to your own blog and social connections. Give the people what they want, and what they want will become you. This is what we call *pull marketing*. You're not pushing sales on people. You're helping people where they are. Do that and they will want more.

Architecting Widgets On-Page

"Widget" is a fun name for those various selector, connector, and content options on the sidebar of WordPress blogs (you know, those classic business case examples of "Joe Smith is starting a company to sell widgets." Personally, I would have called them "gizmos," but I can deal with widgets). We've already discussed some—RSS feeds and social follow—that can be structured as widgets on the page. More widget options include blog categories, tag clouds, and archives (see Figure 4.3). These are great options but they should be architected strategically for what can most benefit usability. For the most part, these have little SEO benefit, so it becomes a focus on the web visitor. But it raises some questions: How many menus, links, and selectors do you need? Are you allowing too many opportunities for the visitor to click off your page? Let's not forget to KISS—*I mean keep it simple, silly.*

Now I like using tags and tag clouds on blogs, but if you feel very confident that your audience will not respond well to or utilize a tag cloud (see Figure 4.3), and if it will just clutter your page, you might not want to use it. But tags themselves can still be shown at the bottom of your blog posts and be accessible for other WordPress blog readers to access when seeking those content subjects.

A list of blog post categories (shown in Figure 4.4) is a good idea, just don't overdo it. Good practice is to have one category per blog post, and 5–10 categories to a blog site.

Figure 4.3   The Tag Cloud and Categories widgets.

Figure 4.4   The Categories widget.

Widgets are critical considerations for the appearance, usability, and traffic possibilities for your WordPress blog and overall social presence. We cover categories and tags in Chapters 5, 6, and 8.

Links and Anchors

"Anchor text" is the text written within a web link (as we've discussed in Chapter 3 on strategy and elsewhere in this book). It is often used in your call-to-action (CTA) instead of the antiquated, valueless text, "click here for more." Your onsite links are also critical to your overall site and blog strategy for SEO (as discussed in Chapter 3). You just don't want to point all your blog posts back to the home page.

Footer menus can be great for anchor text links, but at the same time too many links on a page can dilute the "link juice" (the SEO value of one page's content connected to another). If your primary menu and home page are extremely navigable, I recommend focusing on fewer, poignant footer links and enhancing the anchor text for the important page links you leave therein.

Although it is good to pass link juice within your site from higher-value pages to those of lesser value to give them a boost, at the same time we don't want to be overt transgressors of "link bleeding."

Link bleeding is an obvious attempt to pass valuable link juice from a page with a lot of link juice to a page of little content and no value. It can also occur in pages with long lists of links, which dilute each other's. So how to cure the bleeding? Just as we talk about the pyramid of cards with sitemap architecture, we want to apply some of those same principals here. If the top level of a pyramid has the highest value (link juice or rank), the internal links on that page would theoretically direct the spiders to pages of the next-highest value, and so on. This would enable the crawlers to most easily crawl through your site. Yes, you want to help the pages of lesser link juice, but again, this is a delicate balance. As with so many issues in SEO, I don't believe there is one right, perfect answer (and if there is, it may change with Google's next update), but you should consider and think about this in your SEO planning. Your linking strategies (and even linking campaigns) are instrumental in SEO. We discuss linking strategies more in-depth in Chapter 5 and 6 on blogging and Chapter 8 on social media.

Technical Aspects of WordPress.com and SEO

Yes! Even if you have a free WordPress.com blog you can improve your SEO! But many of the manual, time-required, or complex technological requirements discussed elsewhere in this book are automatically done in a free WordPress.com blog.

 Note

Check to See Your Blog Site Sitemap.xml File

One important element in SEO is generating and submitting the sitemap. xml file to search engines, which is automatically generated for WordPress. com blogs. Want to see it for yourself? Wonder what a sitemap.xml file actually looks like? See it in Figure 4.5. Or if you've already created your public WordPress.com and published content, type in your URL as follows: http://YourBlog.WordPress.com/sitemap.xml.

Figure 4.5 The sitemap.xml file.

There are those who say that if you have a WordPress.com site, you're all set and you don't need any SEO. Well, not quite. As you've discovered in previous chapters, strategy, keyword research, and content focus are instrumental to good SEO. For the technological side of SEO, your WordPress.com blog will automatically do a lot, but there's much you should know about what WordPress.com is actually doing and how you can take more of the reins for your own control.

 Caution

WordPress.com Blogs Versus Customized WordPress Sites

Easier does not mean better. WordPress.com's more hands-off approach to blog creation does mean that you are at the mercy of WordPress.com defaults and controls. For example, if your WordPress.com achieves a lot of traffic, it will automatically place ads there (without your control or revenue for you). The ads will not be visible to you if you're already logged in to your WordPress.com account while previewing your blog. The more you are aware of such defaults, the more you can try to control them yourself, but true control comes with your own domain, your own URL. That is, www.example.com instead of http://yourblog.wordpress.com. Because of these domain limitations and WordPress.com default structures, SEO gurus say that even though you can come up in search engine results, your WordPress.com blog favors WordPress overall—not you and your search goals. The caveat is that if you do absolutely nothing with SEO, a WordPress.com blog will come up with better search results than a customized WordPress site. But *you* are that rare individual—one who wants more! The one who dove headfirst into this book to go from WordPress.com beginner to SEO contender! Right? So don't let me stop you—keep on keepin' on learning and implementing!

SEO Basic Blog Checklist

The following are some good, basic SEO implementations that can be done even to a free WordPress.com blog. They can help your blog be seen by the search engines and get it rising in the SERP *(but those in italics are most important)*. Remember that these must be driven by strategic planning—all that fun stuff we covered in the previous chapter. This is just a checklist to mark off as you conduct your SEO efforts. When is a good time to do this execution? If you're just starting to build your blog, that's the best time; it's easiest to start executing these steps while in development. Although these steps are feasible for both basic, free WordPress.com blogs, as well as developed full sites, the next chapter offers a checklist for fully built WordPress sites and blogs with customization.

- *Google accounts setup for syncing.*
  - Google+ account setup/synced.
  - Google Maps integration on contact page. (These are discussed in depth in Chapters 5 and 6 on blogging and Chapter 9 on mobile and local SEO.)
- *Page text.*
  - *Identify major keywords and populate on page and heads.*
- Images optimized.
  - Image filenames and descriptions utilizing keywords.
  - Images placed on Google+ page.

- YouTube.

  - Host videos on your YouTube channel and drop them into your site or blog post. This is discussed more in Chapters 5, 6, and 8.)

- *Blog SEO setups.*

  - *Tags and categories.*

  - *Set Permalinks.*

  - *Set Akismet.*

  - *Auto tags.*

  - Set author information (We'll dive into this heavily in Chapters 5 and 6.)

- *Create search engine accounts and submit site to search engines.*

- *Set up analytics.*

  - WordPress analytics (inherited from Google Analytics).

  - Google Webmaster tools integration.

  - Bing Webmaster tools integration. (We discuss these more in this chapter.)

- Ask someone (a third party) to submit the site to social search and bookmarking sites.

  - Delicious.

  - Reddit.

  - StumbleUpon.

  - Digg.

  - Technorati.

  - Check and capture SERP results. (We'll dive into results and analytics in Chapter 7, "Analytics for WordPress.")

- **Set up location-based directories if relevant:** Local SEO is instrumental if you have a location-based storefront business, such as a restaurant or law office, or even if you're more of an onsite service, such as a lawn care service or exterminator. Not only are location-based SEO channels helpful to your customers who will search for you locally, their profiles are optimized independently from your blog or website (but link to these) and are easier to set up than full blog or website SEO. Sold yet? We dive fully in to how to optimize for location-based SEO in Chapter 9 on mobile and local SEO.

- **Google Webmaster Tools Setup and Accounts Syncing:** There are many things that WordPress.com does automatically for you or makes easier than full, customized WordPress websites. But Google Webmaster Tools is one of the exceptions. Note that Google Webmaster Tools is not a requirement by any means for your blog. But it is a good thing for search results (and it is good for your overall understanding of how SEO works). This is pretty easy. You can use several plug-ins for custom-built WordPress sites, whose purpose it is to set up these channels. But I still prefer to do it manually (which also works for WordPress.com sites). When I provide services for clients, I always start by generating a generic Gmail account for them and their social sites, WordPress site login, plug-ins registrations, stock image accounts, and so on. With that account, I set up the client Google+ business profile and other Google accounts (as discussed in Chapter 9). At that point, I can easily add the Google Webmaster Tools account. From within Google, I can open Google.com/webmaster/tools, add the website URL, and verify it.

Here's how to set up and verify your Google Webmaster Tools account for your WordPress.com blog:

1. Create an account in google.com/WebMasters/Tools to add your WordPress blog URL.

2. When Google requests you to Verify Ownership, choose the last option, **Add a Meta Tag to Your Site's Home Page**.

3. WordPress supplies you with a meta tag to copy. Select and copy the string of letters and numbers presented between the quotes after ' content= '.

4. With that string copied, log in to your WordPress blog and go to the **Tools** section in the dashboard or editor area.

5. Paste your string of Google content into the **Webmaster Tools Verification** section under **Google Webmaster Tools** (see Figure 4.6).

6. Save changes.

And you're done! After you do this, it will give you more data about your blog, such as search engine impressions. It should also elevate your organic search results (for more on these terms and values see Chapter 7). The more you can figure out and integrate between your blog and Google's tools, the better it will help your search results. For example, you could submit your blog feed as a sitemap (as discussed in this chapter).

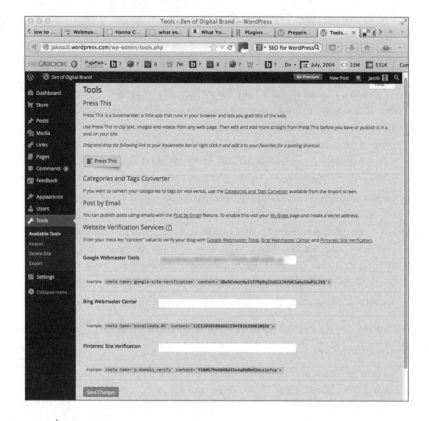

Figure 4.6   WordPress.com and Webmaster Tools Integrations.

Submitting the Sitemap File

Although we know that WordPress.com automatically generates your sitemap.xml file, you can do still more with this. After you've created your Google Webmaster Tools account, you can easily integrate your sitemap.xml file. If you make changes to your website structure, resubmit the sitemap file the same way—the more you interact with search engines, the more they want to serve you.

Here are Google's instructions (Bing is similar):

Tip

Submit a Sitemap With Google Webmaster Tools

Test to make sure your sitemap.xml file already exists on your site (per the note in this chapter).

1. Go to the Google **Webmaster Tools** home page, login, and click the site you want.

2. Go to the left-side menu, click **Optimization**, and next click **Sitemaps**.

3. Click the button to **Add/Test Sitemap**.

4. In the text box, enter your Sitemap filename (without typing the full URL; that is, instead of typing http://www.example.com/sitemap.xml, just enter **sitemap.xml**).

5. Click **Submit Sitemap**.

SEO Ranking Checklist

The following are some positive ranking drivers that you can achieve with your WordPress.com blog:

- **Good in-site SEO execution.**

- **The number of quality backlinks:** One-way links (from other sites pointing to your site) are especially favored, and the more the better!

- **Search engine traffic:** This might seem a bit of a chicken-and-egg thing, but the more visits you get coming from search engines (as well as more visits overall), the higher the search engines will serve you in the future.

- **Mentions:** What is the size of your digital footprint? How many people are talking about you in social media? These issues also positively impact your love from the search engines.

- **Quantity and quality of website/blog content:** How many pages, posts, and content overall? The more relevant content, the better.

- **Freshness of content:** Here is where the advantage of blogs and forums takes over; whereas website content is viewed as more "permanent," blogs are often quickly and regularly updated. Blog reader reviews and commenting also help.

- **Length of words per page:** Different SEOs will say different things regarding how many words to have per blog post or page. It's another indication that search engines don't reveal all their mysteries. A gauge I like says that more than 1,500 words to a post/page doesn't get as much love. I use 250 or 300 words as my bare minimum, but 500–1000 words is a good target for search engine love. (For more on this, see http://www.webconfs.com/15-minute-seo.php.)

- **Local search integrations:** If you are a location-based business, you want integrations with Google+ Local/Maps, Yahoo! Local, and even other local directories such as Yelp or YP. Basically, these further expand your digital footprint and inbound linking. (For more on location-based SEO, see Chapter 9.)

- **Affiliated tools integrations, such as Google Images, YouTube, and analytics such as Webmaster Tools:** The more love you show to Google, the more it will return the favor. Google has a lot of technologies options. Log in and sync accounts to as many as possible (for more on this, see Chapters 5 and 6).

- **Increased rank, authoritative score, and the like:** Tools such as SEOBook Tools will tell you what these scores are (and the factors behind these scores in different tools) for your site. But at the time of this writing, Google is placing less emphasis on its PageRank and hasn't updated it in months.

- **sitemap.xml file submissions to search engines.**

 Note

What's the Difference Between Google, Bing, MSN, and Yahoo?

In this book we put an emphasis on Google because search engine use favors Google roughly as 70% market share, Bing roughly as 20%, and Yahoo! as 10%. But Bing and Yahoo! actually share the same engine. Bing is the product of merged technologies between MSN and Yahoo! about 5 years ago in an attempt to beat Google. The reason we still see separate stats for Yahoo! is because it is helpful to recognize its advertising power, and that some people still use the Yahoo! interface specifically for their search engine use. But Google is the industry leader in more ways than one. From my perception, Google is the one who updates its technologies, algorithms, standards, and criteria, and Bing observes and adjusts based on what Google just did. A prime example is Webmaster Tools. Both engines have it—wanna guess who had it first?

Search Engine Bot Barriers and Other No-Nos

Here's a list of crawler barriers to your WordPress.com blog (or any site)—the features that bots will stumble over. It's important to note that some of these are not in and of themselves bad things, and often there will be other positive reasons to have these features on your site. However, spiders cannot do much with them, and so you have to either replace these with search-engine-friendlier approaches, or else focus your SEO on other aspects of your blog.

- **Flash (.swf) files:** Since the mid 1990s, Flash has been king of the hill for vector animation, video editing, and reduced file sizes. You may remember those mandatory Flash-animated intros to websites that you didn't care about and couldn't click out of. It became a cliché of the era. But Flash itself survived the fall of the dot-bombs (for different uses). In the 2000s it became a staple for editing video files. These days, Apple has barred Flash from correctly serving its mobile products and its web browser, Safari. The new standard has become HTML5 animation files. But this is not retrofitted; HTML5 files will not work with older browsers, particularly Internet Explorer, whereas Flash will.

- **Images, audio or video:** We discuss this throughout this book (especially in Chapter 8 on social media). If optimized with alt tags in-site and planted on channels like YouTube, and integrated with SEO descriptions and filenames, these can achieve better SEO effects than plain body copy on a web page. Videos can be hosted on YouTube, given optimized descriptions and even text-based scripts.

- **Graphic text:** There is text you can build into a graphic file, and then there is your standard blog and website page text. You can identify the latter because you can select the text characters on the site with your cursor. You also can view the source code and see the text coded in the HTML.

- **RSS-fed content:** This is not a bad thing. If you're going to pipe someone else's blog onto your site, you don't want to be penalized for duplicate content. RSS clearly communicates to search engines that this is not original, unique content and therefore should not be crawled on this site.

- **Special file types (presentations, pdfs, and so on):** Certain file types, such as PDFs and MS Word files, are indexed by the search engines, but they require special attention for optimization.

- **Duplicate content:** Just don't "dupe" it.

- **Deep page content difficult to access:** This is where site architecture becomes so important. If your page structure is messy and poor, disorganized, and extremely vertical and deep in links, it's a problem. The search engine bots can't crawl too many links deep.

- **Subdomains:** And as we discuss in this chapter, this is a problem for WordPress.com sites. A subdomain is like a URL extension, so to speak—it's that extra "dot" added in your URL, such as http://yourblog.wordpress.com. Straight URLs, subfolders, and pages are better for search engines.

- **Redirects:** So many people think they can buy a number of domain names and direct them all to the same URL. Sometimes that's necessary, but the search engines don't like a lot of these.

- **Bad, dead links:** If your web visitors are hitting your 404 page (error for "page not found"), it's a bad thing, and the search engines take note.

- **Too many links listed:** In the days of Web 1.0 there were many niche advertising directories. In part, these existed to help supply an Internet of poor search engines with relevant listings. But these days, too many links on a page dilutes the page quality in the eyes of the search engines. Which links should the crawlers follow? The fewer the better, in the search engines' eyes. Again, such listings may be necessary for other purposes. If so, realize that the page won't be great for SEO.

- **Long page-load times:** Multiple factors can contribute to long page-load times: too much page content or copy, too many visitors for the size of the server, too many large media files, and so on. Crawlers don't like long page-load times. Nor do web visitors. And so it becomes a vicious cycle.

- **Irrelevant content or links:** Google likes relevancy. And it doesn't like black-hat SEOs who try to trick search engines by creating landing pages or link lists for myriad other clients. Relevant copy, relevant directories, and association pages—these are the ways to grow positive search results.

- **Keyword oversaturation:** Fifteen years ago people would stuff their sites with meta tags of all the keywords they could think of. Seven years ago, SEOs would stuff the page with their repeated keywords. Google likes natural copy flow. A good general rule is to include your full primary keyword phrase in your headline and two or three times within your blog post or page copy. Overdo it and Google will penalize you. Likewise, you will be penalized for using the same keyword phrase repeatedly across your website. So cool it with the keywords.

Tip

Simple Search Engine Test for Results

It's not enough to search for your keywords in a search engine to see if you come up in results. You have to neutralize your results by dumping your browser cookies and history. The various search engines do this differently, but, for example, Firefox allows you to go to the top menu option for **History** and select **Show All History**—at which point you can select all and delete them, as seen in Figure 4.7.

Figure 4.7   Firefox browser history.

In Google Chrome, you select the top menu option for **History,** select **Show Full History,** and select **Settings** (see Figure 4.8). Then select **History** from the top left, and from the page select the button to **Clear Browsing History** and then **Clear Browsing Data;** then I scroll down to the bottom and select **Reset Browser Settings** (shown in Figure 4.9) to top it all off.

Figure 4.8   Google Chrome history.

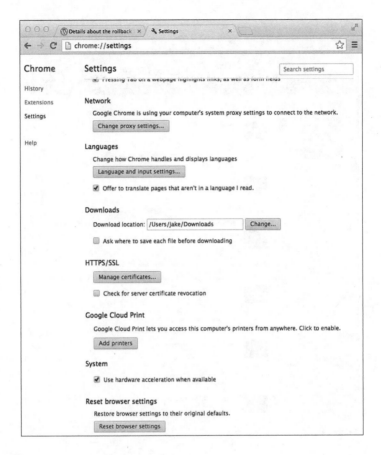

Figure 4.9   Google Chrome Clear Browsing history.

Multiblog Management

One of the things both WordPress.com and customized WordPress.org accounts do well is structure your multiple WordPress accounts. You may have created and/ or managed 25 WordPress sites. You can log in to one of them and the WordPress dashboard can show you the entire list of your blogs and make them immediately available for easy access and editing (see Figure 4.10). So go ahead—start those 30 blogs you've always wanted!

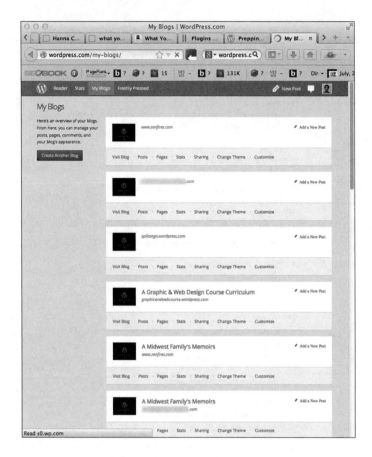

Figure 4.10   A user's multiple accounts listed for management.

 Caution

See Your WordPress Blog as Your Viewers Will See It

You may not realize, but if you're logged in to your WordPress account, even if you're seeing the web-facing design of your blog (in contrast to your backend dashboard), you're not necessarily seeing what your web visitors are seeing. And if you haven't logged out of WordPress after your previous session, you may be automatically logged in. How to tell? If you're still seeing that black admin bar at the top of your blog within your browser (see Figure 4.11), you are logged in and seeing things that only you may see. For example, if you have scheduled posts or drafts that are not yet "live" for visitors, you may see these on your logged-in preview of your blog. Ads won't appear on your preview, whereas visitors may see several. The point here is to always log out of WordPress.com overall to preview your blog as your viewers would see it.

The more often you are logged in to your WordPress account, you may notice that when you access others' blogs you still have your admin bar on top. This is because the site you are looking at is WordPress; it's seeing your WordPress Open ID credentials and is enabling you to readily add comments to the posts there if you so choose.

Figure 4.11   The WordPress admin bar.

WordPress Analytics

Although the default analytics that are built in to your free WordPress.com blog are decent, and based on Google Analytics itself, there are still great differences and limitations. At the time of writing, however, Google itself has been changing things that impact its own analytics in big ways. In the past, Google Analytics did a great job of revealing the counts of specific keywords users searched on to arrive at your website. Now this data is irrelevant for either Google Analytics for your custom site, or for your WordPress.com default analytics. It is still invaluable, however, to do keyword research to see what primary keywords people are searching for, as we showed in Chapter 3. So do your due diligence: Do your upfront keyword research and integrate the best keyword phrases into your writing on your WordPress.com blog. (We go in-depth on analytics in Chapter 7.)

Note

Blog Protection from Spam

As another example of what WordPress.com does to make things easier, Akismet is, in this writer's opinion, a critical integration for WordPress blogs that WordPress.com bloggers don't even need to understand because it's already built in.

WordPress.com Content Approaches

We discussed content strategy heavily in Chapter 3, but one of the realizations in this case is that if you are doing a WordPress.com blog, it is for the purposes of blogging heavily. WordPress.com is not a common option for general company websites. Theoretically, you could use it as such and even architect your WordPress.com blog site by burying the blog and integrating corporate "brochure ware" content, pages, and submenu listings (depending on the theme you choose and how you set it up). But with the common, blogging role of WordPress.com and with the minimized control over technological SEO functionality, content truly is king. And as most regular bloggers would agree, one of the challenges of blogging is coming up with fresh, relevant, constant items to blog about. As we've discussed, WordPress.com defaults help by serving automated suggestions (while you're logged in and in backend content-editing mode within your WordPress.com blog; see more on this in Chapters 5 and 6) for tags, images to use, links, and so on.

 Note

Top WordPress.com Blog Examples and Resources

The WordPress DailyPost is at http://dailypost.wordpress.com/ and has 3 million followers.

For top visitor numbers and topics, you can see the Blogs of the Day WordPress.com posts at http://botd.wordpress.com/top-posts/.

You can also visit the WordPress support communities, such as http://en.forums.wordpress.com

http://en.support.wordpress.com

http://learn.wordpress.com

and the many resources at www.wordpress.org.

Big-Picture Progression of SEO Goals and Achievements

We've discussed the technical implementations of SEO in WordPress.com and the importance of blogging. But more opportunities for good SEO extend beyond, and can utilize, your basic WordPress.com blog SEO.

Here is what I deem a high-level progression of SEO for business websites and blogs:

- Start by working with long-tail keyword phrases for industry niche optimization.
- Optimize location-based directories and channels, if applicable. (For more on this, see Chapter 9.)
- Conduct full technical SEO of your website or blog. (Note that this is limited with WordPress.com for reasons discussed throughout this and future chapters.)
- Achieve a place on the SERP for your website or blog for long-tail keywords searched.
- Optimize social media channels and post (social media can really help SEO; for more on this, see Chapter 8).
- Build backlinks through requests, guest blogging, social shares, requesting customer reviews, and the like.
- Blog and increase digital content.
- Work toward, monitor, and achieve ongoing growing web traffic to your site or blog.
- Achieve several places on the same SERP for previous long-tail keyword searches. (Note that PPC can also help in this strategy; see Chapter 10 on advertising for more on this.)
- Continuing all previously mentioned items, progress toward more/different keywords results, including shorter tail keywords.
- Assess past strategy, tactics, and results. Perhaps research keywords again to set goals for even more, and shorter-tail, keyword phrase search results.

That is a list of fairly standard SEO activities—one I advise my clients with all the time. The only real limitation for a WordPress.com blog in SEO is full technical executed optimization (although that is a big one). This leads us to what's next—such as social media, which is just as important for customized WordPress sites.

We've already discussed in previous chapters the value of inbound links and how you can achieve these by activities such as guest blogging, asking your vendors to link to your site, requesting customer reviews, and so on. Social media is also a great source for inbound links as well as for claiming additional places on the SERP.

Give Me More

As we've discussed, SEO can't be the only focus for your site. What's more, other focuses and approaches can aid your SEO. Focused on good web usability? A more usable site acquires more return visitors and visitors who spend more time interested in your site content without merely "bouncing" back to the search engine. These elements are calculated by Google and factored positively into your blog's rankings. Good writing can also achieve more return site visits as well as shares. Good writers naturally write with "link bait"; the hook that incentivizes readers to keep reading and socially share your content. They may capture the link to your site and blog about it, or share it on their own social media pages and discussions. This, in turn, achieves more inbound links and new visitors for your blog—both of which yield greater results with your search engines.

Along this same thinking, social media use can be an instrumental element for your WordPress.com blog and SEO. You can use Chapter 8 to help you build your optimal social media plan to integrate with your blogging, but that can work just as well for WordPress.com as with your customized site. So many of the important social functionality widgets for social media integrations are available in WordPress.com. Because so much of social media benefit for SEO can occur off of your site anyway, you want to know the options, capabilities, tools, and results.

5

Real-World Blogging

Chapter objectives and questions:

- Blog post architecture
- Blogging why and how
- Pages versus posts for SEO
- The role of social media
- Planning to blog
- Vertical search and authorship

This chapter helps the transition between the WordPress beginner and the SEO intermediate. This chapter is also about coming up with content themes and practicing keyword-driven blogging, as well as the WordPress technologies that you should be aware of and that can aid you in the process. This chapter is beneficial for the WordPress.com blogger as well as a blogger or SEO on a sophisticated, custom WordPress platform site. Although the strategies and some of the technical defaults discussed in this chapter apply to WordPress.com free blogs, the SEO plug-ins discussed here apply to custom WordPress platform sites.

More on Blog and Page Architecture

In Chapter 4, "WordPress On-Page Architecture and Basic SEO Execution," we listed design and architectural considerations in choosing a theme for your WordPress.com blog. Although a customized WordPress.org-based theme site has many more options, you can still use the same principles to reduce your upfront work. In other words, if you don't want to reinvent the wheel, if you want a theme closer out-of-the-box to your final launched look and feel, use those same principles to drive your theme selection (we discussed considerations for choosing your WordPress.com theme in Chapter 4—those same points are also instrumental for WordPress.org-driven customizable themes).

Structuring Blog Post URLs

Ever lay awake at night wondering what permalinks are? Permalinks are the post-level URLs prescribed for your blog—in other words, how WordPress presents deep-down posts as individual URLs or links. For starters, don't use default permalinks; you always want to specify, even if just to choose another out-of-the-box option of WordPress's permalinks structures for your blog. You can access these (depending on the theme or setup) after you log in your WordPress dashboard; select the **Settings** option in the left menu, and from there, select **Permalinks.** For example the data format works well because it is logical, short, and crawlers are not confused by it. The following examples indicate permalinks.

- www.example.com/blog/2010/10-12/post-event-update
- www.example.com/archive/2010/10-12/post-event-update
- www.example.com/category/events/post-event-update
- www.example.com/tags/after-parties/post-event-update

One of the great things about WordPress is that it offers so many ways for users to search within the site for specific content—particularly blog posts. One of the problems, however, is that such approaches enable WordPress to serve content via various URLs—for example, with categories of blog posts (and even tags, as shown next). For each example of multiple URLs for the same page content, search engines can easily get confused, interpret duplicate content, and even penalize your site. The examples above show some potential different URLs which WordPress could assign to the same old blog post.

And if you want even more control over your permalinks, you're in luck. The same comprehensive SEO plug-ins we've discussed in this book, such as SEO Ultimate and Yoast WordPress SEO, have additional permalink options (shown in Figures 5.1 and 5.2).

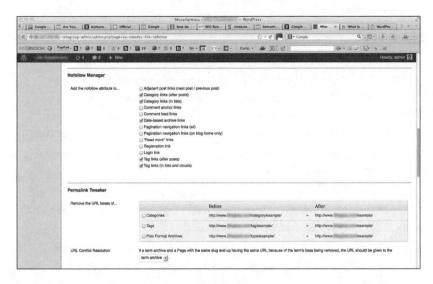

Figure 5.1   SEO Ultimate Plug-in's Permalink Tweaker.

Some SEOs claim that Google will examine the different URLs, assign rank to the non-archived post URL, and do so without penalizing the content. However, I don't like to take the chance nor make Google do so much work. Fortunately, the best WordPress SEO plug-ins make it easy to canonicalize, or structure blog post identifications based on these content issues. And the Yoast WordPress SEO plug-in (as discussed in Chapter 2, "The Search Engines, WordPress, and SEO Tools") has good options to enable you to assign "noIndex" commands to the second through last URL examples listed earlier.

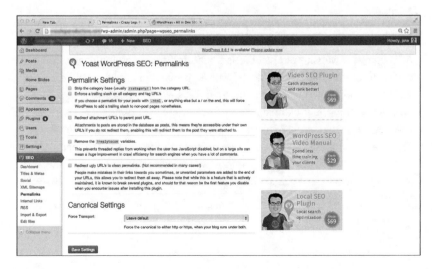

Figure 5.2   Yoast WordPress SEO plug-in canonicalization and permalinks.

Note

Permalinks and noIndex

Still confused about permalinks or the noIndex command? For more on how to architect and choose categories, tags, and archives, as well as how and where to display onsite, and how to set up Yoast "noIndex" options to tell search engines not to crawl archives, see these blog posts and articles:

- How to set up WordPress for SEO success: http://moz.com/blog/setup-wordpress-for-seo-success
- What should and shouldn't you tell search engines to "noIndex" with Yoast: http://wp.tutsplus.com/tutorials/plugins/the-beginners-guide-to-wordpress-seo-by-yoast-configuration/
- Specifying SEO settings in Yoast for archived blog folders to not confuse search engines: https://managewp.com/wordpress-categories-tags-seo
- Why permalinks are important, and the role of SEO: http://digwp.com/2010/07/optimizing-wordpress-permalinks/
- Setting up permalinks: https://managewp.com/wordpress-permalinks-guide and http://codex.wordpress.org/Using_Permalinks

---

Blog posts can be great content elements for SEO, but the added category, tags, and other options means there is more to them than optimizing pages.

 Tip

Architecting Top Menu with Categories

Although your website top nav bar is structured for accessing pages, you can restructure specific blog posts, with a designated category, to be an entire section from your top menu. Why? Take, for example, your blog. A blog is one thing, but company news is traditionally a different matter. So if you have quick company news to post, you could blog about it but assign it to the **News** category, and structure a separate link on the top menu to be News. There it is—an easy-admin news section for your site quickly accessible by all viewers and separate from your blog.

Why Blog?

A great reason to blog is to project yourself as an industry leader, especially if you aren't currently recognized as such. Another reason is because blogging greatly aids social media. A big impact of a WordPress blog's power is that of organic content and organic growth. Unlike paid advertising, content naturally attracts—pulls—web visitors like bees to honey. In other words, the more you blog, and capitalize on WordPress social technologies and connectivity, the better you come up in search results and the more web traffic you achieve. A friend of mine in SEO says the only true vehicle of effective, regular, SEO "maintenance" for small business sites is blogging (with keywords). Organic growth, plain and simple.

The How: Planning to Blog

Blogging is a big undertaking, which is why we discuss alternatives in the chapter, such as guest blogging and RSS feeds of others' blogs. If you want a blog, you have to identify what and who is needed to make the blog happen and be done right:

- **Resources:** Someone's got to do this thing. Who's going to post the social content for your company? Someone internal may know the organization, brand, and messaging better than anyone on the outside. At the same time, someone on the outside may know the media channels better than anyone at your company. Many organizations decide to hire young interns or college grads to do this work, but in that case they are neither an expert in the company content nor in strategic marketing in social media. Keep all this in mind and decide carefully.

- **Time:** It takes time. Who has it? Plan it out in a calendar. Don't blog five times a day this month and then skip it. Blogs are much more informal than magazines and newspapers, but there's still something to be said for consistency of schedule. You should have a well-structured network and schedule of posts between your blog and social media channels and their content. They need to be regular, and the blog is the hub that drives the spokes. So do the job to do it right.

- **Tie-ins with other marketing:** Just as the timing and regularity of fresh content are instrumental between the blog and social posts, the roles of other marketing channels should be considered as well. Do you post similar content or themes to your email newsletter for instance? Do they need to reference each other? Do you blog about your latest press releases or ad campaigns? More specifically, in the world of search, if you have a strategy to either mirror or mix up your keywords across both organic and PPC, this may affect your blog post keywords.

Tip

Keywords, Goals, and CTAs

Throughout this book we discuss the importance of the call-to-action (CTA). We emphasize it heavily in Chapter 8, "Social Media Connectivity." It still has great bearing on blog posts. To really get great SEO benefit, use your blog post's keyword in a CTA link to another post on your site, such as the following:

> *Some say honey from <u>clover is better than from other flowers—read</u> and decide for yourself!*

As you do this, you should have both blog posts use the keyword as the same tag. The keyword becomes the goal you are trying to capture with SEO, and the link is another boost to the search engine value and another means of traffic. But the CTA can also exist in your blog in other media, such as graphic text in a video or audio in your podcast. These aren't as search-engine friendly, but they do represent content served to the web visitor who valued that keyword and content topic in the first place.

- **Content:** Here's the big one: How soon will you run out of things to blog about? One writer recommends structuring full "blog outlines" in advance; even before outlining your posts, outline what your categories and posts will be. So after you've done keyword research and identified what your major keywords and phrases will be, write and sort these into potential blog categories (you can do the same for tags). Then suppose you want to identify 20 posts per category; you can start by writing headlines for each. You can always make changes later, but now you have a long-term SEO strategy for your blog topics and posts (for more on this see http://buildingabrandonline.com/10-out-of-the-box-wordpress-seo-tips-to-dominate-the-front-page-of-google-in-2012/). Then, as the time arrives, you can outline your post content, attach your tags, links, and photos (per the SEO page form discussed in Chapter 3, "A Strategic SEO Upfront Content Approach"). Or perhaps you have a wealth of relevant videos or photos at your disposal. Again, outlining and separating these for posts in advance, while identifying the tags that go with them, can all help expedite writing from the "big unknown" and mitigate the fears of writer's block.

Between those challenges, nail it all down in a schedule for the never-ending world of fun, fun blogging!

Note

Blogging Calendar

The challenges to blogging discussed previously mirror the challenges of social media posting. In fact, your blog should be addressed within your social media plan and calendar. Keep reading to learn how to integrate it all and tackle the issues in Chapter 8, but here's a taste of how to plan:

	Mktg prede-cessors?	Hours (daily/ weekly/ monthly)	Date spread	Short-term objectives	Key metrics & tools analytics	Time/ resource allocation	$ budget	Keywords/ CTA	Segment details
Blog									

When and How Often?

You want to blog with fresh, ongoing, regular content. Some say to blog two to three times daily. That would be ideal, but more importantly, you need to consider all the variables and plan for your blog:

- Your industry thought leaders and bloggers—how frequently do they blog, and what are the length, topics, and quality of their posts?

- Are there industry readership expectations based on the above?

- Are there expectations, or a goal, to write and maintain *more* than one blog?

- What are your resources, budget, and quality of writing comparatively?

- Can you write an adequate amount of quality content without concern for giving away trade secrets, which is a common corporate concern for social media?

- Are additional resources necessary and available, such as a graphic designer or photographer?

- Is there potential and good reason for additional media, such as a video blog or podcasting?

A few high-quality, in-depth blog posts are going to have much more impact than a constant barrage of meaningless content (even though more industry-relevant content is better for SEO). Perhaps more important, the fewer, higher-quality posts attract more followers and shares. Depending on the content topics, you would presumably get fewer opt-outs from blog email followers if you focused on the fewer high-quality posts in contrast to the constant barrage of less-poignant blog posts. In social-channel walls, such as on Facebook, Twitter, and LinkedIn, it is more expected to post unceasingly than with your blog. This is especially true with business-to-business (B2B) than with consumer retail. Quality over quantity is a good mantra. Realize that good SEO has minimum requirements for effective blog post length (and good SEO tools will tell you if you're short of these points; such as guidelines of 500 to 1000 words per page or blog post).

Shared Content Strategies

Directories and listings were very popular in the 1990s and have grown and morphed since then. Inherited from Web 1.0 are Yahoo's legacy directories (such as Local, News, and so on). They are still large; they haven't died like mySpace did. As sites become more versatile in functionality, it raises the question: Will social media eventually supplant these in the ongoing evolution and replacements of social channels such as Friendster, Plaxo, and MySpace? Or do more inclusions of reviews and ratings sustain the directories, as with Yahoo Local, Yelp, Manta, and the like? That which has died away from the Web 1.0 world has been the black-hat directories—channels of metatags for the sole purpose of capturing web traffic to serve ads and impressions for revenue.

Similarly, many people attempt to copy and paste articles or blog posts into their own blogs or websites. Even if giving author attribution, this should not be done. Duplicated content confuses the search engines and generates penalties, although many now say that the spiders are sophisticated enough to discern the originating site and content author versus the attempt to copy. Duplication should not be done, if for no other reason than to prevent yourself from incurring an SEO penalty. The right way to share content like this is either to trade blog posts with another (a good thing for SEO) or set up RSS feeds (which the search engines recognize as nonduplicate content). Similarly, the search engines also know the difference between one-way links (great for SEO) versus reciprocal links (two-way, very little rank value).

Likewise, content-spinning for article posting used to be a popular trick in SEO. You could write a blog post, then change words here and there and re-spin the content to post in free, general online article sites. Today, search engines credit these sites little value, because they're general, with few barriers to posting, and because the habit has been more an SEO trick and less a consumer-writing practice. Hopefully by now you're seeing the long-term trend regarding search engines and SEOs versus consumers and bloggers. Pure, industry-expert, original, strategic content—good. Automated, blasted, re-spun, generically posted SEO content—bad. So are you a good witch or a bad witch? Here's a gimmick to keep in mind when concerned about black-hat SEO or search engine penalties:

Suppose you're at a conference. There are Google representatives there. You walk up to one and she asks you about your web content. What would you want to tell her? That you re-spin articles and trade links between sites that are irrelevant to each other? That you doctor footer links to boost SEO that no reader would ever want to click? If you get this tingly feeling, such as "maybe I don't want to tell Google I'm doing this," then maybe you shouldn't do it. Let your conscience be your guide. We all need our SEO Jiminy Crickets.

As an SEO, you yourself must also be wary of the clients you serve because they can give you a black-hat label for yourself. An easy example of this is porn, or sites promising huge rewards just for taking a survey or revealing your personal information, such as bank accounts.

Opportunities to Occupy More of the SERP with Social Media

Why not dominate the SERP for a primary keyword phrase? It's a good goal. On the one hand, the larger your website and blog, with more content and media utilizing similar keywords, the more opportunities exist for spots on the SERP. But you can also spread your content "wealth investments" so to speak by building up your social media pages and off-site writing or guest-blogging opportunities with same keywords. Although these additional channel options appearing in the SERP have the potential to drive traffic away from your focal website lead-generation page, they *can* help brand your name with the specific keyword phrases to beat the competition that way. And as we discuss throughout this book, your social pages also eventually drive traffic to your goal web pages, such as opt-in forms.

Blog Post/Content Recommendations

So, time to write another blog post. You have a topic, you have a little writing; what about images, additional sources, and more content to finish the post? Luckily, WordPress has plug-ins for that. You may have noticed in the WordPress.com defaults that your basic, free blog includes backend recommendations for web-based images, links, AutoTags, and post tags—the works!

These can all be good content references (so long as you don't infringe on copyrights, such as with images). You also have options within your WordPress site dashboard to select **Tools** to access the **Press This** tool (shown in Figure 5.3), which also gives you these content recommendations. When you build a WordPress website from the ground up on your own domain, these options are not live by default. Luckily, the Jetpack by WordPress.com plug-in is available to give you some of those old resources you miss so much from WordPress.com (see Figure 5.4).

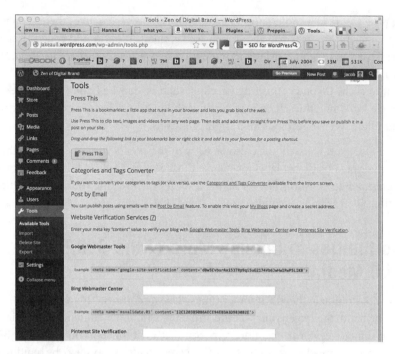

Figure 5.3   Press This tools.

Figure 5.4   The Jetpack by WordPress.com plug-in.

Videos Por Favor!

Videos are a growing phenomenon online for several reasons:

- People don't have time to read anymore.
- Internet bandwidth is getting larger and faster.
- Web development capabilities (such as with WordPress) are getting better and cheaper.
- Videos give sites dynamism and grab consumer attention.
- Videos come up in regular search engine results.
- YouTube is considered the second-largest search engine.

Videos are also growing in other channels' popularity such as Vine and Pinterest (yes, Pinterest accepts videos), and let's not forget Vimeo and Hulu. There are many plug-in options (for customized WordPress sites in contrast to WordPress.com blogs) to easily display videos on your WordPress website hosted from YouTube or Vimeo itself. WordPress websites I've worked on have successfully utilized the Advanced Responsive Video Embedder plug-in. And bloggers on the free WordPress.com can drop videos in their pages and posts via the Add Media option in their logged-in editing section.

But use these video plug-ins! You don't want to upload and host video on your own customized WordPress site. Here are some reasons why:

- You get more SEO benefits by hosting in YouTube (remember me suggesting the "double-the-coverage" theory you get from both Google and YouTube?).
- A big video uploaded to your site will slow consumer website download and display times.
- Many videos embedded on websites are saved with Flash technology to compress size. Flash technology does not display on mobile devices. Flash also creates issues with search engines!

This thinking works not just for one or two of your YouTube videos, but you can have a page displaying whole galleries of your YouTube videos with the YouTube Gallery plug-in. Or you can pipe in entire YouTube channels or playlists with the Sliding YouTube Gallery plug-in. But be sure to use the SEO plug-ins such as Yoast Sitemaps for YouTube to further help search engines acknowledge your content. Be careful when putting YouTube-hosted videos on your sites; you don't want to show YouTube advertising, and there is always the potential for viewers to click out of your site to YouTube.

Podcasting

Podcasts were definitely helpful on websites in the past for media and content variety. But in the mid-2000s, bandwidth wasn't as strong, fast, and prevalent as it is today. With the multiple effects of video, including YouTube hosting and SEO benefits, it dilutes the rationale for traditional podcasting. But if you have podcasts or believe they serve your audience, by all means use them! There are WordPress plug-ins to integrate this media. One of the SEO benefits of podcasts is having them available through iTunes.

Social Community Outreach

If you want more followers of your blog, you have to be involved in others' social communities. There are many interest groups with their passionate online digital communities—everything from pugs to sports fans to travel enthusiasts. Just as with real-life groups and organizations, the more you share others' interests and engage in their discussions, the more they want to engage in yours. In the digital world, this means the more likely they will be to follow your profile back to your own blog (without your trying a hard-sell approach; we discuss all this in Chapter 8). WordPress (although very broad in orientation) is such a community. Your WordPress profile Open ID automatically makes you available for connections to other WordPress users and profiles. When I am logged in to my WordPress accounts, I often notice when visiting other blogs, the black admin bar at the top of someone else's blog, allowing me to automatically leave comments as desired.

As we've discussed, WordPress makes other WordPress writers and content available to you through RSS feed widgets, blogs you follow, suggested content, tags, images, and more. And there is an affinity among WordPress bloggers—a bit of a club for those who are "in the know."

Pages Versus Posts for SEO

It's important to remember that there is a perception of web pages being more "permanent" and less "social" (as in social media) than blog posts are. Hence, blog posts are perfect candidates for web visitors' social sharing activities, and consequent backlinks, and social commenting and rating. All these, again, are great for SEO. You can easily ask your friends to comment on your latest blog post. Web pages don't work this way. I'm a big advocate of putting social share and social follow icons wherever feasible on a website (as discussed in Chapter 4). But blog post content is much more likely to be shared, or followed by RSS, than web page content. So know it and capitalize on it.

Now there is the perceived drawback of potential social bad talk; negative reviews—"talking smack" as some might say. However, that danger exists perpetually online. And if someone is going to talk bad about your company, they don't have much incentive to go to your blog and share your post on their social channels to do it. All they have to do is speak poorly about your company on their own social channels, which is why social reputation management is so important (see Chapter 8 on social media and Chapter 9, "Going Mobile and Local," on local SEO for more).

The same premise for optimizing web pages (as we've discussed throughout this book) works for driving new blog posts (while reducing or scaling down some process elements). Writing a quick blog post is one thing; completely optimizing it requires extra work. But the work is well worth it. Why go to the trouble of blogging if you can't realize the SEO benefits of your writing?

Here are steps to create SEO-ready blog posts:

1. Identify the topic areas you know about for blogging.

2. Ensure these topics are going to be consistent with your personal brand or current blog content; you don't want to promote a "split personality" for a number of reasons, including confusing search engines and causing penalties.

3. Take the list and conduct keyword research. If you've already done keyword research for your website or blog, you can also reference that previous research for your additional blog post keywords.

4. Identify the final keyword topics for your blog posts.

5. Fill out the SEO page forms; one for each post you desire.

6. Use the SEO page forms as outlines to drive your new content posts.

7. Write your content posts to fit the forms.

Blog posts do not generally achieve quite as high SEO as web pages. I attribute this to architecture. Remember our discussions on sitemapping in Chapters 3 and 4? Search engines like the pages closest to top level on the nav. And herein lies the nature of blogs:

- Blogs are structured for ease of user content posting.
- Blogs don't have the formality of web pages.
- Blogs are built on a structure of time-based linear architecture, in contrast to horizontal pages in a sitemap pyramid.
- Because of this, simplified user-based architecture options are included: categories, tags, and dated archives.

If well thought out, these blog organizational options can give readers great options for accessing additional content, more than traditional website navigation. Although category and tags folders cannot be used for sitemapping and crawlers (because of duplicate content issues, as we discuss throughout this chapter and the next), categories and tags themselves can still be great aids to SEO—aids that traditional web pages can't claim!

Keep in mind that blog posts, for usability, should have only one category per post. But they each can have many tags. Those tags, and even categories, should be driven by keywords. That doesn't mean use long-tail keyword phrases as tags, but use the root, shorter, more general head keywords as tags. For example, "film and television special effects and productions" should not be one tag. But one blog post on this topic could include the tags "television productions," "film special effects," "film productions," and so on. One way we can think about blog categories is as if they were the table of contents of a book. (For more on this see www.wpbeginner.com/beginners-guide/categories-vs-tags-seo-best-practices-which-one-is-better/).

Do you want to go back and optimize past blog posts? No problem—just as you can with web pages, with blog posts you can go back and edit the category or add tags to fit your keywords. With default relative links within WordPress, you should be able to change the blog post's URL without a problem as well. In other words, your WordPress blog, sitewide, should be recognizing links as shown:

.../blog/category/bees/honey

in contrast to the full URL:

http://www.example.com/blog/category/bees/honey

You can even set the date for whenever you want with WordPress blog posts. Are you posting a ton of posts this week and want to spread them out over the next year? You can—just use the WordPress publishing and editing options for your posts!

Blog posts can have a casual writing style that is quickly reviewable by the reader, making it easier to skim through such content than through traditional web pages, whitepapers, press releases, and navigation. On all counts, these sound like good things. But keep in mind that all these navigational and user-organizational attributes can cause search engine penalties (as discussed, along with solutions, throughout this chapter).

Keep in mind that since "content is king," search engines still love blog content—the more the better. Ideally, you blog frequently enough that it would be infeasible to include all this content in new web pages anyway. The search engines like content, not chaos. Ongoing blog posts have clean URLs and linear relativity, which is well organized in the long run for search engine optimization.

Pulling from the Kitchen Sink

When you're ready to blog, there are still some things you can do specifically after you're logged in on your post within WordPress. The Kitchen Sink is what WordPress calls its full-content editing bar for editing pages and blog posts. You'll notice that the bar above your text box has an option to click open to show another layer of the toolbar below the first (shown in Figures 5.5 and 5.6). You shouldn't need most of these (if you've built your CSS correctly), but it's nice to know they're there. Remember that SEO feeds off of the "H"s—H1, H2, H3, in that order. The H1 for most WordPress themes is what you specify as the page name (not the browser page title, although these could be the same). It's up to you to write in your own subhead, or H2 within the copy, and apply the H2 CSS style to it. Otherwise, <em> for emphasis is still better for SEO than plain body copy. I like to use <em> or an H4 for my call-to-action and anchor text.

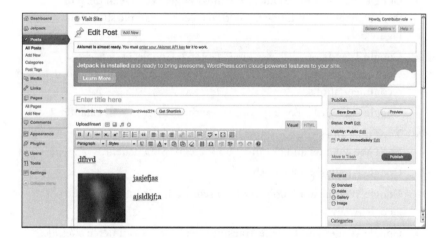

Figure 5.5 WordPress content editing.

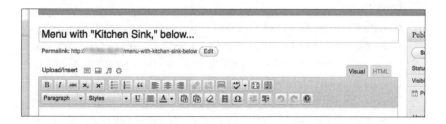

Figure 5.6 The WordPress Kitchen Sink.

Google Accounts List

The list of Google accounts that have merit and which you can sync for potential SEO benefit is endless! NOTE: At the time of this writing, Google promotes its channels such as Google+, Google Chrome, Google+ Hangout, and so on—and Google likes those who play along. Google is always coming up with new tools to experiment with; pay attention to this and play along. Google likes those who like it. Google has integrated its old photo-sharing site Picasa into Google+ pages (and consequent Google Images search results). It has transitioned Google Places into Google+Local. The content has not been lost.

Here's my list. There's probably even more you can add!

- **Gmail:** I always start by creating a new client generic Gmail.
- **Google+ profile:** Google+ requires a personal profile before creating a business page, but flesh out your personal profile and sync that with your WordPress blog post author profile for SEO benefits of author information (as we discuss in this chapter).
- **Google Places/Google+Local Business Page:** We dive in deep on this in Chapter 9 on mobile and local (see the example shown in Figure 5.7).
- **Google Trends:** As discussed in Chapter 2, Google Trends provides great research regarding web searcher locations and keyword recommendations.
- **Google AdWords:** For keyword research, as discussed in Chapter 2.
- **YouTube:** Does your business have a couple of videos? Create a YouTube channel and put them up there for SEO benefit.
- **Google Analytics:** Obviously!
- **Google Webmaster Tools:** As we discussed in Chapter 2 to sync with Google Analytics.
- **Google Wallet and Google Marketplace:** Some eCommerce sites like to utilize these tools again to use "all things Google."
- **Google Alerts:** Use this to monitor social reputations—yours or your competitors'.
- **Google Chrome, Google Drive and Docs, Google Voice, Google Calendar, and the like:** All of these are good technologies that you can make use of, but I wouldn't expect them to aid your search at all.
- **Google Blogger:** Hah! I threw that one in as a trick. You should know by now the platform to use is WordPress! Integrate all your other Google properties and it certainly won't hurt you if you're not in Google Blogger.

Final note: If you want to do the same things with Bing, that's a good idea, too. Just follow the Google list and apply it to all things Bing.

Figure 5.7 A Google+ Business Page integrated with location, what used to be GooglePlaces, and GoogleMaps.

About Vertical Search

In business we often talk about horizontal versus vertical marketing or business models. If you are a vehicle graphics printer serving anyone and everyone, you have horizontal services. If you provide marketing services to dentists, that is your "vertical," or your "niche." These approaches also exist in SEO. On a basic level, the term "vertical search results" represents organic results on the SERP that show more data than the regular search results. One example is images appearing in the SERP among text-based listings (such as the Bing example shown in Figure 5.8). Other examples include "Author information," where the author photo appears within the SERP results for that blog or site. This is another aspect where WordPress rises to the top. WordPress immediately assigns content to a specific "Author" based on user ID. The fuller that ID or profile is filled out and tied to Google+, Gravatar, WordPress user profile, and so on, Google can identify the website content author. This author display info is shown as part of "Vertical Search" organic results within the SERP (see Figure 5.9). It visually pops out compared to other listings and attracts web visitors. This is important to be considered in context of strategy. For an "anonymous" company without a blog or a public persona, such as a bank or grocery store, a specific person's profile may appear odd if the marketing contributor often changes or doesn't have a visible role with the company. However, if the company is the persona, such as a doctor's office or hair stylist, such identification can be invaluable—that much more so with the boost of vertical search results.

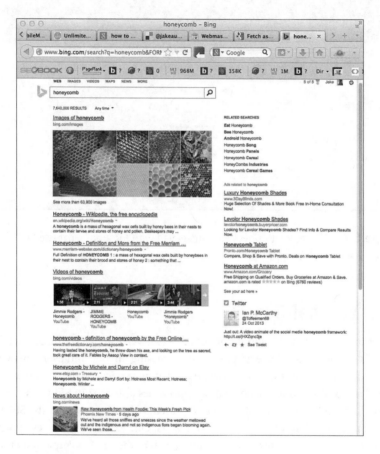

Figure 5.8   Bing rich search results images.

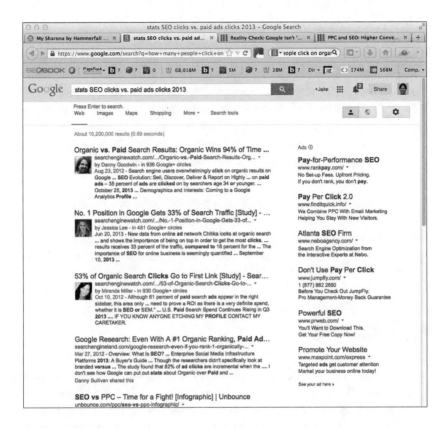

Figure 5.9   SERP author information.

 Note

Author Profiles Are Not Company Profiles

We've discussed the power of an author profile in the SERP as rich content, and how that is tied to an individual and his identity and photo. At this point you may be tempted to think, "Why not use a company logo and write the identity around the company instead of an individual—and beat the system?" One of the ongoing trends of the social media and digital movement overall has been to establish transparency and individual experts and content authors. More and more social channels, from Facebook to Google+, will not allow you to create an individual account if the name "looks fishy." If it reads like a company name, it won't be accepted. These channels also want to utilize image recognition to "find your face" among various social photos. You can choose to avoid Google+ if you want to try, but given the synced nature of Google accounts, I don't recommend it—you need Google on your side. These trends have gone more in-depth over time, and I expect the requirements and technology to continue to get more finite. So what's the tip? Don't try to trick the digital space; even if you were able to beat the system, it would look fishy to your audience. Social and web media are all about authenticity. So make the choice: either be the face of your company, set up someone else as the digital communications face, or neither.

You can read more on Google's author information in search results here: https://support.google.com/webmasters/answer/1408986. Note, however, that author information is not the only kind of vertical search results. Location-based data and reviews are also vertical data for search; read more about these in Chapter 9 on mobile.

Blog, Blog, Blog

To summarize, don't just blog, blog, blog, without strategy and SEO. Yes, make it fun, but when you run out of juice, keyword searches can give you more things to write about. If you're going to blog, you might as well do just a little extra work and optimize it! Blogs are great content in an era when content is king. Likewise, remember that your blog schedule and content affects your social media and other marketing tactics as well.

All the options for a blog can make it confusing. Categories, tags, archives—know what they do and how they can harm or benefit your SEO. Blog posts are different from web pages and require a bit more knowledge to handle.

Finally, a good and a slightly geeky way to end this chapter:

Plan it, Write it, Blog it, Share it. There should be some techno music playing in the background for you to recite this new mantra.

6

Hands-On SEO Execution (Website and Blog Builds Versus Post-Integration)

Chapter objectives and questions:

- Comprehensive SEO checklists and no-nos
- Before choosing and installing plug-ins
- Google and Bing login data
- All-in-One SEO Plug-in for WordPress
- Yoast WordPress SEO Plug-in
- SEO Ultimate Plug-in for WordPress
- The Final Plug on SEO Plug-Ins

You already know about architecting your WordPress site and writing content. This chapter gets into the best SEO plug-ins to implement for customized WordPress websites. This is the heart of the matter—how to execute with SEO! I discuss the features, steps of execution, and the meaning of life. You really don't want to skip this chapter—it's what this book is all about.

I used to say that the best time to optimize a website is as it's being built. But the truth is, with WordPress it's easy either way. The advantage of SEO-inclusion during build is to drive SEO-strategic architecture and URLs. If you're working with an existing site, however, you're not starting from ground zero. You can analyze existing text, images, and video, and tailor keywords to this. I have scanned in old newspaper articles and brochures to convert to text with OCR for clients without existing website content. It can be quite a hunt and extra work.

SEO Checklist for Full Sites

In a previous chapter I offered a checklist of good, basic SEO implementations that can be done even to a free WordPress.com blog. Next I offer a fuller check-off list for fully built WordPress sites and blogs with customization. This list combines the one we previously discussed with the more advanced SEO implementations (***shown in bold with an asterisk).** Don't quite follow it all? No worries—you have the rest of this chapter and the book to learn, and don't forget about the glossary at the back of the book.

- Google accounts setup for syncing
  - Google+ account setup/synced
  - Google Maps integration on contact page
- Page text
  - Identify major keywords and populate on page and heads
  - ***Meta descriptions**
- Images optimized
  - Image filenames, descriptions
  - Images placed on Google+ page
  - ***Alt tags**
- YouTube
- ***Google Maps integration on-page with plug-in**
- Blog SEO setups
  - Tags and Categories
  - Auto tags
  - Set Permalinks
  - Set Akismet
  - Set Author Information
- ***Migrate site from test, check all pages and links**
  - ***.com preferred over .net**
  - ***Primary pages and subfolders preferred over subdomains**
- Create search engine accounts and submit site to search engines

- Setup analytics
  - ***Google Analytics**
  - Google Webmaster tools integration
  - Google+ account setup/synced
  - Bing Webmaster tools integration
  - Yahoo! Webmaster tools integration
- ***Technology and coding implementations**
  - ***noFollows/noIndex**
  - ***Redirects (301s or 302s are best)**
  - ***sitemap.xml (file generated and submitted)**
  - ***robots.txt**
  - ***.htaccess**
- Ask someone (third party) to submit the site to social search and book-marking sites
  - Delicious
  - Reddit
  - StumbleUpon
  - Digg
  - Technoratti
- Check and capture SERP results
- Set up location-based directories if relevant

Make Your Site Speedy!

When we focus on SEO technology factors within the code and page content, it is easy to forget about a broader issue like site speed. The speed at which your site can be viewed depends on a few factors, such as the file size of your content (are your images too large?), the size of your hosting server and plan (is that basic GoDaddy plan large enough?), and the broadband capacity of your website visitor. That last one you can't do much about, but you can be prepared for such problems by taking care of the first two. By the way, site speed isn't important only for the viewer, it matters to Google as well. And we want to make Google happy, right? (Say yes.) Luckily, there are WordPress plug-ins that will help prep your site for streamlined delivery. One of them is W3 Total Cache. W3 Total Cache takes your largest, dynamic, slowest pages and delivers them (via cache) quickly to site visitors, making them and Google both happy. What a deal, huh? (To read more about W3 Total Cache and other plug-in reviews, see: http://torquemag.io/less-is-more-3-wordpress-plugins-for-seo/).

Before Installs

When I implement search engine and social media tools and WordPress plug-ins for clients, I start by creating generic Gmail and/or Yahoo! email accounts for clients, using a consistent client company email and profile and password for access to all. I want to be able to hand everything over to the client when I'm finished, and I want it to be easy for them to manage. Today Google allows multiple parties to be admin of Google Analytics, but in the past only one admin was allowed. I can't tell you how many clients have had old websites revealing Google Analytics in the code, only to indicate they couldn't access it because they didn't have the info. Or their previous agency had access but couldn't give the client admin access because the login was completely tied to all the other agency's accounts.

 Note

Choosing the Right WordPress Plug-ins

Note that this chapter covers a lot of WordPress-specific plug-ins. This is not my endorsement of these plug-ins (some of these I've used and some I haven't). As in all cases, use your own judgment to pick the right plug-in for your needs. Don't forget to refer back to Chapter 2, "The Search Engines, WordPress, and SEO Tools," to the list of items to help drive your decision to choose specific plug-ins prior to install or Appendix A, "WordPress Plugins," for a list of all plugins discussed in this book.

Keep in mind that many WordPress themes will have existing SEO options. For example, Elegant Themes often have numerous in-depth SEO fields. And elsewhere in this book I talk about WordPress total package themes with advertising and SEO options (in Chapter 11, "Bringing It All Together—Testing, SEO, PPC, Social and Mobile, and Analytics"). Go with what you trust—namely, the best SEO plug-ins (which we discuss in full in this chapter). You should be sure to disable all theme inherent SEO options in order to use the plug-ins instead.

Expanded List of Search Engine Bot Barriers and Other No-Nos

I'm sure you remember from Chapter 4, "WordPress On-Page Architecture and Basic SEO Execution," a great list of problem areas for search engines. Now that you have those memorized, here are additional areas of concern **(in bold)**. Enjoy!

- **Code within JSS/JavaScript/AJAX.**

- **Frames:** Modern iFrames are better than traditional website Web 1.0 frames, but even text within iFrames can be search engine crawler barriers.

- **Domain cloaking and masking:** Serving different web content to web visitors versus search engines, and serving the same website through different URLs.

- **Canonicalization issues:** Where the search engines see both http://example.com and www.example.com as two different sites.

- **Forms and content behind forms.**

- **Dynamic URLs:** Sites with moving databases with URLs, such as www.example.com/p=$49T%%x?21.

- **Too many 404s:** And/or old removed content pages without 301 search engine redirects.

- **Don't do single-pixel links:** Seen as an attempt to manipulate search engines.

- **Bad CMSs and/or hosting technologies.**

- **Shared IP addresses:** Especially if it is a shared IP address with other websites of spam or adult content.

- **Shared industry web- and content-hosting:** For example, the same articles shown across multiple industry websites.

  - **Many same industry sites use the same hosting provider:** If all industry sites use the same small hosting provider, the search engines may suspect same ownership.

  - **For content/article sharing:** This doesn't help SEO—namely industry-specific sites; such as shared health articles across chiropractic websites. Even guest-blogging has been over-done and can suggest black hat practices to Google.)

  - **For "proposed" search or advertiser benefits:** For example, industry link-sharing, which can raise flags to Google and in extreme cases cause penalization (this is gray- or black-hat).

- **Poor Authority Score:** Scored by the search engines for web pages.

  (You can research the preceding issues on your site with http:// news.netcraft.com or http://whois.com.)

The following is the original short list titled "Search Engine Bot Barriers and Other No-Nos" (from Chapter 4):

- Flash (.swf) files
- Too many images, audio, or video
- Graphic text
- RSS-fed content
- Special file types (presentation files)
- Duplicate content
- Deep page content difficult to access
- Subdomains
- Redirects
- Bad, dead links
- Too many links listed
- Long page load times
- Irrelevant content or links
- Keyword oversaturation

 Note

Don't Follow the noFollow?

What's the difference between noIndex and noFollow, and why should you care? These are terms used throughout this book, but they are always worth clarifying. NoIndex is a command to assign to website pages and blog subfolders that contain like content, and you don't want penalization from the search engines for perceived content duplication. Suppose you have an eCommerce site with individual pages devoted to the same product in different versions or models (and with copied-and-pasted text), such as for sweatshirts or cars. For SEO purposes, you should pick a primary page for the spiders to crawl and set a noIndex for the other similar pages. Don't worry about the web visitors—from your primary crawled page you can have links to the other models. For another example, suppose you have primary links for your blog posts that you do want search engines to index. However, your WordPress structure also makes those same blog posts available through specified Category Folders and like Tag Folders. Again, there is potential for search engines to perceive duplicate content here through multiple URLs—and we don't want that now, do we?

Alternatively, noFollow is a command allowing you to have links to other pages or websites from your own website or blog. This is explained well later in this chapter with the SEO Ultimate plug-in functions. Basically, noFollow helps you not to lose SEO "value" by passing it on to undeserved sites. Fortunately all these major SEO plug-ins have options to handle noFollow and noIndex commands. You just want to understand the concepts so that you can choose the proper settings therein. So go on and be choosey, just know what it is you're choosing!

 Note

Universal Login, Google, Bing, and Facebook

We talk throughout this book about the importance of syncing channels and Google's universal login. Doubtless you have also noticed Facebook's login and integration features to countless social channels. With Google's integration of Google+ and YouTube for your personalized search results, Bing is left hanging. But you may have noticed Facebook results appearing in the Bing SERP. Facebook also has universal login for Bing accounts (as shown in Figure 6.1). What will this partnership allow for future data exchange? Might we expect Facebook and Bing to grow deeper relationships and data sharing for SEO results in the future?

So we understand the values of Google's multiple properties for your site and syncing accounts. And we have talked about the importance of Google Analytics tied with Google Webmaster Tools accounts for more data, features, and control (particularly in Chapter 4). All these crucial setups are offered by all-encompassing tools, such as Yoast for WordPress SEO (discussed later in this chapter)—so if you're using this and it's easy, then home run! However if you have to add additional plug-ins to solve these issues (for example, the general SEO plug-in SEO Ultimate, also discussed later, doesn't have some of these options) then I would just as soon do it manually and quickly through Google rather than risk plug-in problems or conflicts. Think of it this way: you are going to want to visit Google Analytics regardless to see the data, and you are going to need Google Webmaster Tools integrated to see search engine and other web-source data on referrals. But whether you do it with Google and other tools outside of WordPress, or do it all within WordPress, be sure to cover these most important aspects of SEO.

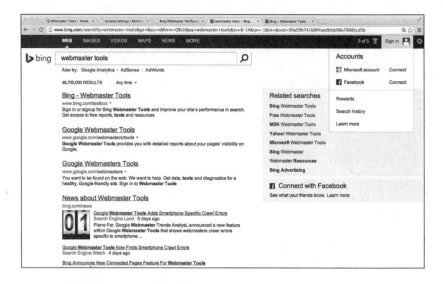

Figure 6.1   Bing and Facebook login.

Hands-On Execution for Specific Plug-ins

These plug-ins excel at offering many of the countless options for WordPress
SEO success! We can't go into every last step here, but note that these tools are
discussed throughout the book regarding important SEO elements, what they
are, and why they're important—and how to execute them via these important
plug-ins. So if you have a specific question about a specific SEO attribute that isn't
covered here, look for another chapter to cover that element. For example, if you
want to know more about these plug-ins' relevance with mobile, look to Chapter 9,
"Going Mobile and Local." Are you curious about social media integrations? Look
to Chapter 8, "Social Media Connectivity." Want to know how to get a ferry to the
Barrier Islands? I can't help you there.

All-In-One SEO

This SEO plug-in is a good one. It has a lot of options for SEO controls for each
page or post—so many that it might confuse you at first. All-in-One has both the
free option and the All-in-One Premium option. The regular All-in-One version is
sound and full of great SEO functionality; I know many who use it as-is (including
myself). So this write-up focuses on that version. However, even the free version
is worth making a donation to. You'll see a place requesting a donation, and such
a great tool is worth "a little something." So don't be a scrooge with the PayPal, if
you know what I mean.

First off, no worries if you don't understand something in the All-in-One SEO plug-in; you can leave it blank. All-in-One's defaults are sound. Even browser page titles are defaulted to unique titles by pulling from page headlines (although this is a common control default). One of the attributes of this plug-in I've had issues with is the menu label field. For pages, it gives you the option to determine unique page titles and menu labels, but I wasn't able to get my menu label to work on a Genesis theme. This is not terribly surprising, however; menu labels are more of a theme- and widget-specified activity. For something as critical to the website structure, menu labels should be controlled in the right place.

Here's how to work with All-in-One for Google Analytics:

1. Install the All-in-One SEO plug-in by logging in to your WordPress Dashboard and selecting **Plug-ins** from the left menu. Select the option from the primary page to **Add New**, and then search for All-in-One. Install and activate your plug-in (as we discuss in this book; see Figure 6.2).

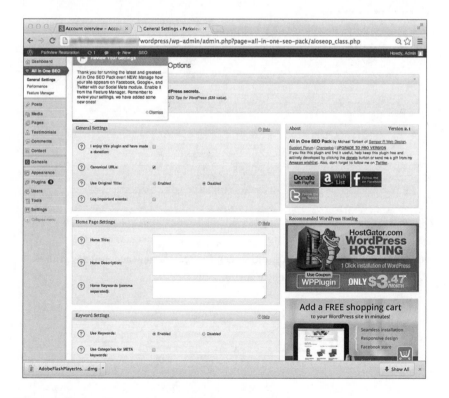

Figure 6.2   Installing and activating All-in-One SEO plug-in.

2. You'll want to leave this window open and create a new tab or window from within your browser for following the steps.

3. If you don't already have a Gmail or Google Account for this client, go to Gmail and create one (as we discuss in this book).

4. Take this opportunity to also create your Google+ business page, as discussed in Chapter 5, "Real-World Blogging," and throughout this book.

5. At this point you can either access **Analytics.Google.com** and sign up for an account (as shown in Figure 6.3), or allow All-in-One plug-in to do it for you (in step 8).

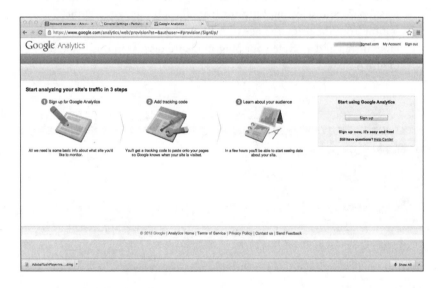

Figure 6.3   Google Analytics.

6. Follow the steps there on the screen to create a new account for your website (as shown in Figure 6.4).

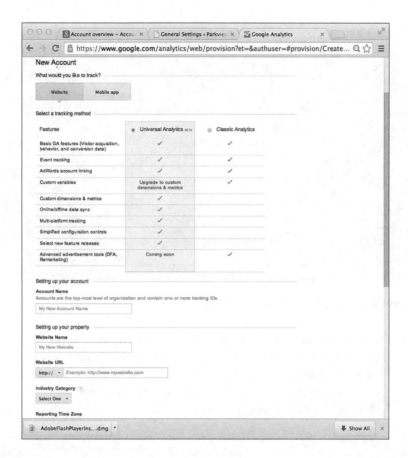

Figure 6.4   Creating a Google Analytics account.

7. Go ahead within Google Analytics and click **Get Tracking ID** for your website (as shown in Figure 6.5).

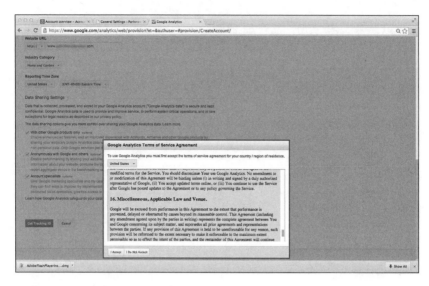

Figure 6.5   Google Analytics Tracking ID.

8. Now go back to your WordPress logged-in access to your All-in-One SEO plug-in. Here you have the option to either input our given Google Analytics code into the Google Analytics ID field, or bypass some previous steps and allow All-in-One to **Connect to Google Analytics** (as shown in Figure 6.6).

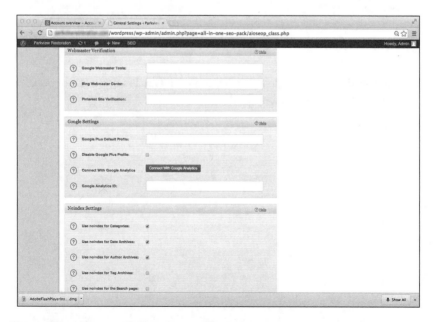

Figure 6.6   Connecting All-in-One and Google Analytics.

9.   Going back to your Analytics.Google.com window, select **Allow Access**
     for All-in-One to view and manage your Google Analytics data (as
     shown in Figure 6.7).

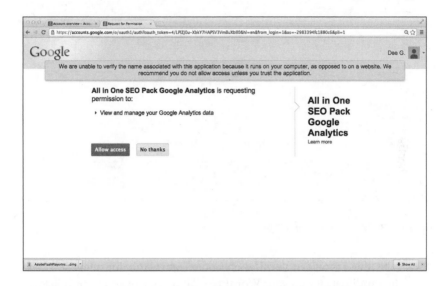

Figure 6.7   Allow Access for All-in-One and Google Analytics.

10. In your WordPress logged-in screen you should see All-in-One show-
     ing a Google Analytics code, demonstrating your success. Take this
     opportunity to also fill out the other open fields, such as connecting to
     your Google+ business page, as discussed previously.

11. You'll also notice a field for **Google Webmaster Tools**. This is also
     a good time and place to integrate that by signing in with your same
     Google account access (as we discuss elsewhere in this book). In the
     Add a Site field, you can add your www.example.com URL.

12. Similarly, you can use **Create a Bing Account** (via the top-right
     settings of Bing.com) and go to **Bing.com/toolbox** to add a Bing
     Webmaster Tools account for your site (through steps similar to
     Google's, as shown in Figure 6.8).

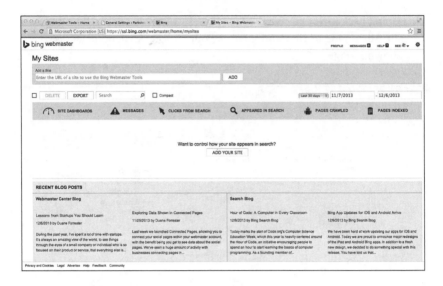

Figure 6.8   Bing Webmaster Tools.

13.   Take Bing's provided Verification Code (from within the quotes)
      copy and paste it into your WordPress All-in-One plug-in screen field
      for Bing (as shown in Figure 6.9). Then, again from the Bing.com
      Verification Tools screen, click **Verify** (as shown in Figure 6.9).

Figure 6.9   Bing verification.

14. Back in your WordPress logged-in access to your All-in-One plug-in, you can also choose **Canonical URLs** to ensure the search engines accurately index your website without duplication (as discussed throughout this book; settings were shown in Figure 6.2).

15. You can also set your noIndex settings here within All-in-One so that the search engines don't get confused crawling your regular blog post individual URLs in addition to category URLs, archive-date URLs, and so on (as we discussed in Chapter 5.

Unfortunately, All-in-One (like other SEO plug-ins) doesn't optimize images on the same page while editing copy. And I wish there were a little more to on-page or on-post image SEO with All-in-One (maybe this is where All-in-One Pro comes in most handy). But you do have two options for image SEO (and yes, you can do both):

1. You can edit alt tags from within the text-editing section of WordPress:

   • Note that this option is vital for specific on-page or on-post image SEO, which is especially helpful when the same image is used within the text on several pages or blog posts but it's limited in possibilities.

   • Select the Photo as placed within the page's or blog post's text CMS (as shown in Figure 6.10).

Figure 6.10   Images within the text.

- Hopefully, you named your photo with keywords prior to upload, such as long-tail-keywords.png.

- Within the text-editing section, choose your image and see the WordPress default "edit" fields.

- Go ahead and fill out with your keyword phrase for this page or blog post (as shown in Figure 6.11).

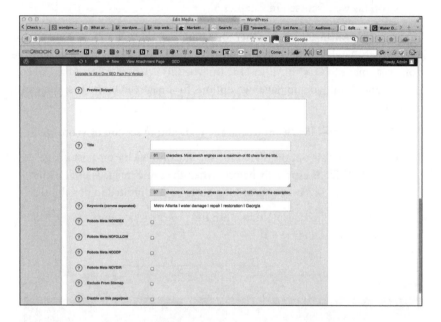

Figure 6.11   Keyword phrase field.

2. You can edit using All-in-One within the Media Library:

- This option gives image SEO options for the overall image media library URL, rather than to the image-specific usage on a page or blog post.

- From the WordPress left-side menu, select **Media**, and then **Library** (as shown in Figure 6.12).

- You will see a listing of images you have used within the site. Select the image you use on the page or post for editing.

- You will see WordPress's default image caption and description fields (see Figure 6.13). You can fill out the Alternative Text field with your keyword phrase.

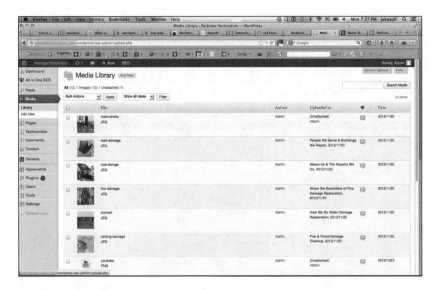

Figure 6.12   Selecting the Media Library.

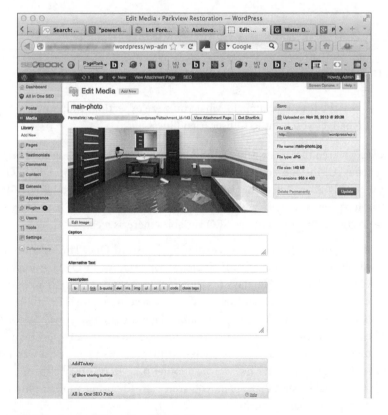

Figure 6.13   Image Alternative Text field.

- Scroll Down to the All-in-One options and fill out the browser Title and Meta Description fields (see Figure 6.14) just as you would for an SEO page (but with slightly differentiated text).

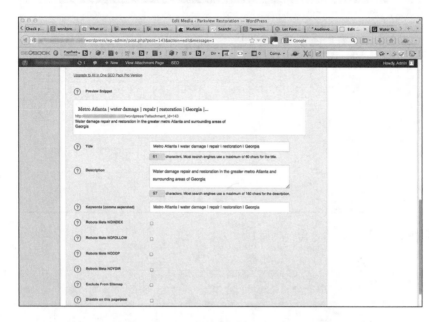

Figure 6.14   Browser Title and Meta Description.

- See the Preview Snippet—what you were expecting? Make any changes you want to fit user friendliness.

So we've covered the major general settings for the All-in-One plug-in. The great thing about All-in-One's organization is that the rest of your important SEO settings are easily accessible at the page level. In other words, while adding/editing content for pages and posts within WordPress, you conveniently have immediate access to controlling the on-page SEO variables there as well.

There are additional features worth exploring for All-in-One. Throughout this book we talk about the role of XML Sitemaps for SEO. All-in-One has a specific feature module for XML Sitemaps (as shown in Figure 6.15). Here is an option definitely worth integrating and setting up (as shown in Figure 6.16). I like to check Notify Google and Bing to go ahead and get the sitemap crawled ASAP for SEO benefit. Regardless of what customization you do or do not apply here, you want to Update Sitemap and check the report that follows to ensure it was a success and that you don't have overlap via another plug-in or sitemap (as shown in Figure 6.17). Just be sure that, again, you aren't already using another plug-in for your sitemap.xml management.

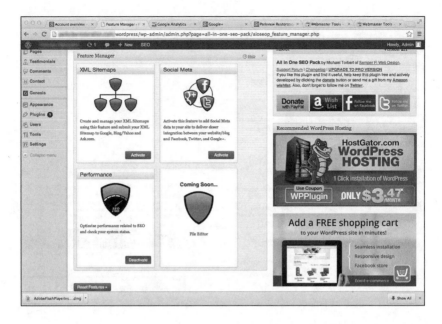

Figure 6.15 XML Sitemaps.

Figure 6.16 Setting up and submitting the Sitemap file.

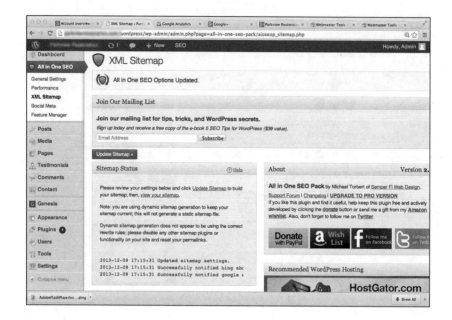

Figure 6.17   Update the Sitemap.

Yoast WordPress SEO

Joost de Valk is the creator of the Yoast WordPress SEO plug-in, and he has a history of creating some great WordPress plug-ins. In fact, Yoast is the combination of several former plug-ins, including HeadSpace 2.

I have already covered some important options and settings for Yoast in Chapter 5. This is the preferred SEO tool for many SEOs. I find that it excels at the SEO options it offers. All-in-One's organization is orderly and user-friendly, and Yoast is also easy to discern and apply. However, it's good to start general and then progress to the page level. But you should double-check all your work afterward, and you will probably want to make adjustments.

1. Just as with All-in-One SEO plug-in, you should start by setting the overall **Yoast General Settings** for your site (shown in Figure 6.18). These general defaults have a number of options and allow you to set up your Google and Bing Webmaster Tools here.

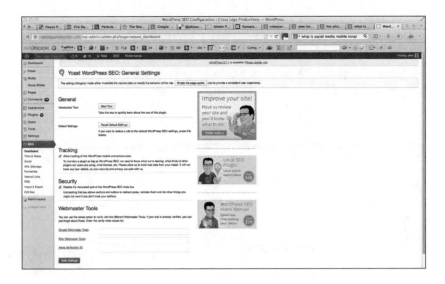

Figure 6.18   Yoast General Settings.

2. The General Settings even allow you to rewrite the robots.txt or .htaccess files if necessary (to direct bots, include 301 redirects, and so on, shown in Figure 6.19). But don't worry—if they frighten you, you can ignore them. These WordPress plug-ins are made to easily facilitate most of those SEO needs through other options.

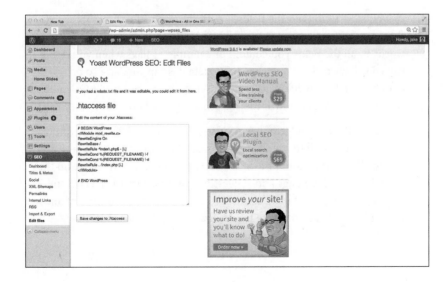

Figure 6.19   Robots.txt and .htaccess files.

3. Next proceed to the page- or blog post-editing level. On that deep-down page or post level, start by filling out the fields with the SEO- and keyword-inclusive information from your written-up SEO Page Forms (from Chapter 3, "A Strategic SEO Upfront Content Approach"). The first field to fill out is **Focus Keyword** (see Figure 6.20).

Figure 6.20   Focus Keywords for pages and posts.

4. As you start filling out the fields, Yoast automatically shows its report (based on your provided keywords) if you don't include those keywords in all the fields you could. For example, it flags when you don't use your keyword in your page title, meta description, and so on (shown in Figure 6.20). This is very useful—even the best SEOs could use an extra eye to confirm they're using keywords wherever they can.

However, the best judge of keyword inclusion is the SEO. Sometimes it doesn't read well to use the full, primary keyword phrase as is within the headline. Nor should the SEO oversaturate the keyword use on the page. But it is these flags and suggestions by Yoast that I referred to in Chapter 3 when I talked about setting up a "test" environment and testing keyword use on-page to get Yoast's suggestions for SEO page documentation and client approval. Again, this isn't how I personally do it; I don't start implementing any SEO until I document first on SEO Page Forms (again, shown in Chapter 3) and get client approvals. It's just that with the suggestions Yoast provides, you could use these to aid those form fill-outs.

5. Yoast even includes advanced options per page and post to control more intricate aspects, such as whether to include within the Sitemap, and page-level Canonicalization (see Figure 6.21).

Figure 6.21   Advanced SEO options for pages.

6. After executing page-level SEO, it's good to go back to the general Yoast Dashboard to see globally how your pages, posts, and their keywords relate to each other (see Figure 6.22). From this vantage point you might decide you have pages that are too similar in keywords or that you're missing an important focal keyword phrase. This combination of page- and global-level visibility makes Yoast truly useful.

Yoast even provides a "migration tool" to migrate your WordPress site SEO settings from using a different, existing SEO plug-in over to Yoast.

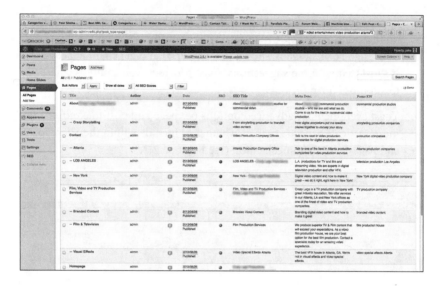

Figure 6.22   Yoast Dashboard.

 Note

Joost de Valk's Yoast and Smaller Plug-ins

The prolific Joost de Valk has numerous small plug-ins in addition to the comprehensive Yoast WordPress SEO. Many of these smaller plug-ins are already wrapped up into Yoast WordPress SEO, so don't install them on your WordPress site—just use the comprehensive version instead. I do discuss limitations with the competitor SEO Ultimate plug-in later in this chapter, so it might be worth researching to supplement with a Joost de Valk supplementary plug-in if you can't execute the SEO implementations without.

Generating and submitting a sitemap file, however, doesn't require a plug-in. In fact, it's quite simple to use an outside site such as http://xml-sitemaps.com to generate the sitemap. If you have already canonicalized your site, be sure to input your canonical URL (for example, http://www.example.com/ instead of http://example.com). This website generates the file and allows you to download and save it in multiple formats for usage and submissions. You can even download the sitemap as a .txt or .html file to see your full sitemap and include it as a page or footer on your website. Sitemap XML file submission to Google is critical for SEO—and be sure to submit to Bing as well. You can learn more about sitemap files at www.sitemaps.org.

- **Google Analytics for WordPress:** Joost de Valk, author of Yoast
  WordPress SEO, also does a great job with the Google Analytics for
  WordPress plug-in (shown in Figure 6.23). Right off the bat this plug-
  in prompts you, and helps you, to notify Google and allow for Google
  Analytics setup for your site. The Google Analytics for WordPress
  plug-in also smartly gives you options for best tracking your outbound
  links and clicks. It's good knowledge to have if you're keeping track
  of these when providing links to other sites and want to show them
  the value of their links, particularly if your site has a directory or paid
  listings.

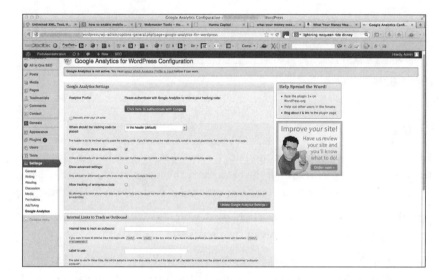

Figure 6.23 Google Analytics for WordPress.

- **The Sitemap File and the Yoast Plug-in:** I wrote previously about the
  value of a sitemap.xml file to aid the robots in crawling the site (discussed in Chapter 4). The file itself is computer generated from a website resource or else from a third-party plug-in within WordPress, such
  as Yoast SEO for WordPress. This tool analyzes the website or blog
  and its pages and generates an XML file (Extreme Markup Language,
  rather than HTML, Hypertext Markup Language) which then needs
  to be submitted to the search engines via the tool. This sitemap file
  generation and submission must be done after the website is built and
  has nothing to do with the information architecture act of designing the sitemap. With this Yoast tool you can check submissions (see
  Figure 6.24).

Figure 6.24   Sitemap file.

SEO Ultimate

SEO Ultimate has a number of modules for you to use for various SEO activities. It's worth checking out right off the bat to have the modules you want available. This and many SEO Ultimate functions are available when you follow these steps:

1. Log in to your WordPress Dashboard, with SEO Ultimate installed (via plug-in install options previously discussed).

2. From the left menu select the option for **SEO**. You will see the SEO Ultimate options, including Module Manager (see Figure 6.25).

Figure 6.25   SEO Ultimate Module Manager.

Tip

See the White Papers

I find SEO Ultimate a bit confusing compared to other plug-ins. Fortunately, there's a whole section of whitepapers available from SEO Ultimate in that left menu (Figure 6.26).

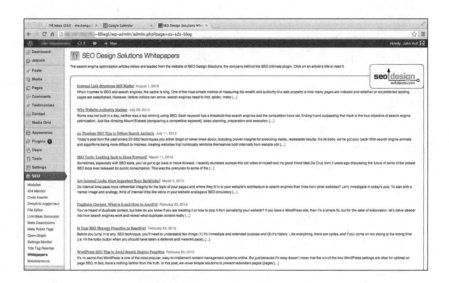

Figure 6.26   SEO Ultimate Whitepapers.

3. As with the previous big SEO plug-ins, after installation you'll want to start in SEO Ultimate by filling out general settings—for example, the Search Engine Webmaster Tools. Setting up Bing WebmasterTools is the same as setting up Google WebmasterTools, within the SEO Ultimate plug-in under the Miscellaneous category (see Figure 6.27). But this isn't much harder than dropping the code, provided by webmaster tools, into the WordPress Head code in the Editor section of your website. Keep this in mind for plug-in conflicts. You don't want conflict between this part of SEO Ultimate and the Google Analytics plug-in (which works well, as discussed earlier).

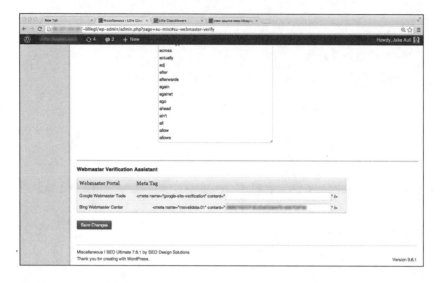

Figure 6.27   Webmaster Tools settings.

 Tip

Paths Toward Canonicalization

If you desire to use a plug-in to manage canonicalization instead of doing it manually via Webmaster Tools, you can use a plug-in such as SEO No Duplicate to control canonicalization tags for your page headers (again, ensure your other plug-ins don't already achieve everything you want). This can be especially helpful for instances of duplicate content pages, such as websites featuring cars for sale where multiple listings have the same descriptions, or manufacturing equipment to serve different audiences, where various product models perform the same operations.

However, I still like to use Google's own tools for canonicalization. Parallel to my Google Analytics account, I can open Google.com/webmaster/tools and add the website URL and verify it. I also immediately ensure canonicalization by adding both URLs, http://example.com and http://www.example.com, and then assign www.example.com as the primary URL.

4. SEO Ultimate does allow applying some settings at the individual page or post level. Personally, I find the interface cumbersome and limiting. Still, you want to work what you've got. Make use of the settings

that are available to achieve good SEO. One of the things I have always found effective is optimizing the browser Page Title with keywords. Luckily, SEO Ultimate has that available right off the top from its page-editing fields (shown in Figure 6.28).

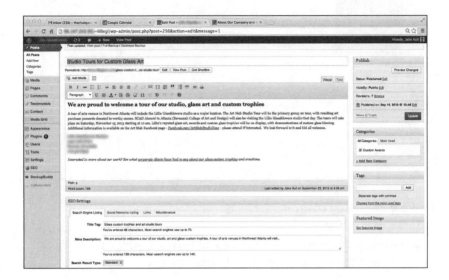

Figure 6.28   Page SEO settings.

Remember to apply SEO settings to the images within your site as well as the content; such technical effects can have greater impact on search rankings then keywords in body copy. But to access these you can't do it from within the page or blog post where your image is placed. Instead, as with Yoast Wordpress SEO, you must do the following:

- Go to the **Media Library** from the WordPress left menu.

- Select and open your image from within the gallery.

5. When you select and bring it up, you'll see several sets of fields—from WordPress, SEO Ultimate, and perhaps your theme or other plug-ins (shown in Figure 6.29). SEO Ultimate provides the same fields for SEO settings for images that it does for content page edits; however, I have had trouble getting them to work properly between WordPress 3.6.1 and SEO Ultimate 7.6.1 (it could have been conflict with my theme or other plug-in).

Figure 6.29   Media Library image editing options.

6. Optimize the image by populating with keywords within the fields, as you would with page content, and similar to Yoast.

So the plan for image optimization is to utilize your same keywords per the page/post (but remember to change your alt description a little from the page meta description). So include them within the Description and Alt Image text fields, which are standard in the WordPress editor.

You also should be able to edit the image-specific URL here, which is another good place for keyword use. This doesn't affect the page/post URL on which the image is placed; this is for the image only. You should have already included your keyword within the image filename itself before uploading.

Remember that the objective of fully optimizing your images is not only to aid the page or post optimization, but to help get your image grabbed by Google Images and other image aggregator sites online. Because plug-ins may be in conflict with each other, and because these WordPress fields can do the trick for image optimization, ensure that you implement the latter correctly.

Linking

One of the more complex elements available with SEO Ultimate is that of Link Masks and Pass-Through URLs. The intent here is good; it is so that when linking to other sites, your site doesn't lose link juice (this is also what the noFollow roughly does). I might add here that if links are shared between you and another search marketer, it is with the understanding that the link juice is also passed between the two, and so to stop your link juice in such a scenario is unethical (you scratch my back, I'll scratch my back). Besides, Google has been advancing ways to identify such tricks and to disregard or penalize them. Be nice. Share your link juice. (See? SEO really is like kindergarten!)

Regardless, the principle still makes sense if, for example, you are posting a link on your site to a directory (such as Yahoo!Local) for reader-benefit info, but without any agreement with the directory. This is a perfect case to do a noFollow to preserve the authority of your own site and content. The way that SEO Ultimate intends to do this is by setting up pass-through URLs—where your chosen outbound links are "passed through" a directory (such as http://example.com/go/) before being directed to the final destination. In turn, this folder directory is entirely set for noFollow. From a technology standpoint it makes sense, and it is certainly easier than going into code and inputting noFollows beside every outbound link in question. However, these kinds of spider manipulations and default, high-volume, potential noFollow commands smack of search engine distrust—if not for now, for the future. I'd find another way to specify my noFollows.

Alternatively, if you want to assign full, individual post noFollow and noIndex commands, SEO Ultimate has a Dashboard to select (from the left menu) with posts listings specifically for that (Figure 6.30). Or, at the page- or post-editing level, you can select the **Miscellaneous** tab for noFollow and noIndex page-level commands (Figure 6.31).

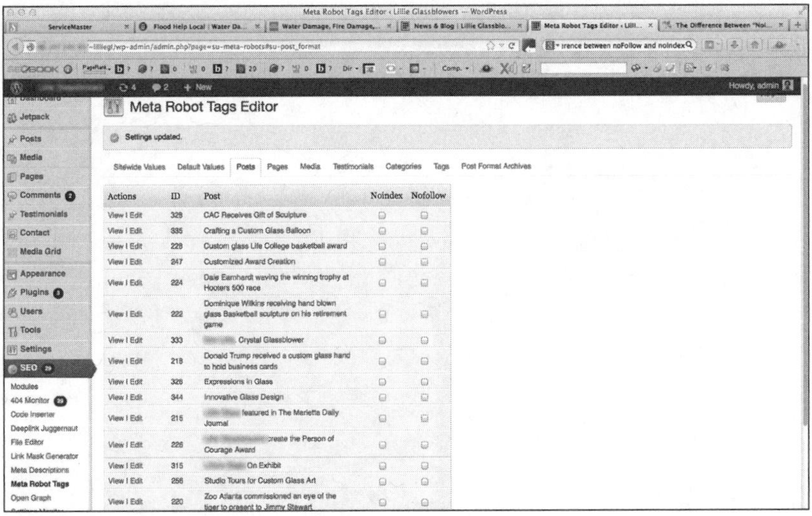

Figure 6.30   Dashboard for posts.

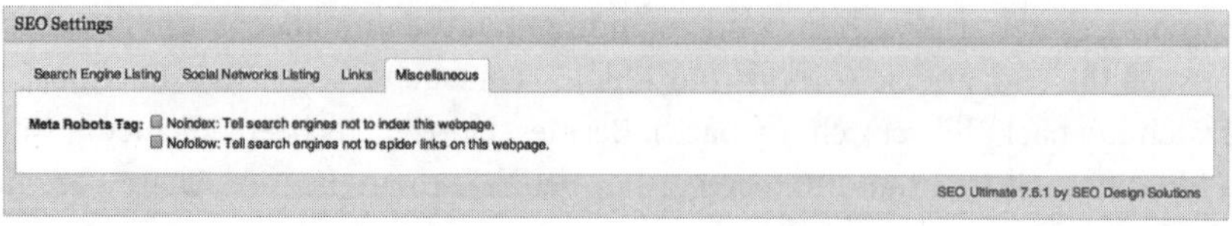

Figure 6.31   Miscellaneous tab.

For Your 404s

I like SEO Ultimate's 404 Monitor to identify all the Page Not Found errors visitors may encounter on your site (see Figure 6.32). The best way to resolve 404s is by setting up 301 redirects, which SEO Ultimate doesn't easily do. SEO Ultimate does have open fields for editing the robots.txt and .htaccess files (where 301 redirects can be coded; see Figure 6.33). A better way is to install the Simple 301 Redirects plug-in, which is indeed simple, and fortunately doesn't seem to conflict with SEO Ultimate. I just wish rush-hour traffic could be fixed by Simple 301 Redirects.

Figure 6.32   404 Monitor.

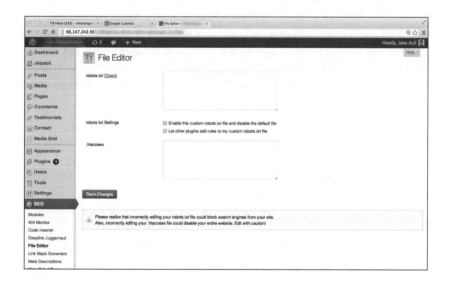

Figure 6.33   Robots.txt and .htaccess files.

The Final Plug on SEO Plug-ins

There are fundamental SEO items that SEO Ultimate doesn't offer, or else they are cumbersome or incomplete in execution, or the features are hidden in less-applicable areas (from my perception). For example, easy integration for Google Analytics. Google Analytics is not difficult to set up manually, and I do it this way all the time. But tools such as Yoast make it incredibly easy to execute within the tool. SEO Ultimate is not so simple.

So SEO Ultimate has a few decent controls and covers SEO basics, but I still prefer tools such as All-in-One or Yoast, because these latter tools have more comprehensive offerings and have more options for optimizing specific pages and posts within the WordPress Editor (believe it or not, SEO Ultimate does not make this simple function easy). Also, I haven't run into other plug-in conflict issues with All-in-One or Yoast. But as I'll continue to say throughout this book, plug-in conflicts are important considerations—and although some plug-ins play nice together, others don't. There may be occasions when All-in-One or Yoast conflicts with your WordPress theme or other essential plug-ins. So it's good to know that plug-ins like SEO Ultimate can still help you execute SEO fundamentals for your WordPress website or blog. Accordingly, SEO Ultimate does things to help such transitions, such as importing meta content from All-in-One SEO. That tree house is only so big, you know—not everyone fits inside at the same time. But between using All-in-One and Yoast WordPress SEO plug-ins? It's hard for me to choose. I've used both on and off for years and like them both. You'll just have to decide for yourself.

7

Analytics for WordPress

Chapter objectives and questions:

- Explanations of terminology
- Immediate, upfront measurements
- Approaches to the measurement plan
- SEO customization versus the "formula"
- Types of results to look for
- Social content and variety on the SERP
- Keywords and rank
- Traffic terms
- Identifying referrals and backlinks
- Best tools for analytics
- Additional analytics options

Note that there are many expensive but good search, social, digital, and email content communications and analytics platforms out there that can do a good job for you. These include platforms such as Omniture, Marketo, HubSpot, and others. The purpose of this chapter is not to instruct based on these. Rather, this chapter is devoted to WP Analytics, Google Analytics, and other free data platforms you can use for your WordPress website or blog.

Number 1 = You Win?

An important thing to remember about WordPress SEO is that so many other platforms have SEO barriers built in—for example, the technology foundation or templates were built for easy, dynamic database access and technology functionality rather than for good search engine crawling. Customized WordPress builds not only don't have those barriers, but they have many options to truly aid SEO. But the old goal of the "number 1 spot" has been made today into a bit of a myth by Google's Penguin update. That's not to say that a number one listing no longer exists, but Google has done two big things to shake up the importance of it:

- For one, Google's increasingly personalized results mean that "number one" and the SERP listings are theoretically not the same for any two searchers. In addition, that number one listing is not driven (solely) by the keyword phrase searched (good thing, considering Google has removed keyword-driver data from Google Analytics, as we discuss in this chapter).

- With combined displays of listings, reviews, images, and more, Google now serves what I like to call the new Google SERP "smorgasbord," which means that a video or an "authorship" listing in the middle of the SERP can jump out and obtain clicks more than the number one listing (as we discuss in this chapter).

So the Google SERP used to be like looking at only one flavor of honey jars for your delight. Now it has clover, orange blossom, white sage, and blueberry honey to boot!

The Terms of Your Terms

Note that there is a difference between analytics, metrics, measurements, and statistics. And the issue of specific terms is critical to this chapter; you have to say what you mean in analytics or else risk comparing Apples to Droids (you know, iPhones to...). For example, the "m" in "cpm" stands for 1,000. But 13.5 MM site visitors means 13,500,000. Website "uniques" means unique or first-time visitors, in contrast to return visitors or overall visits. I have yet to find the "perfect" online dictionary resource for all SEM, SEO, digital, and marketing terms (which is why I've started a basic dictionary in the back of this book). The closest I've found is an ancient online dictionary that is often updated for accuracy—www.NetLingo.com.

The tools you use for analytics will also have some definitions on their sites, too. Referencing these in particular is critical when using these tools, because each tool may have its own criteria for its algorithms and reports. On a basic level, Google's reporting tools will report only Google-specific results, but SEOBook Tools can report aggregate data from Google, Bing, and Yahoo! as well as other search engines.

For some analytics tools, authority is more important; for other tools, rank specifically is tops. And because "PageRank" (in contrast to general search engine "ranking") is Google's own term, the other tools' algorithms and measurements must be different. Don't worry—by the end of the chapter you'll know the important metrics. Although I think of "analytics" as a fairly old term by now, my Gmail still flags this word as a misspell to this day! My definition of *digital analytics* equates to the practice of measuring and interpreting the results of digital activities and channels. More casually, it means the reports—the results themselves for analysis and interpretation. I define metrics as the formulas to apply to data; the formulaic applications to the results at hand—for example, CPM or ROAS (return on advertising spending). Metrics become critical in digital marketing because there are so many different data results, ways to look at them, and there is a need to establish common baselines to logically compare data. Metrics also become critical to make sense of your data in relation to your stated goals. In other words, if your primary digital marketing goal is to achieve more new sales, then what good are social media reports that show only new followers? And identifying your most important and valuable metrics is at the crux; these are your KPIs (key performance indicators).

Let's say Google Trends tells you that the primary keyword phrase you have optimized your website for, 'skull sutures,' is scored at 75 out of 100 (75%) among similar/top keywords (as shown in Figure 7.1). Your reporting analytics has already told you that your website page that is optimized for that keyword receives 10,000 clicks a month from Google. Then if you optimized a page for Google Trends' top recommended similar keyword phrase, 'sutures,' theoretically that page could get 1.33% times 10,000 clicks (if there were low competition and you could get placement you haven't achieved already on the SERP). So from our measurements and interpretations of the analytics, we're applying metrics and common baselines for predictions.

Figure 7.1   Google Trends.

 Note

Statistics or Not?

Through the preceding definitions, hopefully "measurements" are clear. They are the numbers, the data results of your measuring actions. What about "statistics?" Casually, the word "stats" is often used to describe your numbers' percentage results reported. But "statistics" has much more to it than that. I describe statistics as the practice and application of statistical formulas to data for new interpretations. The myth of statistics is that it requires high volumes of data for good applied formulas and interpretations. Instead, statistics is built on randomization. Digital media today can reveal high volume data, but that doesn't necessarily meet the traditional structures of randomization. So what does that mean to you? You probably won't be using true "statistical" analysis of your data for projections. But your measurements, analytics, and metrics are sharp tools for your SEO tool box. Hopefully this helps more than it confuses. But the content in this chapter will strive to cater to those words and their definitions.

In Chapter 3, "A Strategic SEO Upfront Content Approach," we discussed the uses of SEOBook Tools for competitive analysis. These provide great data reports on whatever digital sites you choose to research. These tools can use differing algorithms than what we expect, and they won't provide data as accurate as, for example, Google Analytics. When worst comes to worst, however, these tools can provide a good common baseline for comparisons of competitors' and industry sites—for data such as inbound links, search engine traffic, PPC ad spend, and more.

So how do you travel this sea without drowning in numbers? We start by following these steps:

1. Identifying objectives.

2. Allowing these to drive what data results we focus on capturing.

3. Selecting the metrics to fit our objectives to analyze this data.

Much like the strategic planning stages identified in Chapter 3, I like to start with the digital strategy brief and create a measurement plan to get all stakeholders on board and reports in line. Part of the instrumental value of the upfront digital and competitive analysis is to help identify those goals, metrics, and common baselines for your own site data captures.

The following is an approach for Measurement Plan elements:

- **Campaign overview and objectives.**
- **Communications calendar overview and consumer journey.**
- **Tracking mechanisms** such as Webtrends tags, Google Analytics, Omniture Tags, social media monitoring, Twitter hashtags, and so on.
- **Diagnostic metrics**—for example, CTR, interaction rate, mentions.
- **Success metrics**—for example, ROAS, ROI, conversion rate.
- **Dashboard**—(Not to be confused with the WordPress Dashboard) Showing the key metrics help to understand the performance of the campaign.
- **Reporting frequencies.**

Immediate Upfront Measurements

Chapter 3 discussed the strategy about the value of doing upfront SEO audits of competitors online. But for customers (or new employers) with existing digital presence, we need to perform this activity for them as well. The difference is that for our customers or employers, hopefully we have access to past data via Google Analytics or other reports.

 Tip

SEO Customization Versus the Formula

Throughout this book I have tried to emphasize the value of a customized SEO approach. Not all digital customers are identical—not even if they're in the same industry, which is also why I emphasize identifying upfront digital goals. There are SEO or digital marketing firms that offer the same promotional process to all clients: They'll conduct PPC advertising to a specified, optimized landing page with lead-gen measurement and execute X-amount of social posts as well (more on this in Chapter 10, "PPC and Advertising"). It's sticky business customizing SEO repairs for an existing website. You don't know what you're up against without opening that beehive and examining the honeycomb. But it's necessary, and it's what's best for the client and the client's site long term. This is why analytics is so important to this activity. Or suppose it's a new site. You still want to cover your bases and ensure your optimization is taking correct effect, that Google is reading the site properly, and so on. Customization, personalization, and analysis are at the heart of good SEO—to apply a regurgitated formula of promotion is something else. Who likes regurgitation anyway?

Whether it's a new or old site, here are some of the analytics you want to check for fixing as you go forward (if you're not familiar with these terms, don't worry—this is what this chapter is devoted to explaining—but keep this as a checklist for future analysis):

- **404 pages not found.**
- **Pages blocked and bad links.**
- **301s/302s**—Are these expected? For all the pages you want?
- **Canonicalization.**
- **Number of pages indexed**—Is this all the pages of your site? Are your "noIndex" commands reading properly on the right pages?
- **Pages with duplicate content**—Luckily, your WordPress SEO plugins should tell you this (as discussed in Chapter 3 and Chapter 6, "In-Depth Hands-On SEO Execution").

- **Bounces**—You may consider this a better measurement for post-SEO failure or success, but if there are currently an inordinate amount of bounces to your site, perhaps you need to rethink keywords on the home page.

- **Inbound links**—Critical! Other sites linking to yours can be a gold mine for SEO. You don't want to break these! Identify them upfront and set a plan to facilitate.

- **Form submissions**—Is the form working properly? Are there too many fields for people to fill out?

Types of Results to Look For

Digital analytics is one of these topics where myths seem to prevail and common sense is applied not often enough. On the one hand, digital analytics is a brave new world and requires the re-invention of marketing metrics because it opens up data points that could never be revealed before now. On the other hand, some good principles of marketing measurement still apply, such as the debate on quantitative versus qualitative measurement. Here's my simplified take: When you start out measuring, volume rules naturally. You don't know the significance yet of individual data points, referrals, or visitors by segment. Initially, it is natural to want the most website visitors and blog followers and comments. As you and your WordPress site progress, a better goal is more qualified leads or more qualitative results. Compare, for example, 1,000 one-time visitors to your blog versus 300 visitors who visit multiple times, comment, and share your posts with their own social friends and followers. Or 100 visitors to your eCommerce site who actually purchase. All this is why it's important to set your measurement goals upfront, tie them to your digital marketing and broader marketing goals, and set the plan to measure accordingly.

Although we typically look at analytics for web visitors (quantitative) and, hopefully, referrals (qualitative), and highest-searched keywords for our industry (content demand), there is another way to identify consumer interest—with analytics on your own site. If you have a lot of pages/content on your site, with multiple paths to deep-dive content, seeing what paths those web visitors take can be insightful for what the eyeballs want. In other words, if you're a cupcake vendor, seeing 500,000 searches/month for "key lime cupcakes" would be a great illustration of demand. However, if web visitors continually navigate on your website to your sparse photos and recipes for fudge brownie cupcakes, this could be a great indication of your market brand perception and associated demand (how people see and label you and what they want from you). This provides a great opportunity for multivariate testing, where you can create, optimize, and promote (even with PPC advertising or email marketing; we'll get more into all this in Chapter 10) "equal" landing pages for a new fudge cupcake and one for a key lime cupcake. What gets best results? For best SEO and social media success, you should allow a few months. But the resulting knowledge will give you great savvy for the future of your brand, products, and marketing.

We've talked throughout this book about things you can do to help SEO for your WordPress website or blog. The thing about it is that for everything you try, ideally you measure that for success (or failure). When I perform SEO for a first-time website or for sites previously with no or poor SEO, I see an immediate spike in traffic (a very good thing). From that point on, you have to look long term. If you look at daily rise and fall traffic on a weekly basis, you will drive yourself nuts (I'm already there). Look at the long-term traffic. Is it going up monthly? If not, why? Is your site a seasonal business? Does business or interest historically go up or decrease in your industry over the holidays and New Year? Over the summer? Do your web stats reflect that? Here's a critical consideration: Are you looking at overall web traffic or search engine referral traffic?

If you're suddenly losing overall web traffic, it could be SEO, but it could be other variables as well. Remember we talked about the wheel-and-spoke model in Chapter 3. The spokes drive traffic to the website—it's not by search engine alone (unless you have a new business and new site). Did you stop another promotional campaign recently that would have stopped driving people to your site? Perhaps this is the case. The next step is to ask yourself how expensive was that other promotional campaign? It might have been giving you web traffic, but was the cost worth the return (we go more in depth on these questions in Chapter 10)? An important question—and a way to answer it is to identify the value of your web leads.

When dealing with metrics and measurements, it is vital to consider a number of different factors. Ideally, you can identify your profit versus cost on a per-sale level. In other words, your company has a number of expenditures from production to building overhead to personnel. To simplify things with the examples that follow, we're going to talk in terms of revenue (in contrast to pure profit). We're also not going to try to factor in the cost of time spent; that is, the cost of the marketer's or SEO's pay-per-hour. So we will deal with "returns" metrics; ROMI (return on marketing investment), ROAS (return on advertising spend), and the like.

Let's go back to your digital and SEO goals. We walked through the digital marketing funnel in Chapter 3 (refer back to Figure 3.8); do you remember your "spout?" If the goal was to get more sales via lead-gen form fillouts, then let's focus on that. You have a WordPress form on your website that you drive traffic to. Let's say that historically, for every 1,000 people who fill out that form, your sales/customer service staff follow up with emails and phone calls, and traditionally you achieve 300 new purchasing customers. And each new customer spends on average $10 (ideally you'd calculate average, long-term, customer lifetime value spending rather than first-time spends only, but let's keep this simple for now). Because we've already established that you have a 30% online customer conversion rate (300 buyers out of 1,000 leads), your averaged revenue value is $3.00 for each lead (see Figure 7.2).

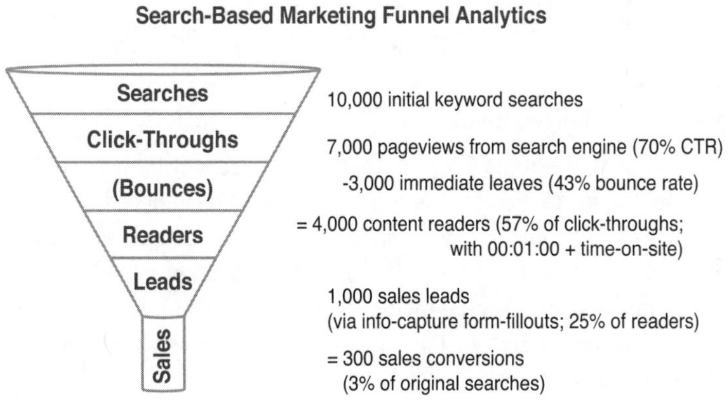

Search-Based Marketing Funnel Analytics

Searches	10,000 initial keyword searches
Click-Throughs	7,000 pageviews from search engine (70% CTR)
(Bounces)	-3,000 immediate leaves (43% bounce rate)
Readers	= 4,000 content readers (57% of click-throughs; with 00:01:00 + time-on-site)
Leads	1,000 sales leads (via info-capture form-fillouts; 25% of readers)
Sales	= 300 sales conversions (3% of original searches)

Figure 7.2   Digital Marketing Funnel.

Social Content and Variety on the SERP

Here's a great way to think about the growing, symbiotic relationship of social media and SEO: Rich snippets, blogger, video, and other social media content become more impactful on clicks from the Google SERP. Hence, the more effort you put into social media, the more effective in the SEO results. If you're connecting to your audience in social media, your social content also has a better chance of being served to your base within the SERP. The more real estate (and images and videos) you consume on the viewer's SERP, the better your brand impression and chance for the viewer to click.

Psychographics

If you think the term "psychographics" means that the men in white coats are coming for you, you're right. In fact, they were notified to do so the minute you bought this book. And they got me long ago. But seriously, psychographics represents the capability to measure or serve content to consumers based not on their traditional demographics, but their interests and feelings. How? Social data. Have you ever visited a website on an obscure topic, only to start seeing ads on it appear in Facebook and everywhere? This is remarketing. But the same concept works via Facebook serving you "Pages you might be interested in," Twitter serving "Sponsored Tweets" and Amazon serving "Additional Products you might be interested in." In fact, you could say Amazon started this whole ball rolling.

Amazon was the first major site with the "recommendations engine" to show you tailored recommendations based on yours and others' purchases and comments. See? There was a reason you were recommended that book on the history of snow shovels after all!

 Note

Bing and Personalized Search

At the time of this writing, Bing still seems to be rooted in more traditional SERP results and rewards for the SEO, as well as consumer browser and search history. Without Google+, YouTube, and other Google access to personalized data, Bing has to serve search results based on other criteria and more traditional search engine methods. So Bing has to place more emphasis on your browser search history to predict your interests and desired search results going forward.

Keywords and Rank

In this book we've touched on Google's progression in analytics and SERP. At the time of this writing, Google Analytics has discontinued showing website owners what keywords visitors clicked on to arrive at their site. Likewise, Google PageRank (Google's assigned rank for the SEO value of a web page) has been diluted of value because Google hasn't updated it as frequently as it used to.

 Note

Keywords for WordPress?

Although Google Analytics has removed keyword-driven data for websites, WordPress.com Stats has not yet (at the time of this writing; as shown in WordPress.com Stats screenshots later in this chapter). But how long, or how accurate, can this data be without Google—particularly because WordPress.com Stats were based on Google Analytics in the first place?

However, we can't throw keywords out the window. Keyword research via Google AdWords Keyword Planner or spy tools is still vital to the SEO process, especially prior to optimization (as discussed in Chapter 3). It's essential to remember that although fewer people may search for your niche, long-tail keywords than short-tail, those who do search long-tail are much more likely to buy from you. See how? If you search for "cold, hard, metal catheters" you already know what you're looking for—rather than the consumer searching for "medical equipment." And it brings us back home again (as we discuss throughout this chapter) to qualitative versus quantitative results.

A Google-based blogger I like to read on search engine analytics topics, Avinash Kaushik, says to use Webmaster Tools data from Google, Bing/Yahoo! and Yandex (an additional search engine, based in Russia) to compensate for the keyword data "not provided" by Google Analytics anymore (for more see http://www.kaushik.net/avinash). I have to wonder, however, how long it will be before those alternative search engines and tools will follow suit with Google Analytics.

 Note

The Role of Yandex

Ever heard of Yandex? It's the fourth-largest search engine in the world! Yandex (see Figure 7.3) is the "Google" of Russia. You can access it via Yandex.com. Yandex also has its own web browser you can install and other software offerings. If your client is in America and focused on American consumers, you may not see much need to optimize for Yandex. But with Google Analytics changing what data it serves and doesn't serve, resources like Yandex can help fill the void. Just take it with a grain of salt to gauge potential difference between its typical audience and that of your searchers.

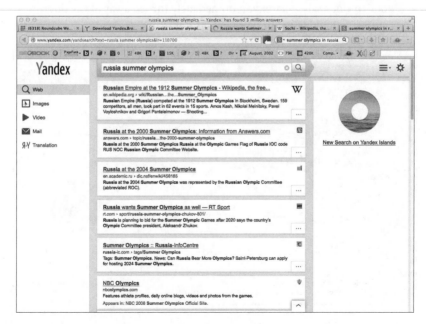

Figure 7.3   The Yandex search engine.

Caught Up in Traffic

Site traffic certainly isn't the only metric (or set of metrics) out there, but these days it's certainly more desired than the classic, vague "impressions." There's a full glossary at the end of the book on all kinds of delightful words (and you can see them in action on the Google Analytics dashboard in Figure 7.4). But here's a few terms related to traffic to tease you now:

- **Impressions are basically "eyeballs."** An impression is exposure; a consumer's theoretical view of a URL, an ad, a brand—whatever. Impressions on the SERP means that the search engine served your listing to a web searcher. It does not mean that there was a click through.

- **Page Views are what we used to call "hits," but page views are better.** Why? Hits can be inaccurate, as when there is more than one linked section on the same web page. A page view represents a visit to the total page.

- **Unique Visitors are first-time website visitors.** This can't be known 100%; instead, it's based on cookies. This measurement assumes the web visitor has visited from only one, primary web browser, which has retained cookies on that visitor's history. If your website has never been in that user's browser history, the user is a "unique visitor."

- **Bounces are website visits that don't stick.** Think of them like the door-to-door salesperson you immediately turned away at the door in contrast your friend who came in and stayed awhile.

Figure 7.4 Google Analytics dashboard and web traffic terms.

- **Visits represent the total visits to your website within the given period.** It's best to have a good balance of both unique visitors and return visitors. What should that balance be? Not to dissuade you, but that's kind of up to you and your goals. If you're just starting out, all your visits will be uniques. But if you're an older company that wants more return business and customer service content, you want more return visits. Simple.

- **Direct and Click-Through traffic are two primary ways a visitor can access your site;** Direct means the visitor typed your URL into the browser instead of searching or clicking.

- **Conversion is what you make it to be.** Just as you have identified your digital marketing goal, you have to identify what your metric will be for converting on that goal. Luckily, Google Analytics offers data surrounding conversion—you just need to identify a page you want visitors to click through the site to land on. But it's a fundamental question—what's your conversion rate? And it's something to build your automated reporting around. Structure reports around your goals and a few KPIs for automated email delivery to yourself, your boss, and—your grandparents! Why not? Get them excited about this stuff, too!

 Note

Want to Learn More?

Want more specific input on the best data points and metrics for you to focus on? Here's a great blog post by Subhash Chandra on Social Media Today: http://socialmediatoday.com/subhashk/1236876/ introducing-five-new-significant-seo-metrics.

Identifying Referrals and Backlinks

I've mentioned that one of the vital elements to good SEO is backlinks. It's time to clarify some terminology. Backlinks are the same as inbound links, which are outside links from external websites or pages linking to yours. They are out there, and if the pages they are on are indexed by search engines, you can measure how many inbound links you have. Note that some of the tools that measure these will also report "noFollows." These are web pages that are linking to you but have told the search engines not to pass any link juice from their own site onto yours. Typically the more websites that link to you, the more it boosts your results in the SERP. But if they have specified "noFollow," you don't get that full benefit. You only get the potential for someone visiting that other site to see and want to click the link to your own site.

When someone does click through to your site, it is a "referral." If the majority of visits to your website come from Google, then Google is cited as your top referral source in your analytics reports.

Because you can have an almost unlimited amount of inbound links or referral sources coming from the same website, it makes more sense to examine "linking domains." Linking domains represent the amount of actual domain names linking to your site. For example, an apartment complex may have more than 1,000 back-links (pages) but only a couple referring domains. How? They use a couple of sites to list and promote their ongoing vacancies for rent.

Here's a deeper explanation: Suppose you are a regular guest blogger and contributor to your industry association's website. You could have hundreds of backlinks from that site's pages and blog posts to your own website. But the industry association website represents only one linking domain. For example:

Pages/Posts with Links:	Website Linked To:
Associationsite.com/blog/12/14	Yourwebsite.com
Associationsite.com/memberslist	Yourwebsite.com
Associationsite.com/topcontributors...	Yourwebsite.com
Tradeshow.associationsite.com	Yourwebsite.com
Domains with links:	**Website linked to:**
Associationsite.com	Yourwebsite.com

I like to take it even a step further than the preceding examples. I'm talking about "Referring IP Address." First, I do like to isolate my clients' domain registration by having them hosted on dedicated IP addresses. When you are hosted on a shared IP address (as many websites are), you probably share the IP address with some questionable sites—sites that are flagged as black-hat or worse by Google. You don't want affiliation with these sites. I mean port sites, scam sites, catalogs that spam, and so on. In my opinion it's best to obtain dedicated IP hosting. It shouldn't be a problem for your hosting provider and should not cost much more.

But one of the big flags from shared IP addresses is that of black-hat SEOs who build up multiple domains just to have them link to their primary site for fake inbound link value. These SEOs may use different URLs, but chances are they're on the same, shared IP address. This is why I like to measure referral IPs instead of referral domains or web "pages" (individual pages that could be on the same domain such as a blog).

To clarify further, here is a theoretical list showing the types of relative quantity differences you may see between these measurement points: www.yourwebsite.com measurements:

- 1,000 backlinks (web pages with links to your site)
- 250 noFollow inbound links (subtract these; they won't help you in Google)
- 250 referral domains
- 200 referral IP addresses

Just Ping Me

Chances are you've seen terms such as "pingbacks and trackbacks" within your WordPress Dashboard and notifications. These are notifications displaying the published use of your own content. In other words, if you publish your latest WordPress blog post, and someone else copies and pastes some of your content onto his or her own blog, you are notified within your WordPress Dashboard (as shown in Figure 7.5). Don't like the pingbacks and trackbacks notifications? You can turn them off. When you're logged in to the WordPress Dashboard, select Settings and then Discussion. From the options shown, select Allow Link Notifications from Other Blogs (Pingbacks and Trackbacks), as shown in Figure 7.6.

Figure 7.5   Pings shown within the WordPress backend.

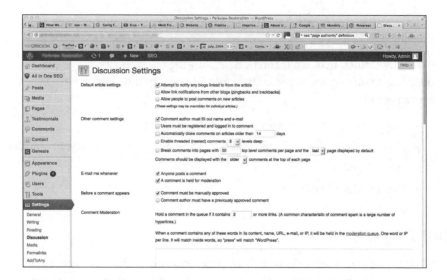

Figure 7.6 Control link notifications for pings.

Which Tools Do You Need for Best Analytics?

As I have throughout this book, I'll mention some of the many available WordPress plug-ins regarding analytics. I've suggested similar questions elsewhere, but here's what to consider before installing those plug-ins:

- Will the measurements from this plug-in be new? Will they give you data that you won't already have from Google Analytics or WordPress Analytics?

- Don't forget that your social share/follow plug-ins probably already include some element of measurement for their user functions. Likewise for form submissions. Aggregate this data if it's valuable to your goals.

- Do these data points really fit to your stated measurement goals? In other words, if your goal is to increase sales leads, are you really going to care much about image clicks from your employee photo gallery?

- Does this data apply to both Google and Bing/Yahoo!? Do you want it to?

- Will the data apply to important metrics you want? In other words, if you're trying to focus on ROMI or blog-engagement metrics, does this data matter or contribute easily to those metrics?

- How reliable do you think this plug-in and data are (for example, based on previous user reviews)?

Jetpack and WordPress.com Stats

Jetpack is a WordPress plug-in that allows for so much of the default functionality from WordPress.com to be used in your customized WordPress website (see Figure 7.7). Customized WordPress sites are great for their advanced options and technological flexibility. But when the simple, easy functionality of WordPress.com is enough, Jetpack conveniently offers so much within one plug-in. Just a few of the options include easy media embedding from video and other sites, posting options direct from email, direct posting to social networks like Facebook and LinkedIn, a widget for displaying Tweets, spell and grammar checking, and a photo-browsing carousel (for more on this see www.jetpack.me).

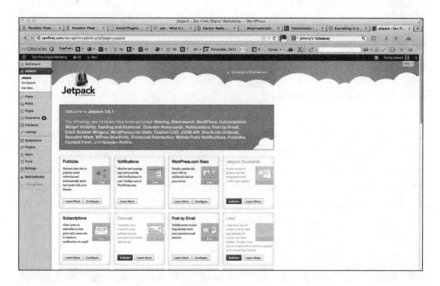

Figure 7.7   Jetpack modules.

The truth is, for a simple WordPress site or blog you may not need all the Google Analytics features. Remember the good ol' days of the simplified stats in the dashboard of your WordPress.com blog (see Figure 7.8)? You can have those again! Jetpack is a plug-in that incorporates so many of those convenient features of WordPress.com within your customized WordPress website or blog, including WordPress.com Stats.

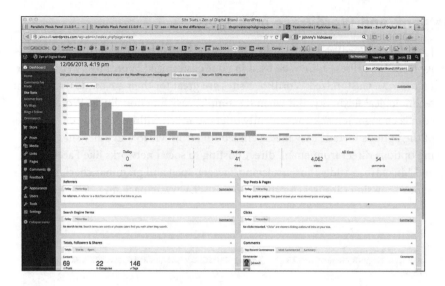

Figure 7.8   WordPress.com stats.

As we've discussed for plug-ins throughout this book, from your Dashboard and your Plug-ins menu options, you'll want to search for, install, and activate the Jetpack plug-in (see Figure 7.9). You will also need to select and activate the Jetpack modules you want from the plug-in's settings (see Figure 7.7). In this case, we want to configure the WordPress.com Stats module to authorize the account syncing and data display (see Figures 7.10 and 7.11).

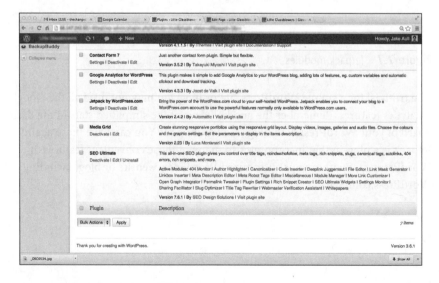

Figure 7.9   Searching for the Jetpack plug-in.

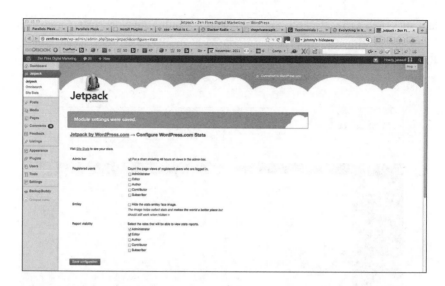

Figure 7.10   Configuring the WordPress.com Stats module in Jetpack.

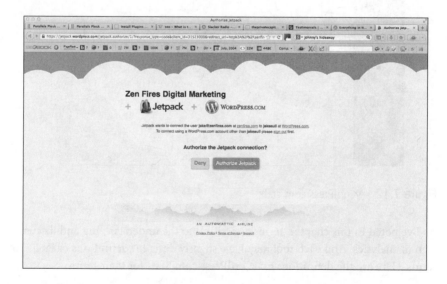

Figure 7.11   Authorization for the WordPress.com Stats module.

The WordPress.com Stats are a good, basic tutorial in blog analytics in and of themselves, thanks to their focused scope of measurements. For the most part, the analytics in WordPress.com Stats have been focused on discovering your blog's most effectiveness—that is, what day did you get the most traffic and what posts achieved the most traffic, comments, and shares. These are obvious blog-centric analytics such as Totals, Followers and Shares, around the blog Posts, Categories, Tags, and Comments. And there are Top Posts and Pages as well as Views and Referrers. This data can be segmented by dates in Summaries (as shown in Figure 7.12).

Figure 7.12   WordPress.com stats.

As I've noted in this chapter, terms are critical to the understanding and discussion of analytics. And each tool may have slightly different definitions of its use of terms. Here are the definitions by WordPress.com Stats for their terms:

"**About the math:** If you try to verify our computations using the numbers in these tables you might get different results. The logic is explained here.

- An average is the sum of views divided by the number of days.

- We exclude days prior to the first recorded view and future days.

- Today (Dec 6) is excluded from averages because it isn't over yet.

- Yearly averages are computed from sums, not an average of monthly averages.

- Averages are rounded to the nearest integer for display.

- Gray zeroes are exactly zero. Black zeroes have been rounded down.

- Percent change is computed from weekly averages before they are rounded."

Google Webmaster Tools

There are WordPress plug-ins that offer to set up your Google Webmaster Tools for you. Personally I prefer just to do it from within my Google Analytics account. It used to be more cumbersome and manual to tie a Google Webmaster Tools account to your website, requiring code, additional to the Google Analytics code, inserted in the website header. Now the Google Webmaster Tools account can be set up, verified, and synced merely by the Google Analytics account admin. A Google Webmaster Tools account for your website is crucial for several reasons:

- For canonicalization—to tell Google that your www.example.com/ URL is the same as http://example.com, so that Google doesn't think you have duplicate content across two different URLs.

- To tell Google your preferred of the two URLs for the SERP listings (generally www.example.com/ over http://example.com).

- To give you vital SEO results in your Google Analytics account reporting.

- To give you additional analytics accessible within Google Webmaster Tools (as we discuss in this chapter and Chapter 10; such as impressions).

- To increase "crawlability" and to give Google one more reason to like you.

Here's how to set it up within Google:

1. After your Google Analytics account is set up, log in to check your website account.

2. On the left sidebar menu, select **Standard Reports, Acquisition, Search Engine Optimization, Queries**.

3. If your Google Webmaster Tools account is already set up and synced properly, you will see data and no error messages here.

4. If not, Google Analytics will display the error message and direct you to set up your Google Webmaster Tools account.

5. Walk through the steps as directed. It will give you several options to set up and verify your Google Webmaster Tools account; choose Google Analytics verification (I find that easiest).

6. Then follow the steps to add and verify both URLs—www.example.com/ as well as http://example.com. These have to be added separately, by the same steps and verification procedures.

7. Google may want a few minutes to conduct these verifications, so have a little patience.

8. When both URLs are added and verified, identify your preferred domain as www.example.com/.

9. Go back to Google Analytics and confirm that you can see the SEO data now.

10. You did it! Now was that so hard? Do some cartwheels or something to celebrate!

 Note

Google Analytics and the Marketing Funnel

I refer in this chapter, and throughout the book, to the concept of the digital marketing funnel. This has direct, applicable meaning and use within Google Analytics, in that Google Analytics charts your digital success by showing how people flow through your website in relation to your website and SEO goals (as shown in Figure 7.13). Charting and instructing on this is beyond the scope of this chapter. Instead, we use the concepts of the digital marketing funnel and customer flow or journey to instruct on digital marketing analytics and SEO thought, strategy, and metrics approaches. However, properties such as Google Analytics' Multi-Channel Funnel (which shows the different digital channels consumers use to access your website, and where; as shown in Figure 7.14) are immensely valuable to know and always worth researching for more info.

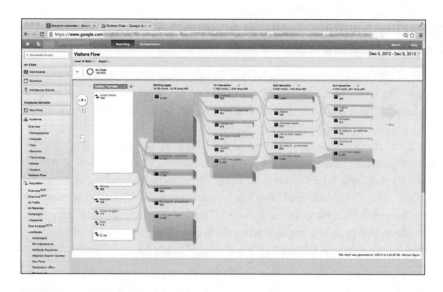

Figure 7.13   Google Analytics and Visitors Flow.

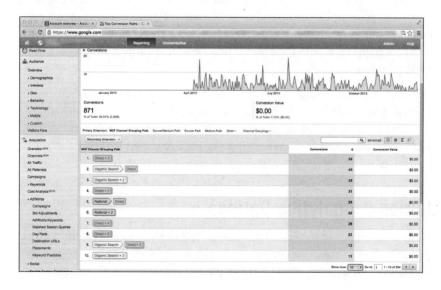

Figure 7.14   Google Analytics and the MCF Channel Grouping Path.

Managing Multiple Website Accounts Within Google Analytics

First of all, be careful! It used to be that Google Analytics allowed only one email address to act as admin for all data, and this admin function could not easily be reappointed to a new user. Many times in the past I have handled clients who did have preexisting Google Analytics accounts for their websites, which were controlled by the outside web designers or digital advertising agency. If clients wanted to change accounts or reclaim admin management of their own Google Analytics, not only did these vendors not want to turn over the admin access and lose the account, they physically could not release admin control. They had all their clients' accounts composed under the same Google account and could not release full admin access to one without releasing access to all (the clients only had viewer access to the data). At the time of this writing, Google has changed this by allowing analytics accounts to have multiple admins.

Regardless, I still consider it most professional to create total, separate accounts for my clients that allow full login admin access to all things Google for their SEO benefit. When I complete my work for the client, I can turn over the Gmail account access and password to them, and they have the option to never let me access that data and those accounts again if they so choose. I do create these accounts in the client names and with their phone numbers for security and password-forget backup options.

However, if I am creating multiple Google Analytics accounts (and Google+ locations, and so on) for one client, I strive to attach those multiple options under the one Gmail (we discuss more on Google accounts in Chapter 9, "Going Mobile and Local," and Chapter 4, "WordPress On-Page Architecture and Basic SEO Execution").

Additional Analytics Options

Want more data, like social analytics? Don't feel like you have to spend a fortune—if your budget is "free," you still have good options. Whether plug-ins, search engine tools, or external sites—there's a plethora of data with your name on it.

- **WordPress Tools:** Google Webmaster Tools verification, Bing Webmaster Tools verification, and Pinterest verification—even within just WordPress.com sites.
- **Google Analytics:** Google Analytics Plug-in (with integrated Google Webmaster Tools) can show where traffic is coming from, including from social media channels. In recent years this has also grown to show more social and reputation data.

- **YouTube Analytics:** YouTube has its own analytics, and these can be integrated with your Google accounts and Google Analytics. Take advantage of this! Create your YouTube channel and sync your analytics.

- **Social Network User Detection plug-in:** Suppose you just want to know what social media channels your web visitors are on simultaneously with your website up. Hello, Social Network User Detection plug-in, which tells us just that. The plug-in has a high user rating and can be good data to drive your own social sites used for social media marketing campaigns. However, as with all plug-ins, you may want to check for plug-in updates and read current reviews for current WordPress compatibility prior to installing: http://wordpress.org/plugins/social-network-user-detection/.

- **WordPress analytics:** You should remember from your free WordPress.com blog that it had some decent analytics in the dashboard behind login. Not as good as Google Analytics, but for free, what are ya gonna do? If you like the filtered results of WordPress analytics, you can still install the plug-in for that on your customized WordPress website.

- **Social media shares and follows:** Okay, so we know of different analytics options to gauge the role of social media in regard to our WordPress site or blog. But perhaps we want to demonstrate our posting success to our readers. Perhaps your company is a no-name startup and you want to show you're here to stay. How about a plug-in that displays your social shares or followers data right on your site? It just might help. One such plug-in is called Social Media Counters: http://wordpress.org/plugins/social-media-counters/.

- **Shortened URLs:** There are a variety of shortened URL formats out there—bit.ly, HootSuite's ow.ly, and so on. Even WordPress has a URL shortener; have you noticed it? Log in to the backend of your WordPress site and pull up a blog post, any blog post to Edit. Under the headline, beside the Permalink, you'll see the option to Get Shortlink (see Figure 7.15; note that this isn't quite as short as what other, true URL shorteners will do). But not only do most of these tools have the benefit of making tighter URLs for you to publish, but if you do so with your account, tools like bit.ly will keep analytics for you on every click. Not bad, eh?

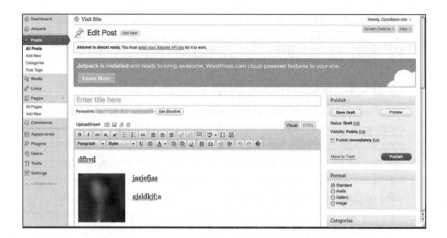

Figure 7.15 Editing a post title and getting a shortlink.

- **SocialMention.com:** I mentioned this site earlier. Don't forget it. If you want a quick count of people who like you and people who don't, pull up SocialMention.com and check your bad self out! This site is advantageous because it reveals your "brand mentions" and not just backlinks!

- **Klout:** Klout has been around since the early days of social media. It is a measurement tool that gathers data from your social profiles and gives you a rank based on its own algorithm. Many social media pros complain about Klout and the supposed methodology behind its rankings. But Klout deserves some credibility for its longevity. For good or bad it is perceived as a type of standard in the limitless world of today's social media.

Shortened URLs

Tiny.url, ow.ly, bit.ly—even WordPress has its own URL shortening options. (When publishing a blog post, WordPress gives you the option for a shortened URL within the logged in editor.) For example, if share your blog post to Twitter via the HootSuite social dashboard, HootSuite will give your link an ow.ly shortened URL, track it, and retain analytics for you on how many click-throughs your link receives from across the web (more on this in Chapter 8, "Social Media Connectivity").

Mobile Analytics

Mobile analytics can be somewhat different from traditional desktop web analytics. For starters, there are apps. Searching for apps is not the same as opening up Google and searching keywords for websites. And of course "app downloads" becomes a critical data point. But app usage is more mysterious and harder to glean. There are reports that say that 80% of app downloaders never use that app again after the first two days. And even with the best mobile app data, how to compare to desktop or web traffic?

Server-Side Analytics

One of the drawbacks of Google Analytics is that if you lose your account access (or never had account access to begin with) you don't have historical data. So don't forget your passwords! However, don't forget about your server analytics. Your web server and hosting provider often includes server data components for showing historical website traffic and onsite search. Don't use this data if it's going to confuse you, but if you have no data alternative, this is certainly better than nothing. As with all digital data, you can find ways to aggregate and baseline with data going forward. Just don't be surprised if you get different numbers from your server analytics than from Google Analytics. The latter will be much more reliable because it has standards regarding bounce identification (what is and what is not considered a bounce and how best to screen them out) and referral click-throughs versus direct access (keyed-in URLs) to the website.

Even SEO Book Tools we discussed in Chapter 3 on strategy reveals data on search engine traffic (click-throughs from search engines to your website or blog), overall website traffic and even unique visitors (but again, not as reliably as Google Analytics).

Final Thoughts on Expanded Measurement

Ideally, you want to try to see data that truly represents search engine and social effectiveness. In other words, if someone is searching for your brand name, ACME Honey Consulting, to find you, that's not quite as significant as someone new searching for "beehive honey extract consultation without getting stung." You also want to filter out visitors from within your own domain name. In other words, if your computer browser is registered to acme.com, you want to filter that out of web visit counts.

8

Social Media Connectivity

Chapter objectives and questions:

- Social media is not just popular—it's required, and WordPress is among the best for social media integration.
- Thinking long-term with social media.
- The power of social reputation.
- WordPress social plug-ins.
- Tying to the wheel-and-spoke model.
- Writing the social media plan.
- See how the power of social integration can also explode your SEO results!

Note

Not Necessarily Endorsements

Note that this chapter covers a lot of WordPress-specific plug-ins. This is not my endorsement of these plug-ins. Some of these I've fully used on a live, working WordPress site and some I haven't. As in all cases, use your own judgment to pick the right plug-in. Refer back to Chapter 2, "The Search Engines, WordPress, and SEO Tools," for the best ways to research and choose the right plug-ins for you, your needs, and your WordPress site.

What relationships exist between WordPress and social media? For starters, WordPress *is* social media. I've already discussed the blurred lines of today's online world of content. When we first stumble upon (or should I say StumbleUpon) a modern website, do we know if it's clearly that or a blog? A magazine or a newspaper? A social media site or a forum? At its most basic function, WordPress's engaging web format is comparable to blog software such as Tumblr or Google's Blogger. WordPress's blog post format easily outputs into Facebook, which can preview great representations of WordPress blog content and format it into an everyday Facebook post. WordPress offers many other options for social media integration. Think of it as a gateway into a variety of social networking roles, content, individual users, and technologies.

Long-Term Social Media Trends

Social media and social networking sites are here to stay. I'm sure this is a shock, but social media is not a passing fad. Now that the cat is out of the bag, what are the major attributes of functionality that consumers use social media for? And what are the big channels today? Believe it or not, there is rhyme and reason; social channels don't just come and go without patterns. People have been using social media for specific operations and purposes since the early days of Web 2.0. If the specific channels themselves have not lasted, they've given way to more streamlined channels of similar purpose and functionality. A lot of books and blogs attempt to categorize social channels differently. Here are my categories based on my own observations on the history of what we call social media and consumer usage.

- Social profiles and posting
  - MySpace
  - Facebook
  - Google+? Will it last? More than just Hangout?

- Microcontent and bursts
  - Twitter
  - SMS/MMS/texting
  - Vine
- Photo sharing
  - Flickr
  - Pinterest
  - Instagram
- Video posting
  - YouTube
  - Vimeo
  - Hulu
- Communities and discussion threads
  - Forums
  - LinkedIn Groups
- Content curation
  - RSS Readers
  - Paper.li
- Video conferencing
  - Skype
  - GoToMeeting
  - Google+Hangout
- Business networking and profile sharing
  - Plaxo
  - Spokeo
  - LinkedIn
- Event sharing
  - Facebook events
  - EventBrite
  - MeetUp

- Content posting/blogs
  - TypePad
  - Blogspot
  - WordPress
  - Tumblr
- Reviews channels
  - Google/Google+/Local
  - CitySearch
  - Yelp
- Local directories
  - Yahoo!Local
  - WhitePages.com
  - YP
- URL shortening and bookmarking
  - Delicious
  - Xmarks
  - Tiny.url
  - Bit.ly
- Social search engines
  - Technoratti
  - Digg
  - Reddit
- Daily Deals
  - Groupon
  - LivingSocial]
  - Tanga
  - Woot!
- Travel sites
  - Expedia
  - TripAdvisor

- Music sites
  - Napster
  - Pandora
  - Spotify
- eCommerce
  - Amazon
  - eBay

These are platform models which have existed long-term in social media and will likely continue to do so. But how they are affected in Google and Bing is another story. The different digital platforms are eternally at war and/or in bed with each other. For example Google versus Facebook, Google versus Microsoft (see a pattern here?), Microsoft ties the knot with Yahoo!, and so on.

How Do Specific, Major Social Channels Impact SEO?

We've already talked about inbound marketing, or link building with the power of inbound links in Chapter 3, "A Strategic SEO Upfront Content Approach." In this chapter we also discuss how social media can be used to build web traffic (very important). But a common goal in SEO is that of total SERP real-estate consumption. That is, how can I have my name on as much of the search engine results page as possible? The answer? Social media (and PPC advertising, but we'll get into that in Chapter 10, "PPC and Advertising").

- **Google+ (and Google Images):** Google likes Google. Google+ was its attempt to compete with Facebook. Although it achieved an astonishing amount of initial individual registrations (25,000,000 within the first two months; far better than Facebook's original 36 months to reach 25,000,000; see Figure 8.1), it has arguably not retained ongoing, active usage. The world is on Facebook, and it isn't dumping Facebook for Google+ anytime soon. But Google has the capability to rank Google+ content much higher in the SERP than Facebook's (even though of course Bing will list Facebook content higher than Google+). So put your company on Google+ and sync the channel with your Google Analytics, Webmaster Tools, YouTube, and so on. You have nothing to lose and everything to gain (see Figure 8.2).

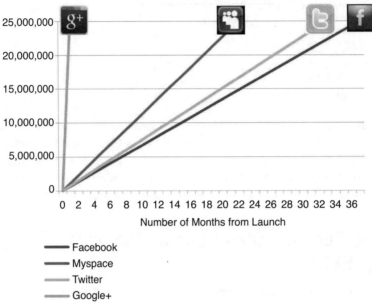

Figure 8.1   Google+ versus Facebook initial signups.

Figure 8.2   Google accounts.

- **Google Maps/Google+ Local (and Yahoo! Local):** What used to be called Google Places is now part of Google+ business pages. Still unsure of what this is? It's the results on the Google SERP when you search for local businesses, such as plumbers, hair salons, or landscapers—the results with a pin beside the Google Map. As I said, Google likes Google, and location-based SEO is very valuable. (We'll get deep into location-based SEO in Chapter 9, "Going Mobile and Local," on mobile and local search).

- **YouTube (and Bing Video):** Remember that YouTube is considered the world's second largest search engine. Its videos don't come up only there, but in the regular Google SERP as well, just as videos also come up in the Bing SERP, as shown in Figure 8.3. Vertical search results, images, and video pop out among regular text-limited results, attract viewer attention, and beg to be clicked (Pick me! Pick me!)—so use these!

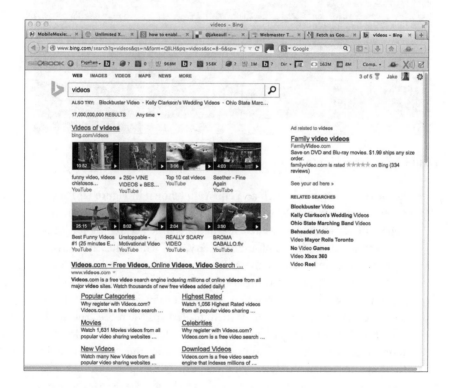

Figure 8.3   The Bing SERP with videos.

- **Flickr:** Flickr.com is a great (albeit old) social media channel (see Figure 8.4), because even though it has fewer social followers these days, it has SEO power. Part of this is because it still comes up well in Google. Google has its own competitor to Facebook, so it won't give Facebook pages good ranking (a point of past lawsuits). But Flickr still comes up. Flickr is owned by Yahoo!, so it will have Bing/Yahoo! search results as well.

Figure 8.4 Flickr's Photostream.

- **Local/review channels such as Yelp:** Yelp (shown in Figure 8.5) and other directories, such as MerchantCircle, CitySearch, and YP, often appear in search engine results—particularly when searching for local keywords, such as "home plumbing, Gary, IN." These sites are massive content repositories, so use them! Even new businesses will be listed in these channels (drawn from business records), but too often with incomplete or wrong information. You want to make full use of these sites and maximize your profiles therein! Perhaps the more crucial aspect of these sites is that of social reviews. Often, businesses don't monitor their social reputation in these and other sites, and believe that there are no "social mentions" of their businesses online. And yet it is all too often for at least one of these sites to have reviews. Maybe good, maybe bad reviews—either way you should know and deal with these reviews in the best fashion.

For more on local SEO strategies, refer back to Chapter 3 and to mobile location-based technologies in Chapter 9.

Figure 8.5   Yelp and reviews.

- **LinkedIn:** LinkedIn, with its business-community targeting, still comes up in Google results (perhaps because Google doesn't have a social competitor to this). And whether it's your individual profile or your company LinkedIn page, you can have helpful inbound links to your website here. And LinkedIn is a great way to post about and promote your business blog.

The Power of Social Reputation

You're only as good as your reputation, or so they say. The social web provides countless opportunities and channels for others to talk about you behind your back on the good, the bad, and the ugly. These reviews come up in search engine results (as well as results within those channels themselves, such as Yelp, shown previously, Kudzu, Angie's List, or even Twitter). You need to be aware of these reviews but also to respond to them. But here's the real power of these reviews: authenticity. People trust more what others like themselves say about a company rather than what the company says about itself. But take it a step further: Any company can have positive testimonials on its website—maybe they're authentic, maybe they dug them up from friends and family, maybe they even made them up. You just don't know, because a website is brand-controlled, not user controlled.

A brand's Facebook page with customer-uploaded reviews is much better— customer reviews are customer reviews. But the Facebook brand page is still controlled by the brand, which has control to filter some items out. However, social review sites such as Google+, Facebook, and YP are controlled by web users leaving reviews. Therefore, these are the most trusted channels by consumers. So treat your online reputation like gold, respond to bad reviews with apologies and efforts to make good on the problem. Remember that even the best companies won't have 100% 5-star reviews; some complaints further add authenticity. For all these reasons, social review sites may be a better option to RSS feed into your WordPress site—better than copying and pasting positive, anonymous testimonials.

Plug-ins, Widgets, and More Plug-ins!

Now you know a thing or two about what social media is and its role in SEO, and you're thinking, "Show me the hands-on tools to integrate with WordPress!" No worries. This section's for you:

- **Social Sharing plug-ins:** Remember reading about Social Share in Chapter 4, "WordPress On-Page Architecture and Basic SEO Execution"? There are several options for these plug-ins. I've used the ShareThis plug-in with great success. However, you can also try SocialShare, AddToAny, and Sociable.

- **Content curation and RSS feeds of social content:** Just as RSS is "content curation," it is not the only such vehicle. You may or may not be familiar with the social site Paper.li, but it is a great content curator, a social site for displaying your own gathered newspapers (see Figure 8.6). Whereas RSS feeds are primarily for your own reading, Paper.li pages are what you publish to the outside world. It is also a good opportunity for your blog or other content to be featured in someone else's Paper.li newspaper. Paper.li sites are promoted via Twitter so it becomes another option in the wheel-and-spoke model we discuss in this chapter. There are plug-ins for piping Paper.li content into your WordPress site. RebelMouse is also a content curation site, which syncs all of your different social networking pages and feeds them collectively into your own online RSS newspaper site. And it too has a plugin for WordPress, so you can display your massive, multimedia RebelMouse content onto a page of your website featuring all of your social content at a glance. Still curious about what the heck this Paper.li is? Open up your own Paper.li or peruse others' and learn!

- **Art Gallery plug-ins from photo and image social sites:** One of the great things about WordPress is that it features a lot of various plug-ins. Take, for example, the Awesome Flickr Gallery.

  As we've discussed, Flickr has been around for eons of Web 2.0, one of the defining channels of social functionality. Flickr has a lot of content; to this day professional photographers keep entire portfolios there. Flickr is also a great resource for finding stock imagery; often images are royalty free for your use (but make sure by reading specific images' restrictions and checking for Creative Commons authorization for free-use imagery). You have the option of achieving double coverage of your art galleries by uploading to a Flickr account and using a plug-in to display that same gallery in your WordPress site. In addition to Flickr, there have been many image-based social sites, and always at least one consumer favorite at a given time. Currently, top (static) image and photo sites are Pinterest (desktop Internet focused) and Instagram (mobile-platform oriented).

  There are also plug-in options for Pinterest. These options include, for example, easy Pin-it plug-ins, such as the Pinterest Pin-It Button for Images or Pinterest Image Pin. These allow each photo on your website to have a Pin-It button for consumers to have immediate access to pin your images to their own Pinterest boards. Although "social share" plug-ins should be able to do the same, this conveniently focuses on your website individual images for the Pinterest world.

- **Third-party social integrations plug-ins for placed content, such as Google Maps:** The importance of location-based SEO, Google+Local, and Google Maps are discussed in depth in Chapter 9 on mobile and local SEO. Take advantage of this—sync your Google accounts and drop your business Google+Local map directly on your website via the plug-in.

- **Plug-ins allowing consumer rating and other rich-snippet SEO and social integrations:** Reviews and comments are one thing; ratings— from one to five stars—are another. Both are shown in channels such as Yelp. You can integrate a WordPress plug-in for rating star options, allowing your WordPress blog or forum readers to rate the content they see on your site (it's a lot of pressure though, isn't it?). Plug-ins such as GD Star Rating easily allow web visitors to rate your website content from blog posts to pages.

- **Social monitoring:** Tools such as SocialMention.com, Google Alerts, and keyword monitoring in HootSuite are great for monitoring your digital presence and consumer mentions. But there are also plug-ins that claim to do this right from within WordPress! If you have stellar mentions online, why not aggregate these and display them on your site? You can do this in WordPress, and such a feed is not "copy-and-paste"—meaning that a web developer can't fake your testimonials. This is the real deal, straight from the posters in social channels. How do you feed all this into your WordPress site? One plug-in is simply titled Social Media Monitoring. Try it! Why have a Testimonials page, which consumers might think you faked, when you can have ongoing, refreshed, authentic, and transparent brand mentions from the real world? See it at http://wordpress.org/plugins/social-media-monitoring/

- **WordPress blog authorship synced with Google for vertical SEO results:** In Chapter 5, "Real-World Blogging," and Chapter 6, "In-Depth Hands-On SEO Execution," we discussed the role of vertical results listings from search engines. The concept is, the more you see in a specific search result description, the more that listing jumps out at you, the more attractive it becomes. The bigger the bait the more you bite.

  These options for vertical results include, for example, "news" or "in-depth articles" and "authorship." You've probably seen Google results where a photo is shown beside the description in blog or article listings (as shown in Figures 8.6 and 8.7). When you properly set up your WordPress profile for your blog posting and sync that with your Google+ profile, Google can attach that to your search results. And yes, there's a plug-in for that! The major, comprehensive SEO plug-ins, such as Yoast, WordPress SEO, and SEO Ultimate, have functions for this. (You can revisit these plug-ins in Chapters 5 and 6 on hands-on SEO).

Figure 8.6   In-depth articles in the SERP.

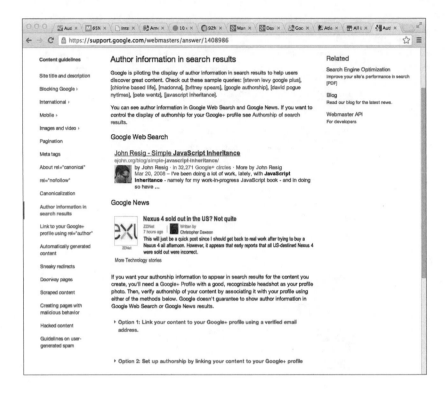

Figure 8.7   Authorship in the SERP.

- **Social community-creation capabilities, such as sharing and discussion groups and community formats:** Yup. You can build 'em with WordPress.

- **Open source community of WordPress support and updates:** As we've discussed previously, you too can be a WordPress theme and/or plug-in developer! This is the open source community—anyone can jump in the sandbox. This is an instrumental, defining attribute of what it means to live and play in the social media age. How about you? *Are you a playa?*

- **Direct push posts-to-social sites, such as with Facebook, as mentioned previously:** Yes, there's a plug-in for that; it's called Social Media Auto Publish. One of the things to be careful about with autopublishing sites and social media add-ons is image display. For example, when publishing a post with a picture from the HootSuite mobile app to Facebook and Twitter, the image comes up as a link requiring an extra click, rather than displaying the picture 100% visible in the Facebook post itself. Fortunately Social Media Auto Publish claims to correct this. (See it at http://wordpress.org/plugins/social-media-auto-publish/.)

WordPress being WordPress, there's always another plug-in option. In this case it's titled the Social Marketing plug-in. In addition to easily blasting to more expected social media channels, it also can post to your Tumblr. You know, for when one blog is not enough (and I say this facetiously: Ask yourself—do you really want to blog post from WordPress to Tumblr? See it at http://wordpress.org/plugins/socialmarketing/.

- **BuddyPress:** The BuddyPress plug-in allows you to generate a full, collaborative social community with your WordPress site.

- **Forums:** You can use themes and plug-ins to incorporate forum capabilities within your WordPress site. These open up the social engagement opportunities. CC Forum is one; it's a good forum plug-in that I've worked with in the past for installing a MyBB forum database and group functionality onsite. Additional forum plug-ins include Mingle Forum and Tai.ki Embeddable Forum.

    Be careful to plan out how to handle forum issues such as these:

    - User profiles
    - Profiles and commenting between the forum and your blog (if you have both)
    - Admin privileges
    - Negative discussions
    - User and content blocking
    - Comment approvals
    - Q&A

As previously discussed, for many reasons WordPress is a modern, socially rich platform—from its open-source collaborative birth to its many social plug-in integrations. But all these inclusions need to be regarded in light of your social media strategy and plan. If Pinterest is not part of your company's social media strategy or interest, there's no purpose in using that plug-in on your WordPress site.

Outside Social Site Usage with WordPress

Plug-ins are not the only way to integrate WordPress sites with other social media technologies. Other good options exist for additional, external social media integrations between WordPress and other social tools:

- **Social dashboard content-posting integrations, such as with HootSuite:** Believe it or not, you can post directly to WordPress from a social dashboard such as HootSuite! If you're going to write long blog posts with image uploads, I don't recommend this—I prefer the WordPress backend interface where you can control everything much more. But if you do quick posts and bursts directly tied to Twitter, Facebook, Google+, and the like, a social dashboard may be your option. If you're unfamiliar, this is what social dashboard tools such as HootSuite do; they allow you to post to multiple social channels, pre-scheduled, synced—however you like! HootSuite is a premium channel, but there are a lot of capabilities built in to the free account options. Try it for yourself. Go to HootSuite.com and open a free account, or use the mobile app. Other social dashboards include CoTweet, TweetDeck, and others.

- **Post-to-Twitter or Facebook:** Your WordPress blog post can be connected to Facebook and/or other channels for broadcast posting from WordPress out across the digital space. (Sounds like science fiction, doesn't it?)

- **Content curation:** In Chapter 4, on WordPress.com architecture and SEO, we discussed RSS feeds options. The same principles for integrating others' blogs into an RSS feed or reader also helps you because others can feed your WordPress blog into their readers and feeds! You can also benefit from other content curation channels, such as Paper.li, which feature your post content with others of similar topics in an online newsletter for all to see.

UPFRONT RESEARCH FOR SOCIAL SITE CAMPAIGNS

We've already discussed strategic planning in Chapter 3, but it bears repeating, particularly here in the specific social technology usage. It's vital to research social channels in advance for any campaign, as part of the strategic planning, for the following reasons:

- **User audience:** If yours is a financial investment social site, for example, you'll most likely have more Baby Boomers than Millennials on your site.

- **Usage and buzz trending:** How new and hot is the social channel? Just because it has buzz right now doesn't mean it will tomorrow.

- **Search-engine friendliness:** Very important!

- **Integrations with other social channels:** Does the channel play well with others? Here are good examples:
  - SlideShare.net feeds into LinkedIn.
  - Instagram and Pinterest feed into Facebook.
  - Twitter and Facebook can post to each other.

- **Integrations and usage in WordPress format:** WordPress is pretty universal, but don't just assume that a social channel can be dropped into WordPress and look the way you want it. When you feed another social site's content into your WordPress site, it may not appear with the native, clean usability inherent to its own original channel interface. So when you want the right plug-in, research, research, research!

Wheel-and-Spoke Strategy

In Chapter 3 we discussed the importance of a hub-and-spoke or link-wheel model. It becomes far more critical with your social media. The tendency has become to show in every channel all the social media channels where your company has profiles. I call this the *loss of multiplicity factors*. We typically think the more social channels you're in, the better. But here's where strategy becomes so crucial. Suppose your company has profiles in Pinterest, Instagram, Tumblr, Flickr, MySpace, YouTube, Vine, Google+, Vimeo, LinkedIn, Yelp, Foursquare, Twitter, and Facebook. But for all of that, you post regularly only to Twitter and Facebook. Regardless, you list, display, and request followers to all channels. In all channels. Equally. Listed by your website. Next to an address to the house you were raised in (okay—well maybe not this last option). Where do the web users go? And if they travel only to MySpace, is that really where you want them? Be strategic. Plan your posting and your ideal digital funnel, and build your social link wheel strategy around that.

1. Suppose you have your latest whitepaper, which is set behind your website contact form on a landing page, so prospects have to opt-in to your site and emails to get the full industry whitepaper.

2. To spread the news and build traffic, you posted a snippet of that whitepaper on your blog with a call-to-action link to the form.

3. Suppose you also post that blog post content in Facebook.

4. You have a goal to get more Facebook "Likes," so you promote and link to that Facebook post from Twitter and LinkedIn.

5. Simultaneously you take the infographic from that blog post and display it (with a backlink) in Pinterest.

6. Later, you want to recycle your social content, so you post the same infographic alone, directly in Facebook, with the link to the blog post.

7. Your salespeople, meanwhile, conduct trade show presentations about the whitepaper content and ask for Twitter questions (and follows, @example) during the presentation (#example); instantly, you're growing Twitter followers.

8. During the presentation you put their PowerPoint slide deck up on SlideShare.net and promote via Twitter @example and #example.

9. The SlideShare deck has a call-to-action link to the blog post.

10. While generating post-trade show buzz, you post a call-to-action link both in Facebook and LinkedIn to the SlideShare deck.

11. You also capture and clean up good video footage of your salesperson's trade show presentation, and you host that on YouTube, with a link to the website landing page form.

12. You promote the YouTube video via Facebook, Twitter, LinkedIn, and SlideShare.

13. It turns out the YouTube video and SlideShare deck reveal some good questions about the content via web user comments.

14. You blog about the answers, and the cycle begins again.

15. Now suppose this original plan occurs over the course of two months (with numerous repeat social media posts—words and tone-of-voice, and time of day, changed here and there).

That provides you with a good digital marketing funnel, a customer online journey via a link wheel. Do you see it? Let's go further, where a customer path can be like this:

1. Prospect reads about trade show in LinkedIn and attends.

2. Prospect follows your company on Twitter.

3. Prospect clicks through and downloads the SlideShare.net deck.

4. Prospect clicks through to the blog post.

5. Prospect clicks through to the website landing page.

6. Prospect fills out the form for the whitepaper.

The assorted social media channels are the spokes (see Figure 8.8). They link to each other to form the wheel. The hub is the website landing page form, or it can just as easily be the blog. Now do you know how to ride this bicycle?

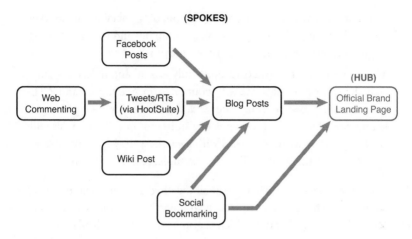

Figure 8.8   A Social media hub-and-spoke.

The Social Media Plan

Social media execution doesn't happen on its own. Just as we discussed in Chapters 5 and 6, it's one thing to identify goals and channels; it's another to identify the intangible needs and roles required upon you and others to make everything work:

- **Resources:** Someone's got to do this thing. Who's going to post the social content for your company? Someone internal may know the organization, brand, and messaging better than anyone on the outside. At the same time, someone on the outside may know the media channels better than anyone at your company. Many organizations decide to hire a young intern or college grad to do this work, but that person is neither an expert in the company content nor in strategic marketing in social media. Keep all this in mind and decide carefully. How about a pet bird? If you look at Twitter and HootSuite icons, birds must be masters of the media.

- **Time:** It takes a lot. How much? How much do you have? Plan it out in a calendar. Don't start a Facebook and/or Twitter campaign without regularly posting to it, for the same reasons you wouldn't invite people to a trade show event and then not put together the trade show. Either do it right or don't do it. However, you can still have a more dormant social profile and some basic, foundational content in channels such as LinkedIn, Google+, and Pinterest.

- **Content:** Will you have the content for ongoing social media marketing? Is there enough to say about your company and industry? What might your customer base want to learn from you?

- **Tie-ins with other marketing:** Now fully extend and hold out your right arm. Now do the same with your left arm. See those hands? They have to each know what the other is doing. Same thing with your marketing. Social media marketing is not an island unto itself—it should work in concert with, or at least with awareness of, your other branding and marketing efforts. Take for example, search marketing.

Okay—so got all the above? Then put it all together in your social media plan. What frequency, what social channels, what objectives, and how to measure. Some call it the social media calendar, which is also a good way to display it.

Table 8.1 shows an example of a social media plan.

Pros and Cons of Social Media in SEO

What's the good news? A strategic social media/SEO plan can achieve crucial backlinks and increased traffic. It also allows customers to leave positive reviews, which greatly aid SEO results (Google+ and Google/Local reviews, for example). The world is on social media; they can find you there as well.

What are the things to watch out for? Social media users can easily click away from a company's social media profiles to other social links, others' social sites and info. And social media is less controllable than other marketing media; you never know what a spiteful customer (or even competitor!) will say there.

The point of social media and SEO integration is to be strategic. Don't run around willy-nilly integrating your website or blog with all social media channels for their own sake.

Get It Goin' On

So there you go—your whirlwind tour of the limitless possibilities of WordPress and social media, including countless WordPress plug-ins, as well as external sites that incorporate WordPress feeds or posting. Use all this power responsibly, with wheel-and-spoke models and social media plans; do your homework upfront first. And don't forget to measure your progress! Now—ready to go posting?

Table 8.1 Sample Social Media Plan

	Mktg Predecessors?	Hours (daily/ weekly/ monthly)	Date Spread	Short-term Objectives	Key Metrics & Tools Analytics	Time/ Resource Allocation	$ Budget	Keywords/ CTA	Segment Details
Blog									
Social Networks									
Microblogging (Twitter)									
Social Press (Bloggers)									
Widgets									
Bookmarking/Tagging									
Crowdsourcing/Voting									
Commenting/Forums/ Wikis/ Rating and Review sites									
Online Video									
Photo sharing									
Podcasting									
Presentation Sharing									

9

Going Mobile and Local

Chapter objectives and questions:

- Mobile trends
- The WordPress editing app
- WordPress mobile sites
- Mobile SEO
- QR codes
- NFC and location-based search
- Daily deals apps and sites

Where's the Web?

There's no doubt that mobile use is here to stay—in fact it's taking over desktop web use as we know it! Consider these stats (at the time of this writing):

- Half of the time spent online by American adults is on mobile, and mobile use is on the rise: http://www.liveintent.com/news/mobile-strategy/american-adults-spend-more-time-on-their-smart-phones-than-ever-before/.

- 65% of overall time spent in social networks is on mobile: http://mashable.com/2013/10/24/content-consumption-desktop-mobile/.

- 55% of overall time in online retail occurs on mobile (especially smartphone), and two-thirds of all smartphone owners use mobile to research products, deals, reviews, and the like. http://www.internetretailer.com/mobile/2013/10/01/its-official-mobile-devices-surpass-pcs-online-retail.

- 40% of YouTube traffic is from mobile, compared to just 6% in 2011: http://techcrunch.com/2013/10/17/youtube-goes-mobile/.

- 92% of the time Americans spend with electronic photos occurs on mobile: http://www.comscoredatamine.com/2013/10/92-of-u-s-time-spent-with-photos-occurs-on-mobile-vs-just-25-for-portals/.

A powerful asset of mobile digital marketing and consumer use is the ability for search, social, and marketing technologies to identify user locations and serve content relevant to that location. Some of this content and identification applies to your laptop as well (thanks to browser and IP address location identification), but the true power lies in mobile device technologies, for both smartphone and tablet. You may have played with location check-in apps such as Foursquare and Yelp, which serve coupons based on location or amount of check-ins (such as for Foursquare "Mayors" and Yelp "Dukes"). You may have seen how these apps, or newer specific area-based apps, such as Banjo, connect you to people based specifically on proximity.

But let's put mobile apps to the side for the moment and focus on the mobile web. Yes, the mobile web is yet a separate Internet, so to speak. If you've noticed the unique domain at the end of sites, .mobi, you've seen a site from the mobile web. You may also notice that some mobile sites come up as subdomains, such as http://m.example.com or http://mobile.example.com, as opposed to http://example.mobi or user-agent-served mobile site on http://www.example.com. User-agent technology is that which helps search engines and mobile web browsers identify and serve your mobile website to mobile device users as needed. Although you have options to structure your mobile site with different domain strategies as mentioned previously, I like the arguments for having the same domain (for example, .com), and the SEO technology and benefits built in to your desktop website there also benefit your mobile search engines. Still confused? No worries. All this same-domain structure is the default for mobile themes in WordPress. So put 'em up and don't worry about it!

Display Trends

Any web user complaints against limitations of mobile usability will surely be changed in the near future. Think the display on your smartphone is too small? The resolution just keeps getting sharper and sharper. Likewise, more and more options straddle the line between smartphone and tablet, just as the Microsoft Surface straddles the line between tablet and laptop, as a tablet with a light, attachable/detachable keyboard. Even the Apple MacBook Pro at the time of this writing no longer makes laptops with a screen larger than 15.2" and hasn't in more than two years.

This technology is older than we tend to think it is, going back to the original iPod Touch, back to the original Blackberries, the PalmPilot, and other handheld electronic devices. Although the resolution of these and app technologies were certainly not what exist today, the physical dimensions and usage have set trends and behavior that have embedded themselves within our society over the years and will continue to do so. Want more proof on user trends? See Google Analytics on your own website visitors' access (as we discussed in Chapter 7, "Analytics for WordPress," and also shown in Figure 9.1). I also highly recommend the demographics web user data available from Pew Internet Research studies at www.pewinternet.org.

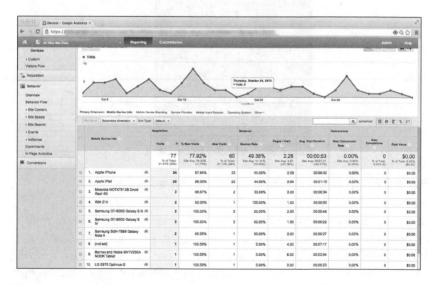

Figure 9.1 Google Analytics mobile data.

The WordPress Mobile App

There are free mobile apps for WordPress software that allow you to post to your WordPress blog from mobile devices. As with many apps, there are some issues. At the time of this writing, the app is not conducive for creating and editing new pages for WordPress. But the app is functional for blog posts—for either the free version of WordPress.com blogs or fully customized WordPress site blogs. The app also manages your multiple WordPress site accounts simultaneously. I can easily access any of seven WordPress sites through my app (see Figure 9.2).

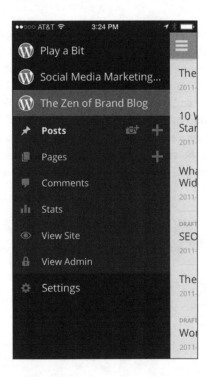

Figure 9.2 WordPress Mobile App for iPhone blog management.

In Chapter 8, "Social Media Connectivity," I discussed social dashboard applications such as HootSuite (which also allows you to write and post directly to WordPress if that works well for you and your process). HootSuite has a mobile app. The same is true for HootSuite's mobile app as it is for the WordPress mobile app in that it's a very constricting method when posting a lot of content, even from a larger tablet such as the Windows Surface. These mobile apps are fine for short bursts like 140 character Tweets (see Figure 9.3), but I try to do my serious WordPress posting from a desktop.

Figure 9.3   HootSuite iPhone app posting.

Mobile Sites or Mobile Apps?

This could be a fun debate for debate clubs: consumer mobile websites versus mobile apps. *"Sites!" "Apps!" "No, Sites!"*—assuming the debate club knew about mobile and web usability and the trends involved. Okay, maybe it would make for a boring or geeky debate. Anyway, since I've pointed to this elephant, let's dive in on full-geek power.

 Note

Why WordPress Mobile Sites Are Winning (or Soon Will Be)

Mobile sites used to present usability issues; websites were built for desktop and compromised for mobile access. Hence, mobile apps were built with full tech functionality and usability. Today we are better and savvier. Websites are built with multiplatform media in mind: desktop and mobile (smartphone and tablet). Functionality and usability issues aside, the practicality of apps has its limitations. With all the various mobile devices, brand names, operating systems, and technology platforms, it gets very difficult, customization-heavy, and expensive to always be updating said apps. Again, this is an important selling point for mobile-responsive WordPress sites. Also making WordPress another leader in industry is that WordPress responsive themes can be as easy as building a desktop website one time, with smart mobile response adaptations defaulted. Themes such as Genesis are careful to clarify—and update—their themes with full mobile functionality.

This is not to say the mobile web is perfect today with perfectly user-friendly mobile web media and results. Even Google doesn't get it perfect all the time with mobile web presentation and usability (See Figure 9.4; this Mobile Web Google page on the iPhone Safari is far too small to be user-friendly). And from Safari (at the time of this writing) Google still displays requests to download the Google app for search. Bing has its app, as well. For these search engines, they expect you to download one or the other to have a monopoly on your search. A good usability question, however, is posed: Why go to a specific search engine app to access Safari results, links, and websites?

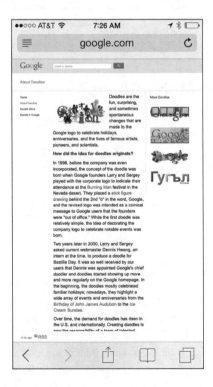

Figure 9.4   iPhone Safari Google poor usability.

Responsive Design and Architecture

Perhaps you've heard this fun "responsive design" buzz word. The idea is websites that "respond" to their environment; software, hardware—even silverware (okay, maybe not silverware). A website with browser detection or "sniffing" can detect the information about the browser in which it is served. Firefox 3.5? IE 7? And then the site can respond accordingly. This is not the only vehicle for response. Sites can also respond to the hardware: Smartphone? Laptop? Tablet?

From an information architecture standpoint, one of the great things about "mobile sites" (particularly those serving smartphones) is the distilled, bare-bones focus on just the most important information of the site (see Figure 9.5). A good mobile site's home page is just the menu—minimized graphics and no complex Flash animations (in fact, iPhones and iPads can't display Flash)—just the most important navigational properties on a site in the display. The flip side is that all the glorious designers' work is practically removed for pure information. And in-site search becomes very important. If you can't show mobile web viewers all the content and navigation options that you can on the desktop website, be sure to prominently give viewers the option to search your mobile site for what they want. (For more good thoughts on mobile website architecture see this blog post: http://www.webcredible.co.uk/user-friendly-resources/web-usability/mobile-guidelines.shtml.)

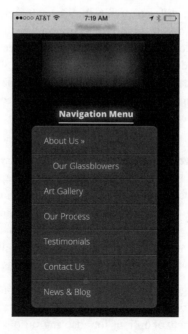

Figure 9.5 Mobile site navigation.

Many WordPress themes come with mobile-responsive adaptations, so your website can be correctly displayed on mobile. If your theme doesn't come with this capability, guess what? There's a plug-in for that. The real trick is in the technology detecting and serving different sites for desktop, smart phone, and tablet. It makes sense conceptually, but it can be limited by the technology and good information architecture to find that "perfect medium" in the structure of the tablet version of a site.

Among all the various browsers and mobile, tablet, and desktop potential versions, there's a lot to test for a new website, and a lot to design and develop for! So keep all this in mind when scoping, pricing, and testing a new site. Luckily, WordPress is making it easier. Just as we are crossing this threshold in web use, where American consumers are using the mobile web (smartphone + tablet) more for certain activities than the desktop web, we should expect to see WordPress themes that focus more on smartphone and tablet sites than on desktop (up to now it has been the opposite for WordPress templates).

Because of this sharpened content and distilled, quick-to-the-point power of mobile sites, the digital marketing funnel we discussed in Chapter 3, "A Strategic SEO Upfront Content Approach," becomes even more critical in the architecture of mobile sites. With the reduction of immediate content, and trimmed navigation options, getting mobile web visitors to your end goal—the spout of your funnel— must be critical with design and quickly apparent to the visitor. However, you may have an understandably different architectural goal for your mobile WordPress site than for your desktop site. If your objective on desktop is for visitors to fill out a full contact form to download a whitepaper, don't expect these for viewers on smartphone. Not only do the small reading and functional accessibility barriers exist, but users on smartphone are typically in transit. That is, they are in line at the grocery store, waiting on a subway train, or, to pull from our book's opening example, sitting in the car waiting to go to work.

Instead, identify alignment between what mobile searchers want from your site and the best thing for you to give them. Couponing is easy but not always practical (nor wise strategically, as we discuss elsewhere in this chapter and in Chapter 8.) Although whitepaper downloads are difficult on smartphone, video viewership has high consumer access (as we saw at the beginning of this chapter, 40% of YouTube traffic is from mobile), so serve them a video and incentivize simple activities such as social media shares, social follows, leaving a review in directories such as Google Maps (Google+Local) or Yelp, or possibly even requesting simple email opt-ins.

There are certainly plug-ins that make transition to the mobile web easy, even with legacy desktop WordPress themes. For example, there's the WordPress mobile pack with a variety of options for adapting various elements within your WordPress site to mobile-friendly options. WPTouch and Mobilize by Mippin are other plug-ins. These allow you to customize how much content—how many menu items, categories, tags, and so on are to be readily shown on your mobile site.

Again because of the real estate limitations, topics as well as copy length are at a premium and have to be served carefully. These and other plug-ins do this. Blog posts, as in desktop websites, can be directed to be previewed with teaser copy— another vital choice for mobile sites and blogs. One thing to remember, even with our progression toward and emphasis on mobile, is that it's still wise to offer the mobile web user the option to click a link (from your mobile site) to view the regular Internet desktop version of your site. The strength of mobile sites is the minimized, focused offerings of pertinent content for the space given. However, there may be web content or options not easily accessible on the mobile version of your site that are still valuable to a few viewers out there. Or if the "mobile" user is on a larger tablet, such as the Windows Surface, she may prefer to view the full desktop web blog instead of the mobile-minimized version. (This is also another argument for different-size sites across smartphone, tablet, and desktop, and specific monitor-sizes.) The book *WordPress in Depth* (second ed., by Bud E. Smith and Michael McCalister, 2012, Pearson, Indianapolis, pp. 340–342) discusses recommendations to include five widgets at most in a mobile theme, and to test your site at Ready.mobi.

Although these limitations for mobile sites are obvious, unique opportunities exist with mobile sites that you should take definite advantage of. The plug-ins mentioned include options for users to immediately respond on your mobile site within their hardware, such as immediate messaging, texting, or click to dial by phone. You can also include direct links from your mobile site to local directories, such as Yelp, YP, or Google Maps, where you might not normally want such links on your desktop website.

Browser and location-detection software also become helpful for mobile because you have the choice to serve specific web content based on location. You have options such as telling your mobile website to display the Chicago-location contact page, instead of the home page, if accessed by mobile devices there.

Mobile Site SEO

Note that the mobile search engines serve different results than desktop web search engines do, so you want to submit your site to these multiple platforms (and design your site for mobile as well as desktop). Google Webmaster Tools allow you to do this and so does Bing. First, ensure that your current WordPress plug-ins aren't already doing this for you. But just as with Google and your desktop website, you want to first generate a sitemap and then submit it. In Chapter 4, "WordPress On-Page Architecture and Basic SEO Execution," and Chapter 6, "In-Depth Hands-On SEO Execution," we discussed the importance of generating and submitting a website sitemap.xml file to Google, and how that could be done either via a WordPress plug-in or from a third-party site such as www.xml-sitemaps.com. This same website can also generate your mobile sitemap file. If given the option to generate as many sitemap file formats as possible, this is not a bad thing. Although some SEO technologies overlap and confuse, having multiple and regular sitemap files generated for your site can only help with multiple search engines attempting to index your site and its pages.

In this case, Google Webmaster Tools has a Fetch as Google option for mobile sites to ensure crawlers index your site. After you log in to Google Webmaster Tools for your specific website account data, select Crawl from the left sidebar menu, and then select Fetch as Google (see Figure 9.6). Enter your exact mobile site URL, even if the domain name and URL are the same as for your desktop site, as we discussed earlier in this chapter. Select your site platform, such as Mobile: Smartphone, from the menu selector to the right (as in the Figure 9.6), and click Fetch.

Figure 9.6   Google Webmaster Tools crawl.

 Tip

Google Webmaster Tools Help Resources

There are many great blogs and online resources to help with SEO issues. So many, in fact, that you want to scrutinize the source. Do they truly know what they're talking about? How old is the blog source? But many of them often reference a Google help resource itself—Google really does have great online help resources—so don't be afraid to use them. In this case, to read more about "Fetch as Google" and additional help resources if you are having trouble with mobile search results, here is the direct Google Webmaster Tools help link on the subject: https://support.google.com/webmasters/answer/158587?hl=en.

We can't talk about mobile search without bringing up voice-activated search. Technologies have made great advances in voice recognition and tying this to existing indexed web-based content. Two major technologies in the field include Google Voice Search and Apple iPhone Siri. Currently, these are tied into text-based search engine indexed content. At the time of this writing, Siri serves location-based search results from its standard iPhone Maps app (powered by TomTom; the Google Maps app is not the default but a separate download) and more information and reviews from Yelp. Nonlocal Siri keyword search results are served by Bing and Twitter. But with technology progressions and the growth of YouTube, the future is voice-activated search.

Mobile Site Testing

Quality assurance (QA) becomes critical for mobile sites because not only do you want to ensure usability is good for the mobile site, but you want to ensure that all links work from mobile web page to mobile web page. In other words, there's something tricky going on here. When mobile users access your site, they are counting on the mobile web user agents to automatically detect and display the mobile version of your site, across all pages, in contrast to your desktop site (I know—obvious, right?). But you still want to ensure that all those links, navigation, search results, and the like work properly and don't serve desktop website content. In case your desktop site content is served in the mobile context, you want to double-check the settings on your plug-ins and mobile theme to ensure all is working and redirecting properly.

There are a number of online resources and tools to help with mobile sites and QA, such as MobileMoxie Phone Emulator at http://mobilemoxie.com, which allows you to test your site appearance across various mobile hardware and from the same site the MobileMoxie Search Simulator tests your mobile site SEO rankings for various platforms.

A Checklist for Mobile Website QA Testing

- Do taps work throughout the site (touch-screen clicks)?
- Is all the content you want shown (and not superfluous content)?
- Is it principally one-column display for smartphone?
- Does the mobile site include a working link for regular desktop website display?
- Do any RSS or social feeds work properly?
- Does video or animation work properly?
- Are photos correctly sized?
- Does the onsite search functionality work?
- Do the mobile search engine results align with desktop web search engine results?
- Does the site work effectively in both vertical and landscape mobile viewing?
- Do there need to be different sites for smartphone versus tablet?
- Finally, do all elements test properly on all major browsers and devices?

A list of major mobile platform technologies (device and OS platforms):

- iOS
- Android
- Windows
- Blackberry

Mobile Analytics

Again, you can integrate plug-ins that focus on WordPress mobile analytics if desired. Google Analytics will also allow this type of data. Some chief metrics you should be concerned with include identifying the platforms people are accessing your site most from (desktop versus mobile, smartphone versus tablet). Then drill down to browsers displaying your site the most. You may not think the Safari browser, being Apple, represents a large percentage of your desktop-web audience. But a significant portion of your target audience may have iPhones where the primary browser is—you guessed it—Safari. As with all digital analytics, keep in mind that if you want more data, it is out there somewhere. A lot of it is free, a lot can be paid for, but it's out there.

The question is, how much do you really need? So many businesses don't know how to properly use their Google Analytics account or what specific data to access there. For many, Google Analytics is an overwhelming sea of metrics. Data options within Google Analytics show your site's audience devices (from which devices people are accessing your site—desktop, mobile/phone, or tablet), and from there the data can be selected to show everything from traffic sources by device (organic search, referral, or none; see Figure 9.7) to screen resolutions, operating system, new visitors versus returning, location of visitor (by IP address), and so on. The Google Analytics spreadsheet can cross-reference any of these and more data points with each other, as well as the data points discussed in Chapter 7 (see Figure 9.8).

Figure 9.7   Google Analytics mobile and device data.

Figure 9.8   Google Analytics mobile data.

As discussed in Chapter 7, identify what data points and metrics are most important to you—what truly represent your goals? Chances are Google Analytics or the
WordPress Analytics plug-in might already tell you that. If not, go searching for
the best mobile analytics tool to tell you what you need to know.

QR Codes

Quick Response, or QR codes (see Figure 9.9), have a lot of possibilities, although
as time goes on, they may be replaced with image recognition software. QR scanner apps are free and quick and easy to download to smartphones or tablets. They
utilize the camera hardware on devices to read the codes and process them via app
software for full functionality. In South Korea and Japan, mobile phones (even
traditional nonsmartphones) automatically come with default QR code scanning
and recognition and have for years. They are also used much more regularly for
marketing. Whole subway walls are printed as grocery store aisles, with shelves of
products with QR codes. Customers scan what they want, enter the quantity, and
create their grocery order—all while waiting for the train. It's important to note
that these activities are not new but have occurred for years.

Figure 9.9   QR code.

In the U.S., QR codes (and even regular bar codes) have been successfully used
by retail marketers for consumers to scan to access more product info. In grocery
stores it is common for shoppers to scan products to gain additional nutritional
information, coupons, or even listings of price comparisons for stores nearby.
Popular code scanner apps include Bakodo and QRReader (see Figure 9.10).
American marketers have also achieved publicity for successfully using QR codes
in museum exhibits, where museum-goers could scan codes beside exhibit pieces
to retrieve more in-depth reading or audio content on the piece at hand. Smart,
huh? So tell me more about this barely visible crustacean imprint in clay?

Figure 9.10   Code scanning apps.

The trick with QR codes is to remember that (following our hub-and-spoke model from Chapter 3) they are a spoke driving traffic to an online goal, not the other way around. I know it sounds silly, but for whatever reason, "newbies" have been tempted to somehow put a QR code on some kind of web display. If you're already online, you don't need to scan a code to access the web. *You're already there. You've made it, baby!* Use links for click or tap—that is how to navigate around the web. QR codes drive consumers from a physical print piece or poster to the mobile web. I know it's simple, but it's an important thing to keep in perspective. I've even seen QR codes on billboards. Not a good idea if you're trying to avoid causing car accidents. However there are still some onscreen uses for QR codes—for example, display screens within retail stores: "scan this code for coupons" or "for more information on the scientifically proven soothing effects of our scented candles," and so on.

Believe it or not, QR codes are incredibly easy to produce—and are even free! My favorite QR code generator is goo.gl. If you create an account and log in to goo.gl every time you generate a QR code, it will keep analytics for you on all clicks. How's that for cool math! Be aware, however, that if you use free QR codes, they can expire over time. If you're running a temporary ad campaign, no problem! But if you're affiliating your brand and long-term promotion info with a QR code, you may want to research and pay for a permanent QR code.

Vertical Local Results in the SERP

We already discussed "vertical" search results (in Chapter 5, "Real-World Blogging," and Chapter 6 on blogging and Chapter 8 on social media)—how various SEO content could achieve more detailed information for a listing on the SERP, such as authorship. Another type of vertical information result is local data, such as Google+Local and Google Maps. Yelp also often shows up in Google results and often shows star reviews of the listing in question (these are called "rich snippets" and also are vertical search results). Reviews as rich snippets can appear in the Google SERP to extend the power of local content (see Figure 9.11).

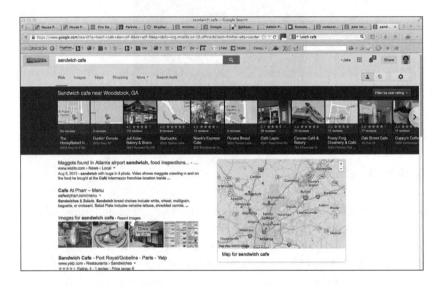

Figure 9.11   Directories and reviews as rich snippets in the SERP.

It's important to recognize that a localized SEO strategy may rely on two very different media: your website's SEO for location keywords, but more importantly, location-based directory sites and mobile apps (such as Yelp, YP, CitySearch, Google Maps, and the like). These latter, myriad channels give you a greater, broader presence on the SERP (as shown in Figure 9.11), a broader digital footprint for your network architecture (as we discussed in Chapter 3), and the crucial platform for customer reviews! The technology for these apps can identify your location via your mobile device in proximity to stores with coupons and also your friends in nearby locations. This technology will only improve, as will newer and improved mobile apps make best and creative use of NFC, as mentioned previously.

Between your website local SEO and location-based directories, I endorse strategic opportunities here to "double and multiply your SEO coverage." What I mean by that is to optimize for multiple search channels simultaneously. (We discussed website local SEO keyword strategy in Chapter 3, so revisit if you need a refresher on localized keyword research and research on local channels for inbound links.) If you have reviews on your business Google+ page, those can also enhance your vertical listing on the SERP. If you host your website videos on YouTube, and optimize those videos, you get benefits for your website SEO as well as within YouTube. Images are similar—if you optimize your images well on your website and in Google+, they will also come up in Google Images searches (and in the SERP, as shown in Figure 9.11). A major aspect of image optimization is to save image files with keyword-driven filenames (with hyphens) as shown:

Filename: your-keyword-named-file.png

You can then upload these image files to your business Google+ page and website and enjoy SEO benefits from both sources. Today, Google+ comprises what used to be Picassa, Google's old social image site, which fed well into Google Images searches. Use that technology foundation to aid your SEO results.

 Note

Bringing It Home—Vertical Business Versus Vertical Search

These are different types of search results touching on rich snippets, ratings/reviews, and location data—"vertical search." Let's reach back here for a moment to our lovely memories of previous chapters where we began discussing "vertical business," and recap and compare to what we've discussed here on vertical search. The two are very different. If your business vertical is in dental, vertical search results are not specific to dentists. However, location data would be much more important to these than to eCommerce. Images appearing in the SERP would be instrumental for businesses such as designers and furniture companies, but less important for doctors or insurance sales. In this way we can still strategically orient our SEO work and potential results to serve the client industry specifically.

Because one of the goals of SEO is to occupy as much SERP real estate as possible (which is also where PPC can help), these other local search channels can be a big aid, and they function with independent profiles. As an SEO working on local search, you have to go to these channels, set up or claim local accounts for your brand, and fill each channel's profile as its own "landing page" for your brand, irrespective of your website. This, by the way, gives power to the local storefronts without a good website or SEO presence; they can suddenly achieve good search-based results by properly setting up these myriad channels.

The ultimate power of results here is multifold: Not only does the brand get automatically served to mobile users on the go via location apps such as Foursquare, Yelp and Google Maps, but these and other local directories results appear in the SERP on standard desktop search for local businesses (hence that whole real estate thing and my previous "multiply your coverage" statement). It should be noted that some of these local directories incentivize brands to advertise with them. Many of these directories will give brands increased exposure and higher listings with paid ads, granting higher appearance not only within the channel itself, but again on the SERP.

These and many other location-based directories, apps, and channels share data with each other. To ensure the correct foundation, the basic search engines themselves must be manually claimed, optimized, and fixed by the SEO or business owner. And because local directories exist in the hundreds, if not thousands, there are channels such as Localeze and InfoUSA that "promise" to blast the correct location and contact info across the board. Some SEOs are in favor of using such services to save time and headaches. Others consider it gray hat and poorer in results than manual pushes. Although we can consider local search as part of "vertical search" because of its deeper, increased opportunities to occupy the SERP, I consider local search to be unique and powerful in itself because of its increased off-page SEO effects (including customer reviews, as we've discussed).

Local Business SEO with Apps and Directories

The point is to go ahead and test all those mobile local apps (what we digital marketer cult members like to call the cutesy SoLoMo—social, local, mobile). So is the info you find in those channels wrong or right? If it hasn't been updated recently, chances are it's incomplete or wrong. Keep in mind the majority of these tools are freemium and offer a lot of quality listing descriptions, photo placements, and even video placements for free. The benefit lies not only in granting customers increased opportunities to find your business, but also for those customers to leave reviews for you (or your client's business) as well.

Directories such as Angie's List and Kudzu are exceptions to the freemium rule—they give you little to no listing options for free (at the time of this writing). *They want your mullah.* The other channels will allow you to claim or create location profiles and verify (such as by phone call) that you represent the business itself and its physical location. Google+Local (at the time of this writing) prefers to send a verification postcard to your specifically stated physical address by "snail mail." This is to ensure that at least the USPS identifies that you are where you say you are. The postcard comes with a code that you enter into your Google+Local account to verify your location. So in case you wondered why Google is kickin' it old school with the post office, that's why.

Caution

Google Places = Google+ Local Pages

If you've managed local SEO profiles in the past, you're probably familiar with Google Places. This was the backend data and accounts that
managed what searchers saw in Google Maps and in the pins listings on
the Google SERP for local search. Google has rebranded Google Places
as Google+Local, but has not done a good job of renaming all backend
account page URLs; nor had it made blatantly clear where settings exist to
make all the changes SEOs need to make. So be cautious of where you are
in your Google account to change the settings you desire. For example, you
may create a Google location account for a business, a Google+ business
page, and multiple address locations. At the time of this writing you cannot
do all this from the same place in the account page (see Figure 9.12).

You can create a business page with a location and verify it via the account
options presented. But then to add additional business locations and verify
these at a later date, you cannot see or access these additional locations.
To control all this location data, the best page to log in is http://places.
google.com, where you can manage all the listings, locations, and descriptions (see Figure 9.13).

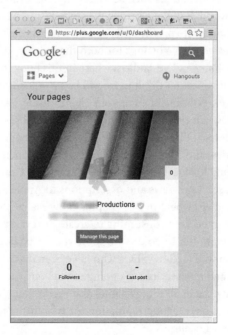

Figure 9.12   Google+ business page management.

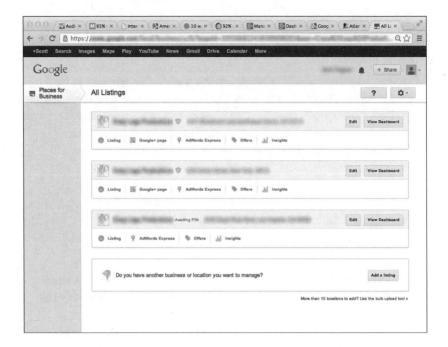

Figure 9.13   Google Places locations management.

Once claimed and verified, tools such as MerchantCircle and Manta will conveniently tell you how much of your profile is complete and what more you need to do to have a 100% complete profile and show you full traffic stats (see Figure 9.14). These directories are the same listings for both the website .com directories and the mobile app versions. As I've said elsewhere in this book, the rising tide floats all boats—so even if you don't think users will be downloading the InsiderPages app and searching for your business or your client, InsiderPages can come up in other search engines, can provide backlinks to your website, and share your location info with other local directory sites and apps. Yelp is one of the biggest of these local directories, and I see Yelp results come up frequently within the Google SERP when searching for local services (see Figure 9.15). Don't forget that Yelp is also the app that serves reviews and descriptions to Apple Siri voice-activated searches as discussed elsewhere in this chapter. Now realize that there are a lot of these tools, and it can be time consuming to create or revise profiles in all of them. There are services that offer to do this work for you for payment. But be careful— many don't work so well (I know SEOs who have been dissatisfied with InfoUSA on these services), and any service isn't going to max out your photos, videos, services—everything. As in all things digital and marketing, there has to be a trade. One service that does have a good reputation for submitting to the list of location directories is Neustar Localeze.

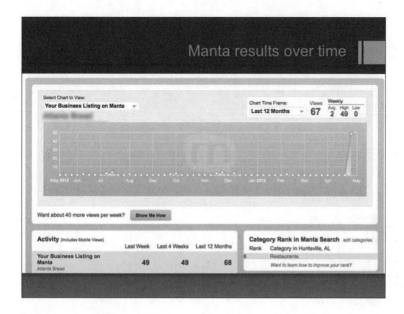

Figure 9.14   Manta stats.

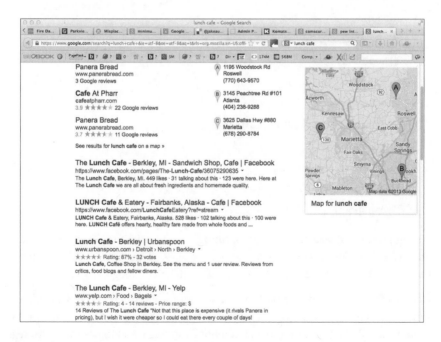

Figure 9.15   Yelp in the Google Local SERP.

So what are these location directory channels? Here's my list:

- Yelp
- Foursquare
- SuperPages
- InsiderPages
- CitySearch
- Kudzu
- Manta
- MerchantCircle
- Google+Local
- Bing Local
- InfoGroup
- YP (YellowPages.com)
- Yahoo!Local
- AOL Local
- Local.com
- Acxiom
- WhitePages
- YellowBook
- InfoUSA
- Neustar Localeze
- UniversalBusinessListing (UBL.org)
- Angie's List
- Judy's Book
- TomTom
- UrbanSpoon

Listing profiles aside, a great way to optimize your website for Google is to integrate Google Maps on your website contact page (see Figure 9.16). Just be sure to use the same Google account as your Google Analytics, Google+, and so on.

Google Maps isn't the only smart integration for localized SEO on websites. It's so simple, yet one of the recurring fundamentals of location-based SEO is the proper utilization of NAP (name, address, and phone number). So long as this is strategically placed on web pages and social media profiles, location-based search channels can recognize and serve the data accordingly. SEO gurus recommend spotlighting your NAP on every page of your site, if possible, and in actual text on the page, in contrast to graphic text (which search engines don't recognize) or dynamically driven text or text within an iFrame (another potential stumbling block to crawlers). So say it loud and proud folks: NAP it is!

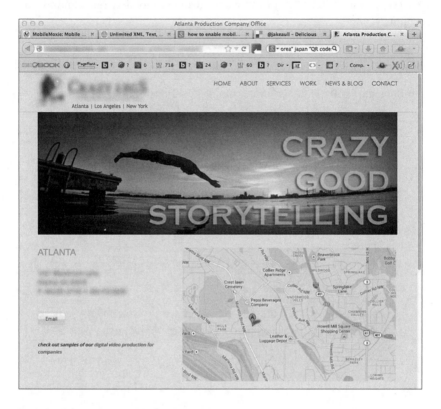

Figure 9.16   Google Maps on a website.

Daily Deals Sites and Apps

There are so many digital marketing options out there that the marketer must be wary of what to utilize in a specific marketing campaign. Think this is beyond the role of your WordPress site? Don't forget your WordPress site or blog acts as a hub that all tactics refer to, whether for landing pages, specific blog posts, your opt-in form, or even just the home page. And like a stone in a pond, the ripples can have extended effects, such as reviews or brand affiliation (with said channels).

Just as I emphasize the value of multiplying your SEO coverage, you can also argue this is the power of local daily deals. You know—Groupon, LivingSocial, and so on—these mobile apps and sites that offer extreme coupon reductions for brands (whether for local storefronts or eCommerce). Offering deals through such channels grants yet another opportunity to appear in the SERP. For consumers subscribing to daily deals apps and sites, there are also the opportunities for increased marketing communications and notifications. For example, apps such as Groupon can send "push" notifications to customer mobile screens and to email accounts.

 Caution

If Considering Daily Deals Offers, Major Questions Should Be Addressed

1. Although brands offer coupons as loss leaders to get new customers in the door (and hopefully retain them in the future at full price), marketing studies have shown that the customers who typically buy such coupons don't want to pay full price.

2. By using such offers, a brand is automatically saying, "Buy me, because I'm the cheap brand!" Is that really the brand message you want to promote? Do you see Mercedes Benz ever offering a Groupon?

3. Then you're repositioning yourself as the cheap alternative in your market. Is that the new market share you want among competitors?

4. Finally, as many of these daily deals offers are structured, you have to ask yourself if your brand can really be profitable at a near 50% discount?

You may get more new customers (many one-time customers) by offering daily deals and occupy more real estate on the SERP for more search effects. What you say about yourself in these channels to customers, however, may be to your own detriment.

Along the same thinking for multiplying search results coverage, eCommerce vendors may list products in eBay, Amazon, or Google Marketplace just to get the brand awareness and potential SEO effects. In those channels you have opportunities to not dilute the brand's price perception.

Bringing It All Home

There are a lot of fun points here to consider on mobile and local technologies and search marketing! We've talked about the differences between the mobile web and desktop web, as separate websites and search engines. We discussed the bright future of mobile sites versus mobile apps—especially regarding great WordPress technologies and themes. We talked about mobile trends overall with hardware and other technologies, where consumer use, hardware options, displays, and resolution are all growing and fast! We covered the pros and cons of the WordPress content editing app for mobile. We got into ways to architect and determine content for WordPress mobile sites—to minimize and distill for the reduced viewing size and available time of mobile viewers. We discussed the importance of mobile site testing and alignment with desktop websites. We dove into mobile web SEO approaches and ways of making Google index your mobile WordPress site. We talked about QR codes and how they can be used to drive traffic to your mobile site or blog from print media. We covered NFC and location-based search directories, sites, and apps, and ways to harness and optimize for all of these. Finally, we discussed multiplying your search power with channels such as daily deals offers or eCommerce options such as Amazon and Google Marketplace. Now go forth and multiply (your search effects)!

10

PPC and Advertising

Chapter objectives and questions:

SEO is for nonpaid, organic content, but what is the relationship between pay-per-click advertising and SEO? Which should I use when surrounding my WordPress site? This book has been thus far about organic search and SEO tools for WordPress, which is a different world than (albeit tied to) online advertising. But it's important to discuss the relationships and possibilities of pay-per-click and display advertising with WordPress websites and blogs. So let's do it! Here's what this chapter covers:

- Types of online advertising
- Advantages and uses for online ads
- Upfront research and planning for online advertising
- Social media advertising
- Monitoring and measurement
- Steps of execution
- A/B and multivariate testing
- Advertising on Your own WordPress blog or site
- WordPress plug-ins for advertising

The Power of Paid

When discussing social media, organic content, and SEO, you may have heard terms like "earned media" or "inbound marketing." The concept is simple: When you post good online content, it earns results, long term. It earns organic search traffic. It earns social shares and reposts. This is inbound and pull marketing because it pulls web users to your hub, your blog, your website, and so on. Your content attracts long-term inbound links and traffic.

On the other end of the scale we have paid media and outbound marketing or broadcast marketing. This is advertising. In PPC we are buying short-term digital real estate, eyeballs, and traffic. It is "push marketing" because we are pushing advertising and sales communications. It is "broadcast" because we focus on blasting our message to the audience in hope of sight and action, in contrast to social one-on-one engagement and connections. The ads and links are there only as long as we pay for them. We don't get organic inbound links from other sites; we get temporary click-through traffic from ad networks. With this frame of reference we can plan for the optimal effects of both SEO and online advertising.

 Note

SEM Versus PPC

From an acronym definition standpoint, SEM stands for "search engine marketing." It used to mean the overall planning and practice of both SEO and search-based advertising. But SEM has been used more and more in reference to PPC specifically, and today it is often synonymous with this. Today when we discuss the overall field, we just say "search marketing." I find it all a bit confusing and silly, but such as it is. So there you go. Call it what you will, but that's the game.

Advantages and Objectives for Online Advertising

Obviously this book is about SEO, and I prefer SEO to search advertising for several reasons. But there are still some good pluses going for online advertising, and the two can be used well together. Regardless, it's wise to know the pros of online advertising, and if planning an ad campaign, which of these to apply as reasons or objectives within your campaign plan:

- Cost control and visible revenue; immediate analytics for ROI/ROAS.
- Location targeting (see Figures 10.1 and 10.2).
- Device targeting (mobile versus desktop).

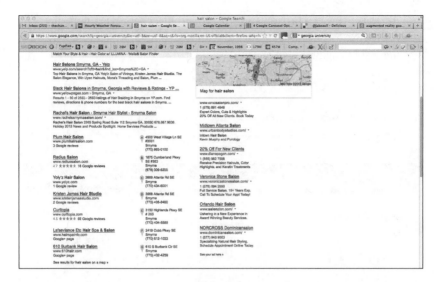

Figure 10.1   Location-based advertising.

Figure 10.2   Location-based advertising on Google Maps.

- Specific keyword targeting (claim even keywords you can't achieve in SEO, such as exact product category names or in some cases even competitive brand names).

- Easy "negative" keyword screening (words you don't want your ad associated with; described later).

- Preview your ads prior to purchase (for example, Google shows you how your PPC text ad will appear before you pay for it).

- Ad placement in a broad variety of, or specific, channels and media (including social and local sites; in contrast to SEO, which is largely for the search engines; see Figure 10.3).

Figure 10.3   Graphic display ads and directory listings on YP.com.

- Website independence; you don't need a specific, large, or even optimized website to do advertising.

- Testing options (which we'll get into in this chapter).

- Microdata (for results and targeting), such as day parting (times of day representing significant digital traffic; described later), keyword effectiveness, locations, and so on.

- Buyer profiling data, such as location and microsegmentation, means a more accurate painting of your customer than what you might get from SEO.

- Exact, and real-time, results (for example, the number of your listing—in an era of Google's personalized, semantic search results and rich snippets to obscure the concept of the "number one listing" organically).

- Full campaign and online multimedia advertising integration (integrate multiple ad versions and media across channels for the same campaign).

- Remarketing opportunities (options for your advertising to consistently reappear in front of the same parties who showed some initial interest in your market, such as by searching and visiting your site or a related industry site).

- Achieve graphics and even animation in listings (in contrast to more limited SEO; see Figure 10.3).

- Build traffic and results immediately, even before SEO or a new site is ready.

- Changeable hub-and-spoke models (point traffic to changeable hubs or landing pages).

- Quickly editable advertising based on results (or lack thereof). Don't like the costs or leads from your online ad campaign? Change the ad parameters immediately, even to the point of bulk editing.

- Options, such as with CPA, to pay only for prescribed user actions such as purchasing (we dive into this in this chapter).

- Options for ad promotion in niche industry sites and directories (see Figure 10.4).

- Magazine and newspaper online plus print coverage; yes, press will let you pay and cover both in one fell swoop.

Figure 10.4   Graphic display ads on the WordPress Dashboard.

Here's the Alphabet Soup

"I would have run a DM campaign, but we've got to go digital! So I looked at PPC but my CPC was too high, and with CPM you just never know what you'll get for click throughs! CPA looks good, but wow they charge a lot per and I really hadn't planned on display and DR! And don't even get me started on bounces, OMG!"

Confused? Don't worry—that's why you're reading this chapter!

Everywhere you go online, a site is willing to charge you money for advertising. The old world model was to sell banner or display ads. And why not these versus text-only ads? Why are the latter so popular, anyway? Text-only ads are the most search engine friendly and compatible with specific keywords and location names.

In the 1990s we all expected the popularity of Adobe Flash (Macromedia Flash then) to provide design-rich artwork that would simultaneously include search-engine-readable text. It wasn't HTML text (and that was the problem with search engines). But it was selectable via your cursor, when on a live website, just like HTML text was. Google and Flash never got on well with each other, and so the dream of display ads with readable text was lost. The irony today is that "the world's second largest search engine" is a visual channel—YouTube.

Online Advertising Models and Uses

As we've discussed, PPC is not the exclusive online advertising option. So what are the online ad media and good uses?

- **PPC ads**, because of their detailed and accurate analytics, are good for lead-gen and testing. If your goal is capturing leads, you need to know your success rate. Similarly, CPA (cost-per-action) ads are good for sales.

- **CPA ads** give you the option to pay only for specified customer activities such as lead capture or eCommerce purchase. CPA ads can often represent pre-negotiated ad contracts based on ad touchpoints, duration of visibility and impressions, costs, and so on. Think of CPA ads as DM or DR (direct marketing or direct response) ads where everything is completely built around a specific, desired customer end action, such as purchase.

- **Rich media** (video or animation) and **display or banner ads** are good for branding goals. If you want to project a strong brand image more than capture leads or sales, these visual ads might be the answer. You've seen video ads in YouTube and popover or overlay ads elsewhere (unlike traditional pop-up ads, these don't trigger a new browser window, but float on top of your other page content). These make you see something you wouldn't have otherwise.

- **Embedded links** are links within regular web content. You pay for the link, but this is a more surreptitious approach and may be effective. This may be a single word link within copy, for example the word "convertibles" underlined as a link within a blog post on consumer favorite car models. The link could go to a profile or website of a car dealership with info on convertibles. Obviously a one-word link is pretty limiting. Regardless, this more informational context (like a blog post, non-salesy) lends itself better to a thought-leadership brand projection than immediate sales growth. Using the preceding example, it's a big assumption that because someone clicks the word "convertibles," the person automatically wants to buy one (see an example of embedded links in Figure 10.5).

- **Directory paid listings** are good for niche industry or location targeting for leads. They can have all the contact info for your company and consequently may yield "leads" without clicks (particularly for location businesses). Directory listings typically may have no real content about the advertiser.

Figure 10.5   Embedded links.

Research for Advertising

One of the main aspects to discuss for PPC advertising is keyword research tools. We already dove into keyword research in previous chapters for the sake of SEO keyword analysis. Remember us talking about the Google AdWords Keyword Planner? The same tool lets you identify advertising keywords—go figure (see Figure 10.6)! But the various keyword research tools are also built to show a lot of pay-per-click intelligence (and the intent to get you to purchase). In fact, when many of these tools discussed throughout this book present levels of keyword "competition," they typically mean advertising competition in contrast to organic. It is not all one and the same. But it is close enough; basically, the companies who want certain advertising keywords typically want those for SEO as well. That's the word.

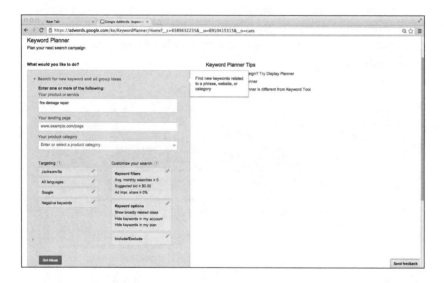

Figure 10.6   Google AdWords Keyword Planner.

 Tip

Quality Score

One of Google's critical drivers for PPC keyword research is Quality Score. For the ads and keywords you want to buy, Google will provide a Quality Score. The higher the Quality Score, the lower your CPC (cost per click). Contributors to a higher Quality Score include the following:

- The sophistication of your ad group and campaign structures
- Quality of your landing page (including its SEO!)

- Ad copy

- CTR (click-through rate)

(For more on Google Quality Score, see https://support.google.com/adwords/answer/2454010?hl=en-uk.)

A good idea is to test your Quality Score-based advertising—by rewriting ad copy, trying similar keywords, and the like. It's also worth knowing that just as much of what Google does influences Bing. Bing has also employed its own quality-based keyword advertising.

PPC Meets SEO Research

One of the great things about adding a PPC campaign to tie in with your SEO strategy is that it reduces upfront work—they both share many of the same prerequisites. Your PPC campaign plan should fit soundly with your strategic digital marketing plan or SEO plan. On a deeper level, the Google AdWords profile and Google Analytics accounts you already created, the upfront competitive and keyword research—all can be executed upfront for both (see Figure 10.7). I still recommend a like strategy of starting long-tail or niche before progressing more short-tail for advertising (for reasons of cost, control, KPIs, and so on). In fact, you can start your PPC campaign with a low budget, monitor daily, and progress to larger spending the more you know what works. Or you can just set a daily maximum budget of oh, I don't know, one billion dollars?

Figure 10.7   Creating a Google AdWords campaign.

When it's time to write your ads, take the same approach regarding writing CTAs that we've already discussed for your SEO copywriting and social posting (in Chapter 5, "Real-World Blogging," and Chapter 8, "Social Media Connectivity"). Be wary of "negative" words along with your keywords. These prevent clicks from unwanted searchers. A classic example is if you're an eCommerce, you don't want searchers inputting keywords like "free giveaway car" if you're trying to sell cars instead of giving them away for free. Google features many instructional guides for your PPC setup and management; be sure to take the online "tours" Google makes available in its tools.

Strategic Research and Planning

Remember all the emphasis I've placed throughout this book on upfront industry and competitive research? Guess what? You can do it for PPC as well. In fact, many of the spy tools were built for this primary purpose. You can not only get a scope of PPC efforts from competitors, sometimes you can even see their actual ad listing copy and offers. So—do you want to compete head-on against competitors in advertising? Or do you want to focus on the differentiated keywords your competitors are leaving behind?

Competitive SWOTs

A SWOT is not a highly trained secret ops team to catch terrorists. SWOT stands for strengths, weaknesses, opportunities, and threats. It's a pretty standard business approach for competitive analysis. And it can also help with competitive analysis in the digital realm—for online advertising as well as for SEO. But it can be based on your own observation or hard data from the outside-looking-in analytics channels we've discussed throughout this book. Either way, the SWOT can also help you look at yourself from the same perspective and identify competitive differentiated positioning, channels, and messaging for your digital advertising and SEO. It's a good tool to put into your digital marketing plans.

Brand or Organization Analyzed: _____

Strengths: Opportunities:

Weaknesses: Threats:

Note

On Online Advertising Planning

We've discussed strategic plans throughout this book. Here are some basic high-level drivers to aid in your online advertising planning.

- Digital strategy brief and USP
- Budget identification
- Business analysis for terminology for keyword research
- Competitive research
- Intensive keyword research for both best PPC keywords and web landing page SEO
- Both overall keyword groups and individual keyword phrases researched and planned
- Keyword phrases identification (as with Google AdWords)
- Campaign/tactics/channels/marketing funnel plan

So what about Google and advertising channels? Note that Google Search Network ads appear not only in Google, but partner networks as well, which is why they are so effective and why Google ads can appear on some WordPress sites. So if you want your ads to appear in older, alternative search engines such as AOL.com or Ask.com, still use the Google Search Network. Bing has similar alternatives—and ties in with the Yahoo! advertising network (in the same way that Bing is the marriage of MSN and Yahoo! organic search algorithms). And there are similar, large-site PPC advertising options with sites such as Business.com.

SMART Goals

Are you smart? (Go ahead, say yes.) Then you'll want to use this motif as well. In this use, SMART stands for specific, measurable, attainable, realistic, and timely (in fact, SMART goal thinking is helpful for social media and SEO as well). Keep these in mind when setting your goals, and then do the work to justify.

Social Media Advertising Options

If you just want ads to appear in social media, you have some good options. Facebook has many levels and types of advertising, such as Sponsored Content listings, where Facebook suggests pages for you to like within your News Feed. This is not to be confused with regular ads shown on the right side of your Facebook home page. You can also pay for contests and other apps on your Facebook business page.

Twitter advertising is not quite as advanced, but like Facebook, also offers Sponsored content. Twitter also features sponsored search results when users search for specific Twitter content. With Twitter, such approaches can be effective and surreptitious because the real-time format is always feeding new organic and sponsored content.

These sponsored listings for both channels are called *native advertising*, because they appear less like ads and more like native content within the channel. "Native" is the latest rage, and it makes sense. As we become desensitized to advertising models that have been around since search engine PPC, content that *appears* more organic is more attractive. I also see a lot of native advertising in local apps and directories such as CitySearch, where again paid content is harder to discern from free or organic content. Watch for more native advertising options to grow in time.

LinkedIn has been running ads for years. LinkedIn has been especially differentiated and effective with running job ads. Perhaps you know someone who got a job or applied for one via LinkedIn ads.

Inputs to Plan and Identify for Your Online Ad Campaign

We've already listed the benefits for online advertising, so those are choices to be considered. More specifically, you want your digital marketing research and planning to include these variables before and while setting up your online advertising campaign. Don't know everything you want right now? No worries! This is the great aspect of online advertising—testing. Plus, setting up and changing online ad campaigns is much, much faster than SEO. These are among the reasons why PPC is great in the interim as you're awaiting your website SEO (or even your website build) to be fully implemented.

The following are the inputs and decisions to identify while planning your online advertising campaign. Because online advertising has different variables than SEO (as revealed by the list of benefits discussed in this chapter), it requires a different list of determinations in planning. But there is an advantage to this—by asking yourself these more specific questions, you can build a more detailed target profile of your prospect. Hence, the list below contains questions worth asking yourself even while planning social media marketing and SEO. So don't downplay the exercise. Not ready to do PPC right away? It's still worth this examination for improved digital marketing plans, even if you change the details later on.

- Targeting:
  - Plan audience specifics such as location, demographics and interests.
  - Device identifications for mobile and/or desktop.
- Tactical options for ads:
  - Display or Text ads?
  - If display, will they be graphic still, animated, or video ads?
  - Display ads generally should be 20–50kb and 72ppi at 100% size.
  - Should they be skyscraper (vertical), horizontal, or all three orientations?
  - Or graphic popovers/overlays (described later)?
  - CPA—will the ads be cost-per-action or PPC?
  - Remarketing—do you want the ads to continually reappear to the same viewers across channels (more on remarketing throughout this chapter)?
- Advertising platforms:
  - Will the ads go through search engines such as Google AdSense network or Bing/Yahoo!?
  - Will they appear in social channels such as Facebook, Twitter, or LinkedIn or other native advertising options (more on native advertising further in this chapter)?
  - Will the ads be placed on same industry or partner sites?
  - Will they be directories listings?
- Budget—such as daily maximum spend?
- Keywords/phrases:
  - Will there be tight or loose keyword relativity? Or more specifically, "broad," "phrase," or "exact" matching?
  - Any negative keywords to specify? (more detail on keyword specifics such as negative keywords and Quality Score throughout this chapter)
- Landing page/URL to direct viewers to (not your website home page)
- Cost-based KPIs:
  - To be traditional Impressions/CPM?
  - Or CPA for clicks to leads or purchase?
  - Or cost-per-click (for PPC)?

- How many ads to push? What ad rotation?
- What will the duration be for the ad campaign?
- Any testing to plan?

If you're concerned about what to do with all of these inputs after you've identified them, don't be. Your advertising channels, like Google AdSense, will request them as you set up your campaign. In fact, just by doing your initial keyword research via Google AdWords Keyword Planner you would have encountered many of these variables already. And Google will show you Quality Scores for the keywords you research for your advertising (to impact your CPC and ranking—more on this further in this chapter).

The Digital Target Persona

Common approaches to both web user experience planning and social media marketing strategy include writing a "persona" or profile of your target website user or social media target. This is a creative exercise; you want to use your research, measurements, and observations thus far about your consumer market to make up profiles on one or two typical prospects—even to the point of finding a stock photo you think fits the bill. Again, this exercise can be valuable across the board, not only for web user experience planning and social media, but for advertising and yes—even SEO!

Here's an example:

> Jennifer M. Smith is a 35-year-old soccer mom in Illinois with a 5-year-old boy. She teaches first grade in a public school in a Chicago suburb. She is Caucasian and is a graduate of Indiana University. She enjoys teaching, but enjoys spending time with her son more. They often go to parks so she can grade papers on her laptop while Roy, her boy, can play. They have a golden retriever and buy ACME dog food. ACME is their brand because of cost—it is the cheapest. She is active on Facebook and "Likes" dog-shelter pages and talks with friends in Facebook about dogs. She's fine with her current dog food, but loves her dog and is researching ingredients and dog health. She is searching Google, pet forums, and wikis for this overall info, but could be convinced to buy better, healthier dog food.

Monitoring and Measurement

As I suggested in Chapter 7, "Analytics for WordPress," the good news about digital marketing is that you have numerous vehicles and metrics for measurement.

The bad news about digital marketing is that you have numerous vehicles and metrics for measurement. It can get confusing. For example, Google Webmaster Tools and Google Analytics will provide you with some "impressions" and other measurements based on your search results in the SERP (as shown in Figures 10.8 and 10.9).

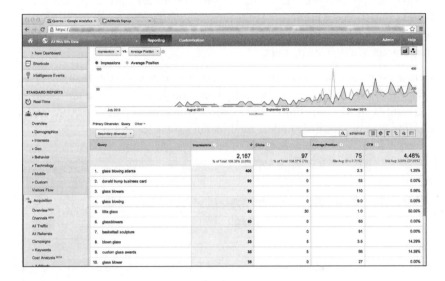

Figure 10.8 Google Analytics Impressions.

Figure 10.9 Google Webmaster Tools data options.

Think about impressions, or visibility, as the power of your brand to project to and influence customers online. If you have a PPC campaign, your website SEO, blogging, and social posts all surrounding the same keywords, and you're achieving SERP results, there's a whole lot of combined influence there. Older advertising metrics (such as impressions or "eyeballs," or the times a brand or ad is seen) enforce the concept of multiple times or touch points for a prospect to notice your brand promotions (typically 4 or 5) before recognition and purchase. With search marketing, you have the potential to occupy their entire SERP for the keywords they search. Multiplicity matters.

Here is the place where PPC can make some measurement easier than SEO (see Chapter 7). When you start a PPC campaign, Google allows you to bid the price you want (against competitors) for keywords you want, and then set your budget cap (for example, for daily budget total spend; see Figure 10.10).

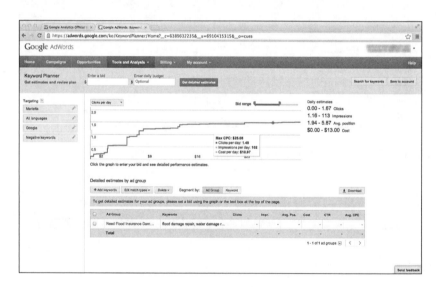

Figure 10.10   Google AdWords campaign setup.

Suppose the following:

1. The keywords you bid on cost you $5 per click.

2. You get 100 clicks/week.

3. Each week you get 20 new purchasing clients (from PPC clicks).

4. Each new purchasing client spends about $100.

Your ROAS (return on advertising spend) is $1,500/week or $15/click. (Note: this ignores the cost of the digital marketer's time to manage the PPC account, as well as your other company production cost factors reducing sales profits).

I have stated previously in this book to be careful about hyperfocus and frequency on all your SEO analytics. You will read things into the data that just aren't so, or that you can't know. If you get 1,200 search-referral visits to your blog on a given Monday, and only 200 the next day, that doesn't mean that Tuesday is a bad day for you to publish blog posts—you're looking at your data within a bubble.

The very next week you might see a reversal. There are things you *can* know, like the seasonality of your business, business holidays, and the like. And there are things you just don't know and can drive yourself nuts trying to. For instance, outside of digital analytics have you had great luck predicting human behavior? Have you really? The good news is that I believe that digital analytics allows for more predictability than most other scenarios of our human existence (except a séance—those are very predictable). But still, if you're trying to analyze WordPress analytics for SEO for rational change on the day level, you may be in for a world of confusion. You can monitor daily; just do so with a grain of salt.

All that said, you might give your online advertising analytics more attention, more focus, and more frequently than your SEO. With PPC you may be getting clicks you can't afford. And you will get much faster results in PPC anyway—real-time in fact—so that's a large plus for the channel. Organic is free; you can "afford" to be wrong or delayed with analysis. PPC costs you moolah. And we don't like to waste moolah.

So be conservative with your daily advertising budget and monitor daily (at the very least for the first couple of weeks) to see the keywords, behavior, cost, and "success." Don't forget that one of the advantages to PPC is that you can quickly change advertising based on results or lack thereof.

Where Metrics Meet Marketing Objectives

These are good places to start with metrics and analytics. But these are also quantitative measurements and metrics. The deeper you get into the analytics you can discover scenarios where your PPC leads cost more, but PPC customers may spend much more on you on average than organic (SEO) customers do. And this is also where your customers' long-term expenditures on your company can matter more than merely first-time purchases. In other words, the longer you keep a specific customer, and the more the customer spends on your products, the more you make.

So what you measure needs to be tied to your campaign objectives. It is also wise to plan your measurements' KPIs and tools while setting your campaign plan. Therefore, what are you measuring? Here are some examples:

- Keyword effectiveness, such as quantitative or qualitative clicks, lead-gen, and the like.
- Short-term SERP results (such as impressions).
- Long-term sales/leads.
- Overall brand or website traffic change (hopefully growth).
- Quality of visitor (qualitative KPIs, such as time on site or page, or pages visited).
- Social engagement (such as social referrals to website or growth in social shares).
- Fresh content and social media content growth.
- Costs or cost reduction. Note: Don't bid on the #1 spot; chances are it will be too costly for your profit level. Let the big brands with all the money take #1 PPC listings.
- Demographics profiling of visitors (see Figure 10.11).

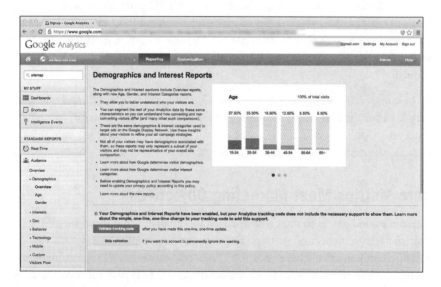

Figure 10.11 Google visitor demographics data.

- Geographic comparisons for visits or leads.
- Day parting—When do the most significant results for your goal achievement occur with your advertising? Times of day, weekends, and so on. Your advertising analytics should tell you this (see Figure 10.12).

Day-parting issues also are important to think about across time zones. Are you looking at significant afternoon data results in the Eastern Time Zone, forgetting that it's morning on the west coast? It's valuable to compare day-parting data to geographic data.

Figure 10.12   Google AdWords Day Parts data.

Going Deeper with Advertising Measurement

The items previously discussed are great starting points for KPIs, but after you understand and can gauge this data, you can do deeper assessment of your valuable analytics. You'll want to know which ad platforms, keywords, messages, and days are most effective to meet your goals. But what is the overall customer journey from your advertising sources? How much customer time onsite did certain ad platforms require before the goal was met? Does the data suggest that certain keywords or ad platforms solicited web users searching only for information in contrast to demonstrating purchase interest? How can this data be cross-referenced with geographic and day-parting data and fit segmentation and customer profiles? What might this data say about your content and messaging available on the destination hub or landing page that should be changed or tested?

With eCommerce, there is a whole deeper potential to analyze data for bounces and shopping cart abandonment against purchases from specific keywords and ad platforms. And finally, with these web user patterns, how can your overall website be rearchitected to serve customer content desires (heck—any opportunity to just scrap the whole thing and start over from scratch, right?)?

Steps of Execution for Your Online Advertising Campaign

We've already talked about the planning stages for your ad campaign earlier in this chapter. Following are the stages of execution:

1. Keyword research and approvals

2. Build and SEO landing page

3. Plan relationship between landing page and WordPress site

4. Design/imagery use

5. Template choice

6. Nonmenu integration (ad landing pages are typically off-menu for clean traffic tracking)

7. Different form/field customer info capture layouts

8. Keywords approval

9. Keyword buys/set maximum budget

10. Structure analytics/marketing funnel

11. Set monitoring plan

12. Write/design/preview ads

13. Get approvals on the ad previews, buys, go live

For more on this, see http://searchenginewatch.com/article/2065989/Setting-up-PPC-Campaigns.

Landing Page Hub Approaches

One of the most important elements of advertising is knowing where to direct viewers—your designated campaign hub or landing page. The ad drives traffic there; your landing page has to cater to your goal to complete the customer journey. Here are a few options to receive your web visitors:

- **Conversion pages:** Often, online advertising campaigns are built to direct traffic to a lead-gen page on your website. This page commonly has a form to capture customer information. The page typically doesn't have menus or outbound links because the purpose of it is to keep the visitor and "capture" that visitor as a lead for you—getting you the info to respond and nurture or sell the customer. Often this page has an incentive for the prospect to fill out the form, such as to enter a contest for a prize or to download a whitepaper.

- **Offsite testing pages:** Because advertising can be more fluid and short-term than SEO, you can test directing traffic to locations other than your website, such as a guest-blog post or test domain. Or perhaps you have a new, separate microsite you want to build traffic on separately from your primary website.

- **Social media hubs:** We're seeing more and more promotions directing traffic to brand pages on Facebook or Twitter. If that coincides with your goals, then very well. But think through your marketing desires regarding customer contact info, the best online incentives to feed your audience, and the optimal control over your digital content.

- **Location channel profile advertising:** Directory channels such as Kudzu, Yelp, YP, and others will allow you to enhance your profile when you do advertising with them (see Figure 10.13). So you can have promotions within the channel itself and a premium profile "landing page" within the channel to receive the traffic and benefits of your advertised listings.

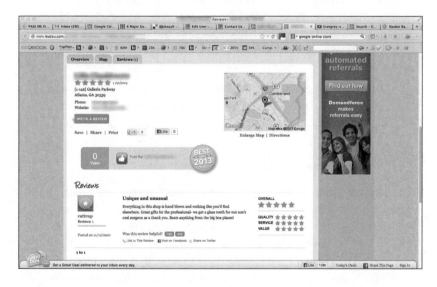

Figure 10.13   Kudzu display ad and profile.

Testing 1-2

Testing is yet an alternative, very different goal for digital marketing. The effects for this type of optimization are quite different. Testing requires a clear, controlled environment. Often, such search marketing testing requires subtle differences between isolated, singular web landing pages, such as for campaigns.

When we talk about testing in search, we talk about A/B (two-pronged) or multi-variate (for more than two comparison subjects) testing. This approach to search marketing testing is inherited from direct marketing, catalog mailing, and market research statistical tactics. Two or more similar audience segments would be chosen (perhaps at random), and each would receive subtly different offers to test results. Perhaps the promotional headline and subhead were changed. Perhaps the primary image and artwork were changed instead. Regardless, if statistical significance was attached to the winner, that was the offer used for greater market audiences. (Read more on testing approaches in Chapter 11, "Bringing It All Together—Testing, SEO, PPC, Social and Mobile, and Analytics.")

 Note

The News on Google AdWords

Believe it or not, Google has been running PPC keyword auctions since the year 2000. And as we've discussed, as of this writing Google is driving its keyword research tool more toward advertising and away from organic search. What is now the "Google AdWords Keyword Planner" promotes "Ad Groups" of keywords and advertising solutions. But this is not a new thing; Google has been promoting and advancing a confluence of its offerings in recent years:

- Less on its traditional organic research keyword tool over the years (for example, fewer updates on its organic PageRank)
- Increased offerings under the AdWords brand name (its advertising component)
- More fodder for commerce (for example, Google Checkout)

This does not mean Google only focuses on, and rewards, paid content instead of high-tech SEOs. Rather, I would say, Google wants to reward the many individual content creators for organic content. Google+ and its positive SEO effects are proof of this. Google has been diluting tech tools for SEOs; besides the organic keyword research, it has also removed the available analytics data to observe the specific organic Google keywords users click to visit your website. (For more on this, see http://searchenginewatch.com/article/2301719/6-Major-Google-Changes-Reveal-the-Future-of-SEO#!)

We talked in Chapter 7 about the "myth of the Google #1 spot" due to several reasons:

- Google has placed less emphasis on specific keyword SEO.
- It has placed SERP visual emphasis and variety on rich snippets (attracting eyeballs and clicks beyond the #1 spot).

- With "semantic search" results, the #1 spot is different for everyone and is dependent on the web searchers' social preferences, profile info, browser history, and so on.

Search marketing gurus suggest that these additional changes also represent Google's push for more importance on advertising. Whether we like it or not, online advertising may be a growing necessary option for search traffic.

So then, what next? How to set goals and benchmark results? This is more of a social content approach encouraging one-to-one digital encounters. In other words, the more socially engaged a brand is with a consumer, the more likely the brand is to come up on that consumer's SERP, and in multiple spots (thanks to various social channels and blog posts).

How Can I Have Advertising on my WordPress Site?

Keep in mind to be conscious of the different tools between ad buying versus ad selling. Yes, you can sell ad space on your blog, directory, or other type of website. We've already talked about how Google is great for advertising by sheer volume and options for targeting on niche sites. Just remember that AdSense is your ad-buying platform. Google DFP, or Double-Click for Publishers, is your ad-selling platform. If you want to be available to a huge amount of ad buyers, DFP is a good way to do it. Google will walk you through what you need from an account perspective, as well as from your website perspective, to sell ads.

So yes, if you're seeking to manage placed ads on your own blog or site for revenue, you can do it with WordPress and WordPress plug-ins! Here are some things you need to keep in mind:

- What's the nature of your site? Would advertising be appropriate? If it is your corporate brochureware, there's no role for others' ads.
- You'll want a visual balance between content and advertising. Too many ads will turn off readers (and advertisers).
- What quality will the image advertising be? Cheap ads will, in turn, cheapen your site. And might your brand be tainted via others' advertising anyway?
- If you can identify and sell specific advertisers relevant to your blog content, then you keep revenue that you would otherwise lose to Google.
- Remember at the beginning of the book when we identified the nature and roles of websites? What is yours? And consequently, what

advertising fits that? If you are a magazine-style blog, then magazine-style display ads are appropriate. If you are more of an industry resource and directory, then directory listings are the way to go. And if you are a 404 page you should just go fix yourself.

Plug-ins to Manage Placed Ads on Your WordPress Site

Here are capabilities to look for in a WordPress plug-in to do your ad management:

- Keep track and notify when ads expire
- Facilitate ad placement, order, and rotation
- Analytics, such as impressions and click throughs

Here are a few plug-in options you can read more about on the topic:

- **AdRotate** is described as a good, flexible vehicle for placing ads on your WordPress site. (http://wordpress.org/extend/plugins/adrotate/)
- **Amazon aStore widget** allows you to show Amazon products similar to the category that you promote or sell on your site. (http://lifefusion. hubpages.com/hub/How-To-DIY-Install-An-Amazon-aStore-On-A-Wordpress-Website-Create-An-Online-Retail-Store-Easy)
- **BlueHost Affiliate** plug-in is an opportunity for WordPress professionals who host with BlueHost.com to receive revenue via BlueHost banner ads. (http://partner.bluehost.com)
- **Chitika Premium** is an alternative to Google AdSense for search-targeted advertising (yet still compatible with AdSense). (http://wordpress.org/extend/plugins/chitika-premium/)
- **Easy AdSense** is a plug-in that simplifies having Google ads on your blog or website, assuming you have enough traffic for Google to desire advertising on your site. (http://wordpress.org/plugins/easy-adsense-lite/)
- **Max Banner Ads** manages plug-ins for rotation and placement on your site. (www.maxblogpress.com/plugins/mba/)
- **Useful Banner Manager** is part of a series of "Useful" plug-ins for WordPress. This particular one strives to do as it is named. (http://rubensargsyan.com/wordpress-plugin-useful-banner-manager/)
- **WP125** manages 125x125 ads for your blog and will rotate and remove older ads automatically. (http://wordpress.org/extend/plugins/wp125/)

- **WordAds** is an option for managing Federated Media ads on WordPress.com (see Figure 10.14). (http://en.blog.wordpress.com/2011/11/29/wordads/)

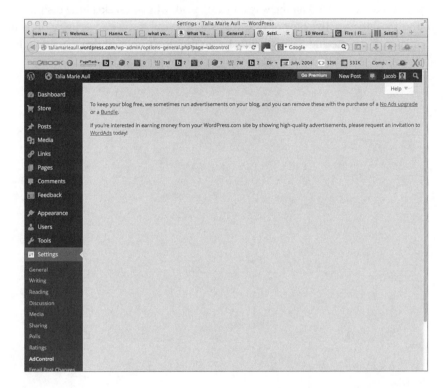

Figure 10.14   WordAds options within the WordPress.com Dashboard.

It's a Wrap

So how'd we do? Did we go from thinking SEO was the be-all and end-all to becoming a PPC convert? The beauties of online advertising show that there are a lot of options. But online advertising (especially PPC) and SEO can aid and complement each other—particularly with ad campaign landing pages, Quality Score, and testing. And upfront research between SEO and PPC can be similar and cross-referenced.

Google drives the boat for online advertising, but there are other ad platform options, and the more you know about them (and about Google AdSense) the more power you can have on results and cost-reduction. Including social media advertising—social isn't just organic anymore! Which brings us to measurement.

PPC brings some strong analytics options to the table that your SEO might not have (again, making testing so powerful). And the data can give you deeper info for your customer profiles and personas.

If you're a die-hard SEO all the way and anti-paid, why not seek a little cash for yourself? With an active blog or directory site, you can feature advertising on your own WordPress site and have income. If you just don't want all that extra dough, you can just send it to my PayPal account. I'm here to help.

11

Bringing It All Together—Testing, SEO, PPC, Social and Mobile, and Analytics

Chapter objectives and questions:

The preceding chapters of this book have been structured to give you a progression of learning. Whether or not you were previously a complete novice, this book was written to start you with the basics of what is SEO: to what is WordPress.com, to SEO options for a basic WordPress.com blog, to blogging approach and SEO plug-ins for a customized WordPress site, to analytics, to social media, to mobile technologies and strategies, and to advertising. So now we bring it all together. We show you how to use this knowledge for your WordPress site or blog and build a digital marketing strategy around it—with your hub-and-spoke model.

Welcome to the chapter where we turn it up to 11! Here's what this chapter contains:

- Media beyond search
- Integrated marketing campaigns
- Hub-and-spoke overall models
- Channels deeper in the marketing funnel
- Overall search strategies
- Drip marketing campaigns
- Customer life cycle

- Backlink strategies
- Testing
- Online audience optimization

The Digital Model

We've talked about the difference between traditional broadcast advertising approaches and today's digital inbound marketing. But we can't forget the search engines as powerful lynchpin in all of this; like it or not, they have goliath impact on the digital world. And Google's changes over time show a definite trend toward serving specific, tailored content to the best matches. This is especially true these days with PPC advertising advances and social content emphasis. To do good digital marketing, we need to think like our audience, but we also need to think like our search engine.

Putting It All Together

A phrase important to the concept of this chapter is *integrated marketing campaign*, or IMC. Why are multiple channels and IMC important? Because at its best, promotion works by hitting consumers on multiple touch points. When a prospect sees your brand from every angle, she remembers it (called "brand recall") faster and persuasion to purchase sets in. Or more to the point of where SEO meets PPC, stats show that that combination of promotion on the SERP can achieve up to 89% more clicks than organic alone (For more on this concept visit http://searchengineland.com/the-holy-grail-of-internet-marketing-owning-the-whole-serp-155232).

Media Beyond Search?

By this time you're likely thinking of ways to integrate SEO, social media, and online advertising. But what about email marketing? Believe it or not, it still has a lot of relevance and effectiveness, and by planning testing schemes, you can test the effectiveness of different ads driving traffic to a landing page one week and different emails the next. The big value here from an SEO perspective is to repurpose that content! In other words, if you output an email newsletter, great—but that in and of itself has no additional value to SEO or social media except to maybe drive more clicks to the website (if it's effective). So, place the newsletter on the back end of your website or in a blog (yes, you can still email it, too). Many email packages, such as MailChimp, offer WordPress plug-ins with capabilities such as direct publish to a blog simultaneously with email content production.

In addition, don't forget about your brochures and other promotions. You've already written the content—why not convert those to PDFs and post them? We've all seen these on some websites, yet it's surprising how many other companies still don't post them. It's relevant content. The search engines will be kind to you. Don't leave them hanging.

What about press releases? Most people know to put press releases in a media section of their website. Just make sure that both it and your newsletter are in formats that search engines can crawl. Remember, search engines love content. Yes, search engines can crawl PDF files (and PDFs have settings for saving with SEO options), but don't get rid of those older press release and other content files. They may be ancient, but the search engines have already indexed them. Don't lose that traffic and have your clicks otherwise replaced with 404 error pages.

Errors and Additional Integrations

Speaking of which, you should have a customized 404 page for your site to offer navigational options for your web visitors. The default 404 page from your hosting provider will look like an error page or that something is wrong with your site. A customized 404 page, branded to your site, with your site's navigational elements, will make more sense to viewers and give them opportunities to still journey through the site. If building a custom 404 page is difficult for some reason (or if you're waiting for one to be built), you can redirect 404 errors back to your home page. Don't forget that your WordPress plug-ins or Google Analytics and Webmaster Tools accounts can show you your 404 page hits (as we've discussed previously).

Yet another way to look at IMC is with our old hub-and-spoke. All pieces are "integrated" by pointing to the hub (as shown in Figure 11.1). Between that and print pieces with URLs, direct mail pieces with your URL, printed QR codes, print ads, they can all work in concert to meet your marketing goals.

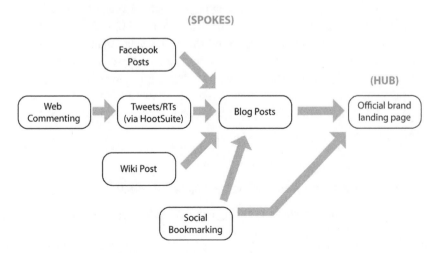

Figure 11.1   Hub and spoke diagram.

Getting Centered

In this book I've discussed the value of SEO to attract searchers with your relevant content, social media to achieve interaction and involvement, and PPC to drive traffic to a designated hub. I've talked about the necessity to architect your WordPress site, blog, and greater digital network to serve your audience and achieve your goals. The greater trick then is to identify how all these tactics need to work in concert and feed off of each other along with other media, including—dare I say it—offline media! (Eeeah! Gasp!)

So much of this comes back to strategic, central hub identification. Although we want it all to work together, the unique power of SEO lies in its permanence (or at least semi-permanence). Wait, you say, you thought nothing online was permanent? Online advertising stays up as long as you're paying for it. Social content stays up until the social wall or feed refreshes. Website or even blog content that is optimized and architected properly remains searchable for as long as there are spiders to search it. Let me say it again: Live web content that is optimized can be crawled as long as the engines can see it.

So if you tell me you have great SEO I'll ask you how good is your hub? Want to know what you could do better? The answer lies in your analytics; what do they tell you? Should you grow your content? As long as it's strategic, nonduplicated, relevant, and valuable to visitors and search engines, then yes. But you want to know the best place to put it.

 Note

Reminder Steps for Campaign Hub-and-Spoke

Whatever you designate as your landing page or hub for your ad campaign, don't forget to optimize it. Just because you're doing PPC, it doesn't mean you can forget SEO—quite the opposite! Optimizing your landing page can allow for it to come up on both organic and paid-ad sides of the SERP (that whole, total real-estate domination strategy). But a well-optimized landing page and hub can also reduce the cost of your PPC ad! Google has been said to favor pricing for sites it trusts (again, based on SEO drivers).

Steps for identifying your campaign and hub:

1. Identify goals and digital strategy brief.

2. Conduct keyword, competitive, and audience research.

3. Build campaign plan and timing (start conservative; it can be reviewed and extended after results).

4. Should include a landing page (with SEO) and ads to point to this.

5. Online advertising can be fruitful, but which media best fit the end goal of the campaign?

6. Could/should include social media posts.

7. Plan ad placement around budgets and relevance.

8. Google is king, but smaller/alternative engines can also be effective and charge less for advertising.

Don't Forget Your Funnel

Think with the digital marketing funnel (as I've discussed throughout this book):

If you're not getting enough eyeballs at the mouth of your funnel, such as when your website first starts up, this is the time to dive heavily into your SEO efforts, social networking awareness, and maybe do some PPC advertising. Just achieve awareness (see Figure 11.2).

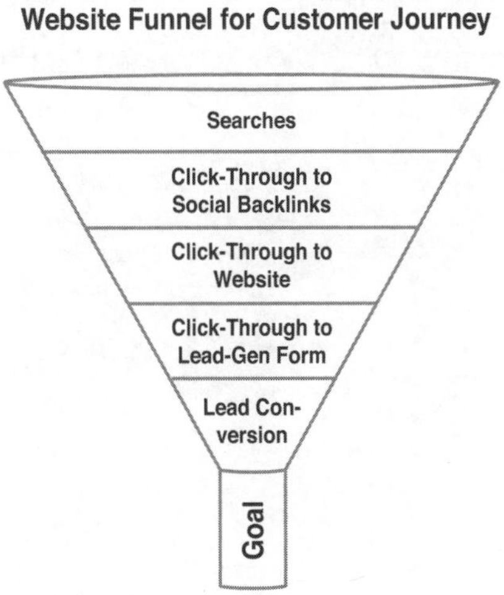

Website Funnel for Customer Journey

Searches

Click-Through to
Social Backlinks

Click-Through to
Website

Click-Through to
Lead-Gen Form

Lead Con-
version

Goal

Figure 11.2   Marketing Funnel example diagram.

Are you losing a whole lot of people in the middle of your funnel? You might consider having more middle-tier content on your site or blog. I am referring to nonsales content, but still rich with desired information for what people are searching for. If people want to know more about honey, tell them everything there is to know about bees. Show them how to cook with honey. You can sell them honey later.

Maybe you're just not getting enough visitors before that middle tier? This is where social media and blogging might help. Social and blog content can help attract visitors and incentivize them deeper into your funnel. How can you get more positive reviews in online channels? How can you achieve more overall content online? Lead your audience in a journey to your deeper site content. Do you have videos on your site's pages about cooking with honey? Promote them in social and blog posts.

Or are you losing everyone before converting in the funnel spout? Then try ramping up your incentive—why should people opt-in to your lead page or buy from your eCommerce site? Give them more to get more from them. What would it take to incentivize you or your friends? If visitors don't want to opt-in to get your e-book on the flowers, bees, and honeys of the world, then give them that for free and offer a free honey sample for opt-in. Draw them in all the way. Optimize everything along the path. (See the visitor path from Google Analytics shown in Figure 11.3.)

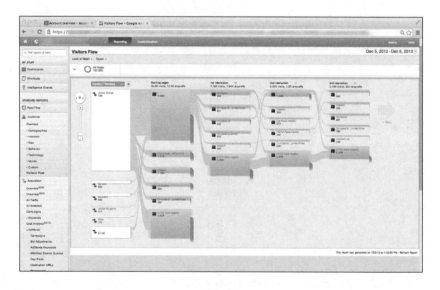

Figure 11.3   Visitor flow through the website.

Remember, there's a perfect model for your site and goals. Work with it until you find it.

KNOW YOUR OVERALL STRATEGY

A lot of SEO firms will promote their overall digital marketing services under the guise of SEO maintenance. Whether it's digital marketing or true SEO, it's no good when clients are getting no results and pay money for nothing.

Here's a commonly promoted service: Some SEO firms will build a landing page for the client on the firm's own web server/IP. The firm will SEO that page and set up a PPC campaign to drive traffic to that landing page. They have some kind of end-customer info capture and results measurement; maybe they have a special phone number for tracking, or they measure the emails or form fill-outs (and, of course, web traffic). They charge monthly for this, and when the client decides to stop paying, the client loses everything. Because the client never "owned" the landing page (it wasn't on its own domain or server), the client doesn't own any of the SEO or future results. True "SEO maintenance" should comprise maintaining your overall organic search results for your own properties. My personal preference for SEO maintenance is to build/boost client social media and/or blogging. Build additional pages on client websites and SEO them. Optimize all the local profiles. Find SEO problems or shortcomings on websites and boost them (that's a better definition of "maintenance").

If you are paying for a temporary landing page on a third-party's server to be optimized and receive short-term PPC ad traffic, only to see those effects gone when you stop paying, that is not long-term SEO growth.

These services are easy to rehash, requote for any new prospect—no focus on the specific client's needs, just "here's what we'll do for you, here's our quote for you, you'll have all this work done." And if it's their own landing page and PPC campaign, it's much easier to show cut-and-dried analytics than it is for me if I'm repairing a page or two of your website SEO at a time (actually, I can prove results: That page goes from not showing up in first page Google to suddenly showing up first-page Google for a keyword phrase). A friend in digital marketing, whom I really respect and from time to time get input from, says the only way to really do ongoing SEO maintenance is to blog. I think there's a good, hard truth there (not to say that other digital marketing efforts are ineffective, just that SEO maintenance after initial site SEO is strongest as blogging).

Be wary that many location-based directories will also provide search marketing services. Channels such as Yelp, CitySearch, or Kudzu may offer paid services to enhance your location profile (on their directory) along with advertising or sponsored listings for more traffic. The problem can be that it all stems from that one channel. Is enough of your audience really looking at ads in CitySearch and Kudzu? If this is what you want, very well. Just be sure of what you're getting.

Overall Search Strategies

Alternatively, search engines *do* like longevity of URL ownership, and stable, relevant content without complete content overhauls (and consequent new 404s) every year or two (or more). Past content can still achieve traffic if it's archived properly.

Online advertising is a tactic within your overall digital marketing planning including SEO. Strategies that marry everything together can include the following:

- **Multichannel campaign for the digital footprint:** This would be ad placement in a broad variety of channels (including social and local sites, in contrast to SEO, which is largely for the search engines) or a multichannel/multitouch campaign. So if you sell port-a-potties, if someone searches for these in Facebook, you're there. Bing, you're there. Instagram and Pinterest, you get the picture (pun intended).

- **Footprint consolidation:** Perhaps you need to gather and redirect your total digital footprint and inbound links. Suppose you've acquired 50 subsidiaries over the years, and all have their own websites, social sites, social mentions, and inbound links. You've got a messy plate of spaghetti on your hands (see Figure 11.4)! Probably a lot of broken links and 404s. We don't like 404s now do we? (Say no.) And 301 redirects are only part of the equation. Remember, the web is full of social mentions and profiles! So you need to do a heavy strategy even between your various web properties to direct links and traffic.

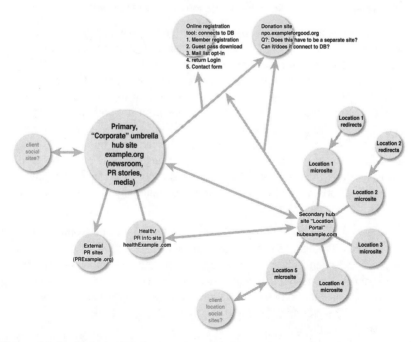

Figure 11.4   Multiple digital networks and linking.

- **Data mine campaign:** Get the real-time, microsegmentation, and keyword data you can't from SEO or other tactics—mine that data! Through social content sharing/reposting and PPC advertising results, you have great opportunities to mine data you wouldn't get from SEO in Google Analytics or WordPress analytics alone. To form a deep, full profile of your best customers, it may be worth executing a heavy campaign in various channels for such data. This data can, in turn, help you tailor organic content and SEO keywords and approaches more specifically.

- **Testing:** Testing can help you mine data, as we've mentioned, but it can also help you identify your most effective channels and approaches. What campaign will be most effective for the next slow summer? Test now to help you plan accordingly.

- **Deep-Niche Coverage:** You might want to maximize options for ad promotion in niche industry sites and directories. Go ahead! Advertise those gorgeous port-a-johns in construction directories and building catalogs!

 Tip

Choosing Niche Advertising Platforms

Large advertising resources such as Google, Facebook, and Business.com will give you good targeting options for your advertising. But you may want to advertise in industry- or target-specific channels, online magazines, or blogs. If these are your considerations for digital ads, you have some more choices to make and things to think about. Is this channel complementary to your own business and audience? If you sell quilting supplies and you're looking at a trucking magazine, you may reconsider. What kind of competition to you is already on there? Will you be drowned out?

- **Microtargeting and day parting:** Day parting represents the time of day for targeting your prospects. You can get deep, as deep as you want. You can target specifically and test the results and try again. The end goal is to spend less effort and money in the future for deep niche targeting for maximum result for your best micro segment. Your best customers aren't women age 20–50; they are Caucasian single moms with children in elementary school, age 30–40, who search for shopping between 3–5pm weekdays.

- **Location-based targeting:** Let's say you're a local storefront, such as a restaurant or hardware store. Location-based search, social, and mobile targeting can have a lot of effect for you (as I discussed in Chapter 9, "Going Mobile and Local").

- **Broadcast blitz:** Perhaps you want no holds barred—you don't want a rifle, you want a tank! For a heavy broadcast/push digital marketing blitz, such as for brand awareness, with display or multimedia advertising. Hit everybody everywhere with everything. It will cost you an arm and a leg, but hey—if money's no object... It's at least worth considering if you need maximum, immediate results and can scale back after a short time. But be careful here—this was the approach of so many big name (and low deliverable) dot-coms of the late 1990s!

- **Multisite traffic:** For good SEO it is often recommended to build content on a large site rather than a number of smaller sites. But if you have to drive traffic to a number of smaller or new sites, PPC may be smarter than organic. Separate landing pages, blogs, social sites, and so on. Drive the various traffic with advertising.

- **Remarketing:** Remarketing, or retargeting, represents a continual push for consumer top-of-mind and incentivization. It's a constant hit of advertising to the people who saw or visited your product or category once already. Did they search for port-a-potties? Keep blasting them with your ads everywhere they go online.

- **Incentivized customer action:** Perhaps you want specifically to achieve isolated customer action, such as with CPA or PPC for social follows. Want prospects to download an e-book for lead-gen, buy a nonselling item? You can center efforts around this and structure a cost-per-action ad campaign for the goal specifically. No messing around!

- **Couponing:** Perhaps you want coupons or short-term sales—or bumps to meet quotas or quarterly expectations. In other words, digital "daily deals," such as Groupon, to achieve first-time buyers (as a loss leader). I'm not a big advocate of this because it conveys a brand image of "cheapness" to first-time customers, who often won't come back to pay full price. Special first-time offers also often create confusion for existing customers who can think, "Well what about me? I've already bought 200 port-a-johns from you, and now you're selling the first 50 a new customer buys at half off?" I see it everyday. Port-a-john envy.

- **Retention:** No, not that kind of retention. Customer retention. Digital customer rewards accounts are growing more and more common, and it makes sense. Like airlines miles, everyone wants to accumulate them. Rewards or credits are a great incentive and can preserve a "quality" brand image.

- **Multidevice or mobile coverage:** Okeydokey, so you've noticed in your Google Analytics that a whole lot of folks are searching for your port-a-johns on tablet and smartphone. But you really haven't done much to service mobile platforms. So do it. Make sure your site is responsive; make sure your sales centers are optimized for SoLoMo (social, local, and mobile) channels like Yelp and YP. Got people demanding great product shots in Instagram? Serve them up!

- **Dominate specific keywords or phrases:** Build PPC ads on your same SERP with your SEO listings to achieve maximum real estate. So you want to dominate the SERP for keyword "industrial toilet paper"? SEO your site, social sites, and fill up PPC ads with everything centered on that keyword. Dominate!

- **The balanced and differentiated total campaign:** Suppose you want PPC ads based on keywords or phrases different (unachievable) from your SEO (such as competitor words or product labels). Try as you might, you just can't beat your competition for organic SERP listings on keyword "industrial liquid soap." No problem. Buy the PPC ads instead and focus your SEO on other product category keywords instead—a balanced strategy.

- **A build or startup campaign:** Build traffic and results immediately, even before SEO or a new site is ready. You should know this one already. If you're starting from ground zero, definitely build up your SEO, but now is also a good time to do an awareness thrust in PPC, social media—everything—just get your name in front of eyeballs. Even to the point of buying ads with your brand name!

- **Serving the long sales cycle:** So you want a strategy to fit the long customer journey or sales cycle. We see this in B-to-B all the time: customers who need a lot of information, multiple stages of approval, and long times to consider and compare the purchases. So how can you serve them the marketing funnel content they need for decision makers along the way? How can you cater to each phase of the cycle? (See the marketing funnel discussion in this chapter).

- **Affiliate marketing:** Perhaps you want to build your partnership marketing and cross-promotion or cross-selling? Perhaps everything in your digital footprint is hunky-dory and you're getting the traffic you want and meeting your objectives. How can you branch out? Promote other offerings and digital results. Selling out on those port-a-johns we mentioned? Now promote toilet paper. Work with a partner vendor for advertising and a piece of the action. Of course, you can have cross-sell strategies for your own brands and not exclusively affiliates.

- **eCommerce Awareness:** At first this doesn't sound like an SEO strategy per se, but believe it or not, if you're in eCommerce there are several options where you can use "online sales" as a means to gain product or brand awareness and even search effects and rank! I often tell startup clients that building an eCommerce site can be very costly, but if you want to start achieving immediate revenue and growing awareness, you can use existing channels now (just at a cost to you). For example, you can promote and sell your products on eBay and Amazon. You can even expand your Amazon offering to pages and hosting. Google has its own options for eCommerce for your use— namely, Google Merchant/Google Shopping. All these megastores easily come up in search engine results currently, making them invaluable for search effects and awareness. Remember how we've discussed that Google loves Google? The more Google channels you're in, well, you know where I'm going. Otherwise, it's good to know that back on the WordPress front, eCommerce tools such as Shopify have plug-ins and easily adapt to your WordPress site.

More on Search Marketing Strategies

We've covered some good overall search marketing strategies so far, but more is definitely better, right? I thought so—so are more approaches with depth.

Reputation Management—Planning for Reviews

I've already discussed this for location-based search strategy and in Chapter 9. For example, don't forget the power of the "Review us in Yelp" sign. You've seen restaurants with this (or "See us on Yelp") on the outside door. Problem is, customers won't give you the full benefit—writing you a review—until after the coffee is served or after the dinner. That's when you want to hit them with the sign (which they won't see because it's on the other side of the front door). Are you a doctor's office? Put the sign on the desk for payment so they see it as they leave. Include handouts that show customers how to leave a review for you online. It's a simple concept but very helpful for SEO. Get customers to give you good reviews online in Google+ Local or Yelp to boost your overall SEO. Remember that I said the rising tide raises all boats? Those reviews show up in vertical results on the SERP (as I discussed in Chapter 5, "Real-World Blogging," and Chapter 9) as well as boosting your overall website search engine results. The concept of IMC is an old one, but this manifestation of it is pure SEO and social. Companies like Demand Force make strong monthly revenue from doctors' offices and auto shops by following up with every customer after an appointment to specifically request an online review, and it works!

On the flip side of reviews, you want to monitor and respond to those you get (both positive and negative). It will help you appear relevant to the reviewers and readers alike. And as we've stated elsewhere in this book, it will boost your overall search results. Plus from a customer support standpoint, you need to be monitoring your mentions online and reviews to see how you can solve your customers' problems. If a customer complains online that your product broke, you need to respond to keep that customer and as demonstration to prospects. But there's an added bonus to all of this. Reviews channels like Yelp will reward you for your activity therein. Even if you have many "filtered" reviews there (visible to you but not the public), if you engage and respond to those reviews, Yelp can acknowledge and release more of your hidden reviews.

Drip Marketing and Marketing Automation

Drip marketing is a campaign strategy, typically for email, where prospect and customer communications are sent based on timing intervals with strategic messaging. Often testing is used to help identify the best patterns and frequencies for goal achievement. In this context we often hear references to "marketing automation," because you can use email software to automate this process. You may have heard of solutions like MailChimp, Marketo, and ConstantContact. These technology platforms allow you to best control and measure results for opt-in emails and sometimes even social integrations. What's the impact on search? A lot if your search strategy is to capture more lead-gen via opt-ins. And if you are trying marketing automation, think back to how it will best fit within your hub-and-spoke and marketing funnel models. The channels all touch each other sooner or later.

I've talked throughout this book about the value of driving traffic to a customer form to capture info on your WordPress site for lead-gen. But what's the next step? After you have the lead, you can follow up directly with the lead or employ an ongoing drip email campaign. But when you have an opt-in for your email list, how best to technically harness that opt-in for your marketing?

Again, WordPress has the power of plug-ins. Many companies use services such as ConstantContact to manage their mail lists and email campaigns. These services can also have WordPress plug-ins to best incorporate WordPress form data in with total email lists and minor customer resource management (CRM) services. So this is worth researching more prior to setting up customer forms or buying email management services. (For more on ConstantContact's own WordPress plug-in, see http://marketplace.constantcontact.com/Listing/applications/katz-web-services-inc/PML-0172.)

Round Pegs, Square Holes

When we strategize on the IMC scale, some pieces might not fit together. For example, if you want to trend growth for the future and appeal to the more "innovator" target audience, you might like the idea of placing emphases in your integrated marketing campaign on both mobile and video. Well, although video comes up well in the desktop Google SERP, at the time of this writing, I'm still not seeing it come up a lot in Google and Bing apps' SERPs on mobile (whether iPhone, Windows Surface tablet, whatever). Part of the reasons for this would undoubtedly be concerns over traditional .swf-compressed Flash files not appearing correctly in mobile (HTML 5 is the new thang). And there are concerns over bandwidth, immediate/easy access, YouTube app versus the YouTube site on desktop web, and so on. So if these two tactics (video and mobile) are your two biggest focal points, they may not play nicely together. *Bad mobile! Bad video! Play nice!*

Another example could be merging email marketing and Twitter. If you're using Twitter as a means to solicit email opt-ins for your email newsletter, it may not be the best mirroring of channels. Twitter has been around for a long time (in social media years), but the biggest use of it is immediacy—freshness of content and interactions. Follows, retweets—all in real-time, especially for young adults who have dropped Facebook in favor of Twitter for their online social interactions. And Pinterest or Vine. If you use those channels to promote traditional, slower, bulky email newsletter marketing, you may not have an obvious pairing. LinkedIn might be the better social channel for requesting opt-ins, or SEO for the email opt-in landing page. So place close attention to consumer behavior regarding digital channels prior to cross-channel promotions!

Customer Life Cycle

When we talk search marketing, we typically talk about prospects, not past customers. Because past customers already know us, they know our products and our website (if we've done our job right). But these are assumptions we should not rest on. For example, with the impact of online reviews for SEO (as we've discussed in previous chapters), we need to get existing customers to leave those reviews in the first place! So messaging and giving past customers incentives for such goals is vital to our ongoing SEO (and business) success!

There are other cases where SEO goals regarding existing customers are instrumental. Suppose your business is doing a rename, rebrand, or buyout. Or your name in general is hard to remember, and you want your online content to continue to be available to past customers (such as for customer support issues). Serving past customers via SEO and even PPC for the keywords they might search becomes a vital strategy.

Don't forget about the value of a customer rewards site—both for your custom-ers and ongoing purchasing and retention for your products (as we discuss in this chapter). If your customer from two years ago goes back online to search for such products again today, you want him to know that he can have rewards points from what he previously purchased from you!

The Viral "Plan"?

So what's your "viral plan"? Well, those words don't go together very well. The most successful viral videos and campaigns could not have been predicted for results. That's the point. "It went viral" is a phrase emphasizing unpredictability! In other words, you can't really plan viral success, which makes it a poor goal for strategic planning. Just by use of the English language, when someone says they achieved "viral success," they typically mean unprecedented growth beyond their wildest dreams. I'm all for reaching for the stars, but what goals are you work-ing toward that you *know* are achievable? This is more the approach for SEO and digital business, even in a viral world. After all, you can optimize all you want. But if people don't want the next hot video on a chicken that dances to your text commands, then what good is it all? However, we could think of link baiting as a minor viral strategy—writing copy specifically with the hope to achieve shares and backlinks.

The Strategy of Speed

Load time is important! This in and of itself is not a typical search marketing strat-egy, but the search engines do like smaller sizes and fast delivery and will penalize sites that don't have it! So perhaps your existing digital footprint is endless, cum-bersome, and slow, with large videos and images, and it just doesn't have enough server speed to accommodate the traffic you get these days. Fix it up! Another reason for this to be a primary focus might be for competitive edge. If you're a car lot and all your competitors have endless photos and videos of their cars with slow load times, poor servers, endless links, and poor usability, you've got a great com-petitive opportunity!

Budgeting

Here's a good question: What's the best way to manage your budget for search marketing? Obviously this can get very industry-and company-specific. One starting point is to analyze past digital marketing time and budget investments. If a specific channel worked well previously, be sure it's not "maxed out" before investing more. For example, you may not be able to see any additional return on increased advertising investment on the same keyword if you currently have good proliferation.

Many advertising budgets are structured as a percentage of sales or projected sales. Likewise, percentages of overall budgets are portioned to various digital tactics or media. Or you may find yourself in a tight budget, but in a high manpower and time availability scenario. This is why you're in luck here, because organic—SEO and social media—is "free." So amp up your content strategy as we discuss in this chapter.

Backlink Strategies

Let's say you've been asked to be in an interview or write an article for an online magazine. Great—use it! First, no you don't want to plant a link from your website to the magazine; you want it the other way around. Regardless of whether people see and click or not, this is about search engines recognizing that there is a reputable site on the web (the magazine) that has a one-way link to your website. You can *mention* on your site and social media sites that you have an article in the magazine, and can mention the date, and so on, but you don't want to plant a link for them. You want it the other way around. The way to do this in your planted article could be to say something like, "To see more about this topic see www.ourwebsite. com." Or "You can read more about so-and-so and her contributions at www.ourwebsite.com." Do that every time you have an article on another website.

You never want to duplicate the article word-for-word on your own site, but this is an opportunity to have more content on your site. So you could reword and paraphrase that article for your own website blog post or news section, as something such as, "Recently we were lucky enough to have so-and-so join our team and had a feature article on such-and-such a magazine. To paraphrase that,…". Just things to think about for the future.

Testy, Testy

I briefly covered A/B and multivariate testing in Chapter 10, "PPC and Advertising." But can it work for SEO as well? Yes, if two different primary keyword drivers are used for similar/same web page offers, then best keywords can be identified. Or perhaps primary keywords are changed once every 6 or 12 months (while all else remains the same). It would be more expected to run search marketing PPC ads for such experiments, but SEO tactics can complement the campaigns. Is there statistical significance? In my marketing research studies, statistical significance begins to emerge with a base of about 600 (random) persons. As an SEO, you have the opportunity to bump a small business's new website from 0 to 400 impressions in a day. SEO analytics are best put under the microscope over a one-month period (possibly several times if you want to drive yourself nuts), and click-throughs (and other metrics) are more valuable than impressions (eyeballs, viewer exposures on the SERP), but the point here is to strive for statistical significance. Which keywords convert to click-throughs from impressions over a one-month period? Which PPC ads? These can be tests worth running.

Potential Control Test Variables

Here we get into the fun of scientific method—controlled experiments and testing (aren't you glad you read this far?)! So for good A/B or multivariate testing, you want to have common variables with one element of change. With like conditions for two or more ads to test, what might be good elements of alteration? Here are some possibilities to test for best ad success:

- Ad body copy or headline
- Promotional offer/incentive
- Ad CTA or link
- Landing page layout/design
- Landing page imagery
- Landing page text
- Landing page site location/content
- Landing page SEO/organic inbound links
- Ad audience targeting
- Ad days/times placement
- Ad keywords
- Advertising source channel

As stated, only one of these variables should be changed at a time, and that list only scratches the surface of testing potential. (For a good reference scorecard for change variables, see http://unbounce.com/a-b-testing/scorecard/.) Alternatively, here are variables that might not allow fair results with drastic changes between the test subjects:

- Ad run duration
- Medium (for example, outdoor board versus PPC text ad)
- Impressions only (nonclickable ads) versus click ads
- Overall product category or market changes (for example, cleats versus trash bags)

- Drastic usage and behavior changes (for example, B-to-C versus B-to-B)
- Different sites with different media (for example, SEO drivers for one site versus display ads to a very different site)

So test strategically but scientifically, accurately measure the outcomes and test again. This is the never-ending circle of test.

Comparing Big Pictures

Think of A/B and multivariate testing as comparing one cell's honey to another in a honeycomb. We can't do that until we've already built the honeycomb itself. But after our builds and testing, we still want to pull back to look and compare one honeycomb to another and inspect even the flowers producing the nectar in the first place.

I've talked about testing approaches utilizing search marketing. And it's a given in digital marketing that overall you want to be cognizant of what's working and what's not. As I've said before, the glory of digital is the capability to have more data than ever before. We can lose ourselves endlessly in a niche if we so choose (and I've discussed that can get very dangerous if making SEO strategic decisions based on minute daily fluctuations in traffic). But we also have to be able to step back above the fray and be savvy about the overall approaches and strategies that work or don't. Sure, file that under marketing "common sense," but all of this does take a different shape in this digital age. Above the microscope of landing page testing, we have to ask if our customers are making their biggest decisions based on location-based search channels and our profiles there (and reviews), or on our viral videos across the web and our YouTube channel. As SEOs, we have the abilities to improve and expand search for our presence in those places. Our traditional website doesn't *have* to be the exclusive SEO grand slam. This is new SEO thinking. And how does WordPress help? WordPress can help collect, stream, connect to (and even support, if the case may be) these "hero" channels.

How Does Your Best Audience Use Search?

Sooner or later our digital marketing itself has to be about serving the customer! What's working? Yes, ask the question of your analytics, testing, and so on. But "what's working" should be about what works for the customer. How are we best serving our customers in digital content, service, and interactivity?

The old focus of SEO was to make a website come up in search. There's much more to it than this now. And if you're still not buying it, look at all the recent search engine and social changes discussed in this book.

The old focus of SEO serving your website content in Google and Bing depends upon two criteria:

- That your customers are searching primarily in Google or Bing
- That they want website content

Get out of that frame of mind!

Search Marketing on the Next Level

Part of what testing and PPC help with is to identify specific data about your best customers (even down to the microsegment if you want) and their product research or purchase behavior. So the next question (or perhaps the question in tandem) is: *Where* are these folks searching for content, and specifically *what kind* of content are they searching for? Do they primarily want videos? Reviews? Blog posts? e-books? In business you are trying to serve your targets with a product or service they want, but the next step for digital marketing is to serve them the content they want and *even the digital experience they want*! Do they want social engagement? Forum collaborative response? Infographic and statistics research? Use testing not only to flesh out your customer identities, but to identify the content and experience they want.

And guess what? Your keyword research can help you with this!

Let's say your business offering is the 1970s classic: pet rocks (you're really hoping for a comeback). When you do your keyword research, you want to identify not only the relevant keyword phrases people search for (as I've discussed throughout this book), but information and media that are being searched for in context. How many searches are there for "pet rock videos" versus "reviews of pet rocks"? "Pet rock Q&A" versus "e-books pet rocks." In the end you want to give the people what they want, but you also can give them the content they want about what they want. Right? Make sense? Again, think of *the product they want* as the spout of the marketing funnel (purchasing; the goal), *the content they want about it* as the middle of the funnel (for product consideration), and *the way they search or find out* about the content as the entry to the marketing funnel.

The Real Power of Multiple Media on the SERP

We know now that you can even tailor the specific media and content to the SERP itself. Remember all the various media options, which we've discussed throughout this book, now appearing on the SERP with rich snippets? (see Figure 11.5). Authorship information and pictures, the Google Carousel, "in-depth articles," the growth of video results, the growth of Google+ Local—and Bing is keeping up—to the point of logging in with your Facebook accounts! (See Figures 11.6 and 11.7.)

If your audience reacts well to blogs, optimize a lot of blog content with authorship. Do they respond well to reviews? Optimize and push your reviews channels' profiles and sync with your Google+ account to aid SERP placement. You get the picture—go to it!

So how does this thinking impact our concepts of hub-and-spoke marketing? Sure, you want to be strategic in identifying your plan and landing page or hub site, direct traffic there to meet your goals, and the like. But if your customers don't want to interact with a traditional landing page, then all your efforts don't matter much, do they? So plan a hub that both your target customers will respond well to or engage with, and that can likewise meet your goals, without creating a messy digital network architecture (or lack thereof) for yourself!

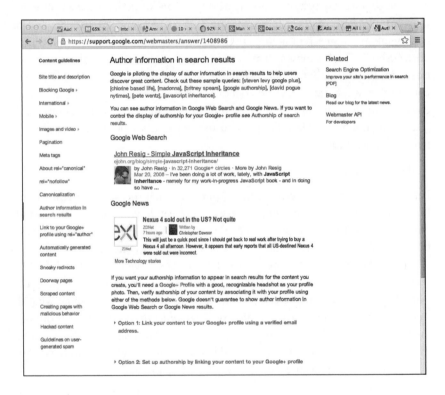

Figure 11.5   Google rich snippets.

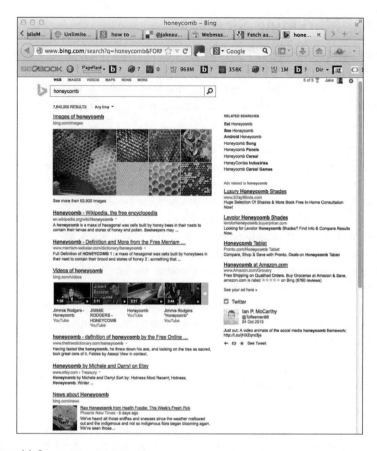

Figure 11.6 Custom SERP media results.

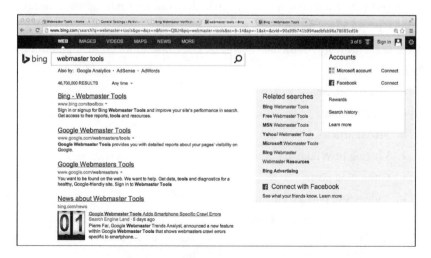

Figure 11.7 Bing Login with Facebook.

Content Marketing Strategy

What's your content marketing strategy? In truth, that's just another way to pose the questions and approaches I've been raising throughout this book. But the alternative vantage point can be helpful food for thought. Also it is the question more immediately raised by a web or social copywriter than an SEO (so yes, it's still valid).

We can begin with an assumption that a traditional SEO might not make—that we have the complete capability to produce any great content. Therefore, what content should we produce, and where should we put it? As we discuss in this chapter, definitely serve the content that the customers are looking for in the channels they want. But we also have more opportunities to think strategically on behalf of our company: What content, where, can best represent our brand and move customers to our goals? We can achieve the essentials of giving the customer what the customer wants (priority 1), and accommodate the luxury of producing brand-, product-, or company-centric messaging. And just because it might be company-centric doesn't mean it can't be optimized. What if your brand messaging *is* your search strategy, such as with reputation management or brand awareness goals? You have the means to the end.

Content Forms for Digital

With content marketing we have some additional considerations, such as increased opportunities for link baiting; we want to bait web users to help us market ourselves with social share and conversation. And the sites we use, such as PR and online article sites, we want to ensure will not be off-topic to our own brand or be red flags to the search engines. So we go back to our research tools and research these relevant sites for credibility and link authority.

Here are some forms of digital content we can consider for content publishing or recycling:

- Newsletter/email.
- Press releases.
- Placed articles.
- Writing in Wikipedia, About.com, and other content sites.
- Guest blog posts.
- Videos and podcasts in audio/video sites.
- Alternative, more niche social channels, such as Tumblr or Vine—maybe not the first choices for your business or customers, but if you have the content and can try some testing, what's to lose?

As with so much of what I've discussed, analytics is key and should drive your strategic digital plans. So what analytics can inform your best use of content production capabilities? For one, refer back to our discussions in this chapter on the customer path and marketing funnel. You can create content to serve the drop-off points within your funnel for the total sales cycle or even total customer life cycle (aw heck—let's go even to the customer bicycle!).

Online Audience Optimization (OAO)

I've talked about the issues of ever-changing SERPs and the myth of the number-one Google result. So what replaces it? Perhaps Online Audience Optimization, or OAO. Just as we've mentioned that there has been a growth in search engine importance for social content, as well as customized results, we can label this under the concept of OAO—the latest blog buzz among SEOs.

Think about it this way: "Number one SERP position" relies on the assumption that it will be number one for a broad base of searchers, excluding individual search habits, social interests, and search engine bookmarks. After all, remember the old-world way of proving number one results was by deleting cookies to neutralize the browser prior to search. It's a myth because nobody searches from a neutral browser with neutral results anymore. There is a new path for Google (and all those who follow goliath Google).

We have to put more emphasis on the marriage of specific digital web users and their behavior, media, and content desires. After all, if you are selling pet rocks, and you have a great social presence with Joe Blow as a "Like" and social follower, when Joe Blow alternatively goes to Google to search for pet rock content, you want to be the one who comes up. And when you do, it will be because of one-to-one relevance, history, and overall digital context as opposed to "neutralized search engines." I've already seen a number of online articles about OAO titled "SEO is Dead." I have a good hunch there will be more. (For more on OAO see http://www.clickz.com/clickz/column/2320639/top-search-marketing-trends-of-2014.)

The Changing Changes

I've written quite a bit about the changing SEO landscape, particularly on the channels level. Location-based directories that traditionally offered free business profiles and consumer reviews are now finding more ways to charge for services and rankings. Google places less emphasis on the classic number-one organic SERP listing and keyword click data. Social channels such as Twitter, which traditionally had no advertising, are now piloting the way for a newer advertising model—native advertising. You know enough, if you're paying for advertising or sponsorship, to watch where your money is going. But you might start paying attention to where these channels' revenue is going. After the crash of the dot-coms in the early 2000s, everyone was afraid of trying to make money on the Internet. Now, as we've just discussed, there are more and more creative ways being explored to do just that. These channels will continue to try to make money from you. So be smart about where these channels are going (and definitely don't put your entire budget in one basket). Ask yourself what the channel wants. Want some local social channel examples from my own observations? CitySearch and Kudzu want your advertising. Demand Force (a search and social reviews directory for medical services) wants your contracts for their services. Yelp wants the world very active in Yelp—it offers more unfiltered reviews and higher results for increased business and consumer profiles, reviews, and activities there.

Oh Yeah, What About WordPress?

So, let's bring all this big-picture thinking back to WordPress! WordPress makes content output simple. And it is an easy conduit, via its SEO, social integration, and other plug-ins, for content-based SEO and digital marketing success. Blogs, categories, tags, and onsite search; easy social share, stream, and follow integrations; and simple content editing and adding for a variety of media. Whether it's a blog, website, eCommerce site, community, or direct-to-social-publishing platform, WordPress feeds the content search engines crawl. As you architect for your WordPress technology, strategize your organic content. It all works together to serve your customers and meet your goals.

The Total Package

There are also total WordPress systems that are meant to function as complete digital marketing packages. I've already discussed concerns with WordPress themes that include and promote their SEO features (discussed in Chapter 6, "In-Depth Hands-On SEO Execution"). But there are many other features that people like and desire to be all-inclusive. One example is real estate themes. Real estate sales and rental sites have a need to be very fluid with integrations with other homes listings and advertising. To serve these markets there are comprehensive digital marketing themes such as Optima OmniPress complete WordPress sites. OmniPress goes beyond the limitations of traditional WordPress themes and manages whole databases of images, such as real estate photos, across the WordPress site as well as other social and advertising media. The theme system can even manage text content comprehensively across the different channels. Note that the catch here is that you pay monthly for these package services.

It's All About Priorities and Focus, Right?

Over the past couple years, SEOs have become more social marketers; social media has become more like search marketing, and mobile marketing grows for everything. Many call this the era of "content marketing" and say that this is the new label for SEO. Maybe so. But whatever you call it, don't forget the principles, priorities, and effects of the good work.

In the next chapter I talk about the future of SEO and digital and social channels. This is a point that many folks get concerned about. No worries—just focus on where your customers are. What digital tools do they use? How many places do they really "search" and what words do they use there? I'm not saying don't pay attention to new technologies and channels, I'm just saying focus on what's most important. Focus on your customer base and where they are. You may see competitors heavily invested in the latest, hottest channel. Okay, but does it give them anything? Are customers involved or searching there? Remember this and let it guide your thinking. *And with that, I invite you on to the future!*

12

What's Next? The Future of SEO and WordPress

In the future we will all drive flying cars, have our own personal robot to serve our every need, and our TVs will be 3D and take up entire walls of our house. Virtual reality will be our home environments. We will teleport to work and vacation on the moon. We will have microchips in our wrists and QR codes on our foreheads. Isn't that about right? Well, maybe, but that's not what this chapter is about. Besides, those mall rent-a-cops don't look much cooler on Segways, so how about we focus on search engines instead?

SEO Next Steps

So let's say you've done the basics of SEO, you've got it working, and the search engines are recognizing your site and giving you first-page results for at least some keyword phrases. Good job! Now it's time to reevaluate your goals and research more digital channels. Here are some options worth considering for next-level goals:

- Occupy more of the SERP real estate with additional text listings, videos, images, or other vertical results or PPC ads.
- Go after broader "head" or "short-tail" keywords.
- Go after new niches and long-tail keyword phrases.
- Improve location-based SEO and channels

- Focus more on smartphone and tablet search.
- Do multivariate testing.
- Build ongoing traffic via analytics and successful triggers.
- Pursue social-media savvy goals, such as growing social commenting, reposts, building community, and the like to empower your social audience to market for you.
- Further optimize the marketing funnel of your website; reduce bounces, emphasize customer-important content or reduce clicks to the goal (how many pages consumers have to click through to get to the landing page or shopping cart).

I've mentioned long-tail digital marketing. When we discuss aspects of niche positioning, data and content marketing, it is merely the old battle of qualitative versus quantitative strategy; the rifle versus the shotgun. In more primitive years, marketing promotions required broadcast advertising or anonymous junk mail. When promoting brand awareness, marketers didn't have deep data CRMs or micro-targeted email lists. They had a few TV stations to advertise to the masses and general address lists. Today's increased options in digital consumer data means an unprecedented quality of market data (read: higher likelihood to purchase). Sure, everyone watches Super Bowl commercials, but can you afford the cost of so many off-target, unqualified prospects for your business? The increased quality of data and communications will only continue. We see it in social, so we'll see it in WordPress.

Be My Fortune Teller

"What is the future of SEO?" is the wrong question. SEO is the constant adjustment and adaptation to the digital market forces that drive results. By results, for the sake of brevity, I mean results on the SERP—results served by the search engines to consumers in need. SEO itself is a service—the act of getting desired information served to those who search for it. So, there is no "future" of SEO besides serving future digital searchers within the new technologies wherein they search. You want to know the future of SEO? Look to the new technologies and serve the consumers where they search. That's it. Since WordPress is such a large portion of the web and digital content, WordPress itself is part of the future of SEO. Kind of glad you have this book now, huh?

So the right question to ask is, "What is the future of…"

- Google advancements
- Changes in SERP display
- Online advertising

- Alternative search engines and their emphases
- Digital content creation, repositories, and service
- Digital marketing and social analytics
- Mobile usage and technologies
- Social media search
- Users' alternative vehicles for finding content

Remember, the process of digital marketing and SEO is to set goals and plans, enact them, measure and evaluate, and revise for next steps. This is all common sense. But it is also important to look at the industry trends and drivers of general consumer usage. As we've discussed throughout this book, mobile usage (particularly mobile web and mobile websites) is in high growth and is overtaking desktop web usage. Videos continue to grow in consumer use for reasons of bandwidth technologies and capabilities and channels, whereas traditional television usage has been reducing long-term accordingly. Watched anything good on Hulu lately? (Even a year ago, 18–35 year olds spent 41% of their viewing time on digital streaming in contrast to traditional television, and now we are seeing Internet-connected television. For more on all of this, see http://www.factbrowser.com/facts/10107/.)

Some trends for the future of SEO aren't necessarily "new," they'll just have a more entrenched and obvious presence in the space. Content strategy continues to be critical, along with its integration in social media. Throughout this book I have discussed SEO keyword research and strategy to drive web, blog, and even social content.

On one hand, we've talked about how Google Analytics removed data regarding keyword drivers to website traffic from search engines. On the other hand, Google AdWords Keyword Planner has added more data regarding location-targeted keywords. Because we know people speak differently in various regions of America, why wouldn't their search terms be different as well? If the keyword data changes, that means the content changes.

Likewise more and more tools appear to measure social media content, sentiment and keywords. The accuracy and awareness of social sentiment technology increases (as we discussed in Chapter 8, "Social Media Connectivity," social sentiment is the simplified but true identification of positive, negative, and neutral social statements by digital users). Just as I have stated that keyword research uncovers "content demand," we can expect the accuracy of this to continue, which means deeper delves into the long tail.

I believe the long-tail theory to be truer today than ever before. Niche continues to be a vehicle for us to define our business and online representation. We can expect niche product demand and digital purchasing to continue to grow. Mega-trend economics aside, I'll go so far as to say that brick-and-mortars will continue to suffer if they can't find ways to compete with the infinite niche marketing capabilities of eCommerce.

Semantic Search

Hopefully by now you're seeing that Google steers the boat. At the time of this writing, the news within recent months has been updates to Google's search algorithm technology, Hummingbird. It continues to value social content, not only for SEOs and bloggers, but for web searchers. That is, Google uses the searcher's social media profiles, browser history, and universal login accounts data to tailor search results semantically. Semantic search is nothing new—it has been the next step up since contextual results (which represented web searchers' keywords written and searched in context). But semantic search has represented an ongoing progression towards psychographics, or data based on consumer interests, social information, and identity, in contrast to just demographics or purchase history. Semantic search aside, we've already discussed how Google's removal of keyword-specific data in Google Analytics might represent its trending emphasis on PPC advertising revenue. Perhaps, but this won't keep searchers from clicking on organic results. (For more on this, see http://www.steamfeed.com/google-hummingbird-mean-future-seo/.)

Helping drive psychographics results is the data available from universal login. Google's universal login is a piece of the technology trend in cloud computing and storage. Think about your Google Docs, Google Calendar—all the Google technologies we've discussed throughout this book available with one login. It's all stored in the cloud for free. WordPress is also a perfect example of cloud content. All your blog data, comments, prescheduled drafts, database items, and more—in the cloud and accessible via login anywhere. Cloud has definitely changed the roles and even the face of computer use today. Watch for game changing trends like this in the future. Google's apps and personalized or "secure" search results (as we discuss throughout this chapter) matter more to SEO than you might think (see Google's attempts to gather more of your personal profile information in Figure 12.1). This means that if Bing/Yahoo! can't gather more of your logged in, secure, semantic social data, it will be restricted to providing you search results by browser search history (as shown in Figure 12.2). With this growing trend, we can only hope that these digital power houses don't end up fighting over semantics. (Yes, I just had to go there.)

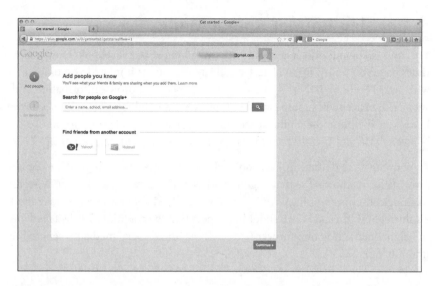

Figure 12.1   Google universal login and profile information seeks to gather more about you.

Figure 12.2   Bing serves personalized search results via search history (in this case with Flickr).

The Ongoing Role of Social Media

We can't talk about universal login without talking about Facebook. How many times have you pulled up the latest social site-du-jour as it invited you to log in with your Facebook ID? And to access all your personal profile information and friends? By Facebook's mere global web presence and billion+ users, it is a force to be reckoned with in the digital space and has consequent relevance for SEO. *"I mean OMG did U C that photo Lisa posted on her wall this morning?!?!?! 'Like!!!'"*

As with the phrase "once in Facebook, why leave Facebook?" the content keeps growing for its internal search engine (and even if you rarely see Facebook results in Google, they are in Bing). And just as we've talked about hub-and-spoke models throughout this book, we shouldn't expect that the traditional website will be the digital marketing hub forever (especially as brand social media presences keep multiplying).

 Note

Google Versus Bing

A common question regarding search engine activities is on the use of Google versus Bing. Bing/Yahoo! (because Yahoo! uses the same underlying engine) has represented a combined, nearly 30% usage for years compared to Google's approximate 70%. Within this flat trend, Bing and Yahoo! themselves have traded percentage points up and down (as the face of the search engine access). Ironically, just as Google+ can't seem to knock off Facebook as the social networking 800lb. gorilla, Bing/Yahoo! just can't seem to knock off Google.

Digital channels, just like brick-and-mortar stores, obtain a brand perception from we the people. In other words, to some extent, we determine what the social channels actually "are." Remember when MySpace got relabeled as the channel for rock bands? And Pinterest as the new hot site for women's dresses and shoes? Public perception of use runs deep: YouTube is a social media channel, but we don't think of it as such, we think of it as a viral video site. LinkedIn is a popular social networking site, but we think of it as a business networking site, and so on.

In some ways I think Google+ is still awaiting user branding (aside from having a 68% male audience). Right now it has two commonly used features: Google+ Local, maps for location-based reviews and search results (formerly Google Places); and Google+Hangout, video-conferencing software. At the time of this writing Google has integrated Google+ with Google News (and with news results on the SERP; see Figure 12.3). We'll see if any of these become the new primary face and identity of the Google+ experiment. Considering Yahoo! news sites have still received good web visits since the late 1990s, the additional news spotlights on the Google SERP may not be a bad idea (as shown in Figure 12.4).

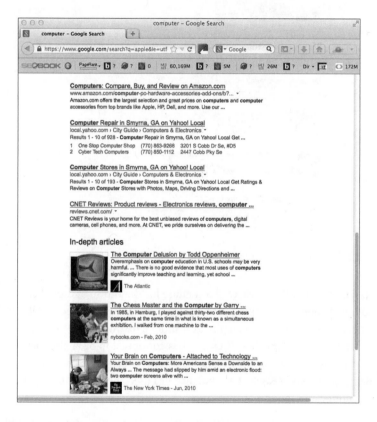

Figure 12.3   Google+ News profiles and the SERP.

Figure 12.4   Google News rich snippets and the SERP.

All this is to say that if you seek a good guide for the future of digital channel use, look to how people are thinking (and using) the channel right now. Although Twitter was initially built as a channel for mobile texting (SMS) communications, people rarely used it in SMS. It was, and has continued to be, a channel of social post sharing. Investment and banking community channels have been used most by older generations because that audience has used those resources most and has had the money and investments to track.

After so many bad investments with heavy losses during the dot-com bubble of the late 1990s, and with the state of the economy since, many Internet business people are banking their money on more incremental, small, but recognizable financial gains instead. Apple itself helped put this into play with iTunes. In a world of late 1990s free music-sharing habits (think Napster), iTunes began selling songs for $1 each. People could justify that cost and did. These incremental charges have helped pave the new eCommerce. With the reduced costs (per the reduction of brick-and-mortar store requirements on the web), businesses could sell incrementally and pay small fees to many resellers or online advertising channels for promotion. This world of digital low costs and gains is continually reshaping the way we think about business.

Social channels should be looked at for target industry use. High school and college social networkers have been transitioning from Facebook use to Twitter, while their parents (and grandparents) have been growing in the use of Facebook. Pinterest since its launch has had an 80% female audience but is still a high-consumption channel and is showing more and more male-oriented content. (See more on Pinterest and other social channel statistics on www. business2community.com/social-media/103-compelling-social-media-marketing-statistics-2013-2014-0679246.) So research social channels and communities before using them in your business. The resources we've discussed throughout this book will help you.

Meanwhile, social channels seem to grow all the time around facilitating "sharing": ride-sharing and car pooling, time shares, even couch/room sharing. So we can expect more social channels facilitating industry-specific content sharing as well—for example, guest-video-blogging. Think eLance consultants and content on the extreme niche level. ChristmasTreeLance for bloggers, anyone?

We should also expect social media optimization (SMO) to grow in sophistication. Searching from within social channels should get better and better, just as more and more incorporate search/social capabilities such as tag words. Twitter began the #hashtag use craze, but since then Facebook and Instagram have incorporated #hashtag use for posting and searching. Facebook and other social channels continue to negotiate with search engines to make their content appear within the SERP. Facebook results appear often in Bing. LinkedIn appears in both. Google, of course, serves Google+ results in the SERP. These listings give more presence and validity to the social channels themselves, their user profiles, and advertising.

What is lost from Google Analytics can be rising somewhere else. What isn't surprising is that in recent years Google has incorporated more social media data into Google Analytics—namely, Google+ and YouTube analytics. Perhaps data such as these and other social media analytics will step up to provide more important metrics and data points for search marketers to capitalize on in the wake of lost keywords (see Figure 12.5). With the continued growth (and chaos) of social media marketing and demand for sensible analytics (beyond Klout), we will have to see more social analytics integrations for WordPress.

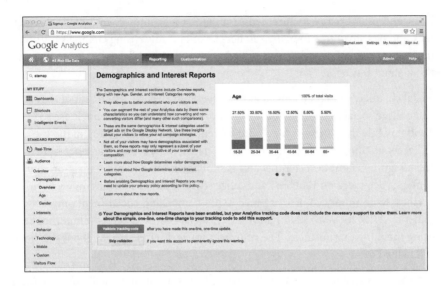

Figure 12.5　Social media and other web visitor data within Google Analytics.

Video Content and SEO

It should be a big red flag that in recent years Google and Bing have delivered more and more multimedia or rich results on the SERP. More videos, images, and local data on the SERP could be a good indication that the dynamism of appearance of the SERP will only continue. And with these needs and rewards for more content, it is natural to expect more offerings in this department, particularly with Bing, which has to catch up. I've personally already noticed "Bing Videos" and "Bing Images" showing up more and more in the Bing SERP (see Figure 12.6). However, this content can't be from the content farms and gray-hat copy spinning of the past; search engine trends have progressed to penalize these up to now, and we should expect that to continue.

Other technologies applicable to SEO in the immediate-and-growing departments include HTML5. This platform allows for more searchability with different technologies such as animations and videos. In the past, animations were executed primarily with Adobe Flash, which could have actual keyed-in text, selectable within a browser, but not searchable by spiders. And Flash was not accepted by Apple's Safari browser and consequently could not be viewed on iPhone. HTML5 gives us new options for animations, video, and apps, but is not omnipresent because, as is always the case with web technologies, there are many people still using older browser software and versions. Eventually, however, HTML5 will be the expected standard. Even a year ago, 50% of app developers were already programming in

HTML5 (see more on HTML5 and use on www.html5report.com/topics/html5/ articles/328645-html5-ascendent.htm).

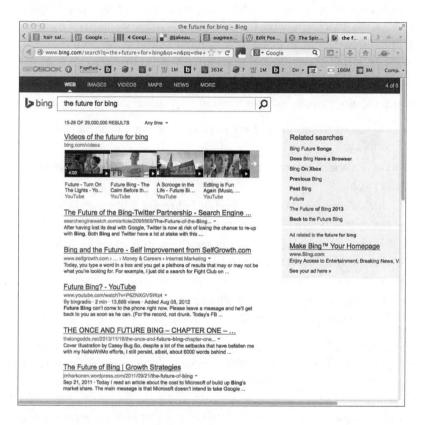

Figure 12.6   Bing Videos in the SERP.

Content and Collaboration

Other important, advancing technologies with impacts on content and search include near-field communications and geo-location digital directories and apps. If you as a marketer can cheaply communicate to a surrounding area that you are a shop specializing in high-end, used Mazda racing parts and repair, then you have a sales and marketing reach and low spend that you could not have had ten or 20 years ago.

One of the fascinating things about search is that not only does the technology change over time, but the usability and user-focus changes, as does the consumer behavior. So search engines learn from us, but we also learn from search engines. It is a marvelous, reciprocal learning relationship over time and this is a relationship we can expect to continue.

An amazing thing in keyword research that continues to surprise me is when specific keywords being researched have long-term downward trends (such as viewing the 4-year option in Google Trends). This goes even for niche. For example I did an SEO audit for a client in the CNC machine (stands for computer numerical control) industry, and the simple keyword "cnc machine" has been in long-term decline for search—even though the industry itself for that has been in constant, high growth! Why and how can such anomalies exist?

To help identify for your industry, you can ask yourself the following questions:

- Do you search words in search engines today more than you did five years ago?
- Do you search longer or more specific terms? Or shorter and broader keywords?
- Do you ever quickly search a keyword phrase, not like the kinds of search results listed, and change your search terms to search again?
- Do you search including different search words if you're ready to buy something online versus to just boost up on your knowledge or to get an answer to a question?
- If you think your own search behavior has changed, how do you think it goes for the market overall?

So as digital searchers learn more about how to use search engines and find the content they want, the keywords they use change. If the phrase "cnc machine" is in search decline, but the industry is growing, chances are that consumers are using different, more varied and specific keyword phrases to get the content results they want. This makes sense also from the perspective that as markets grow, customer awareness and savvy will also grow. I think about the early 20th century when auto drivers were labeled "motorists." Today we all drive and have basic understanding of car motors, parts, and operation. So there is no reason for the word "motorist" to be used.

From a content perspective, all of this increases the keyword phrases that we want to be responsible for covering. We still focus on the same "theme" of content to a targeted market, but our keywords increase and then so does our content.

More on Local

Another aspect to look forward to is growth in NFC-local data social channels. (We talked about this technology and use in Chapter 9, "Going Mobile and Local"). But social channel identification of "friends near us" is still growing and will continue to do so. We see it in our traditional mobile apps for channels such as Foursquare and Facebook, as well as channels exclusively built on NFC and identification of people we know within geographic proximity. And if other technologies can identify and respond to digital users within specific locations, why not have your WordPress site content do the same? From keywords, to maps to location info and specific sales reps—it makes sense that WordPress would grow on that going forward. So we should expect these WordPress opportunities to multiply. Meaning, more plug-ins for the aforementioned channels to be integrated somehow with WordPress. Want maps and reviews fed onto your WordPress site? Google is not the only answer. Why not feed your Yelp or other channel reviews directly into WordPress via plug-ins with options? Even targeting specific locations?

 Tip

Google Local Keyword Recommendations

As technology, data, and sophistication grow for location-based search, there is another gap filled. We have discussed how Google has removed keyword-specific click data within Google Analytics for websites and blogs, and likewise how Google has moved its keyword research tool behind AdWords accounts (although still free). With this keyword tool move, Google has likewise provisioned it with more location focus. Now Google tries harder to recommend best keywords on even smaller city levels (We discussed local SEO in depth in Chapter 9; see Figures 12.7 and 12.8).

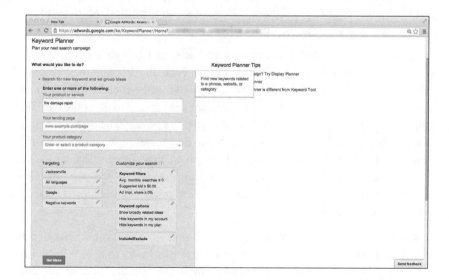

Figure 12.7   Inputting locations within the Google AdWords Keyword tool.

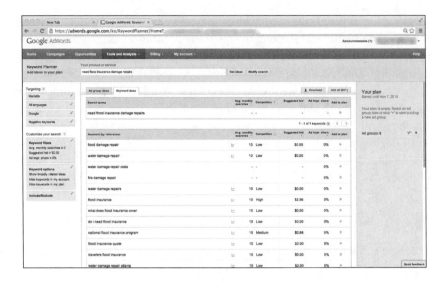

Figure 12.8 Keyword recommendations from Google for locations.

Because the digital space overall is still an experiment in progress, analytics have been inconsistent and all over the board. Just as with the recent growth of "big data" companies, we should expect to see analytics offerings continue to grow, and standardization efforts become more visible. Klout has been a long-standing social software standard projecting metrics and measurements for registrants (although many social media gurus have distrusted its seemingly random assignment of <100 point, or more accurately <60 point, scores for social identities). More standardization options should rise as the dust settles.

The hands-on SEO is already (theoretically) disappearing—just look at WordPress—and there is less website coding in general. Although they are not all to be trusted, there are more and more automated tools, especially from your web hosting providers, which are meant to supplant the manual work of the true SEO (not that web hosting provider tools do it right). Resources like Localeze submit local profiles to countless other location-based directories in substitution for the search marketer needing to do these by hand (as we discussed in Chapter 9). *And as we've discussed social media grows in importance and SERP occupation, making the "content marketer" a more valuable achiever than the traditional technical SEO wizard of tricks and tools!*

And it is the nature of technology, regardless, to replace the manual work of programming in general. Again, WordPress is a great testament to this. With so many preexisting themes and plug-ins, nonprogrammers can suddenly create websites. Graphic designers, who decades ago had to do manual illustration, comping, and lettering, today can be replaced by the average user with lite versions of Photoshop (now a household word). With these progressions, why wouldn't the SEO be replaced as well? Time will tell. Until then, use these principles and do great SEO work!

 Tip

The Role of the SEO as Strategist

Remember that one trend with Google is to continually try to weed out black-hat SEOs and instead reward the individual, savvy, niche industry expert blogger, content creator, video producer, and so on. Expect that to continue. Today's white hat becomes tomorrow's grey hat becomes the day after's black hat. Expect Google to try to find ways to reward content creators and move away from tricky SEOs like us. Yet this is a delicate dance; there will always be the more technological savvy persons seeking new ways to beat out (or at least better execute the technology than) the creative, nontechnological writers. Whichever way the search engines and SERP sway at a time, there will always be a need for strategy, which is perhaps the greatest strength of the good SEO. Call it SEO, digital or content strategy—this is a role vital for us to understand and execute (which is why Chapter 3, "A Strategic SEO Upfront Content Approach," is devoted to it).

Local SEO has trended for more targeted identifications in recent years. I've seen local SEO results and Google Maps pins go from general metropolitan areas down to specific ZIP Code centers. As more businesses achieve more detailed local SEO information, we can expect even deeper targeted data and results.

Geolocation data and channels continue to be enhanced technologically—NFC information being only one aspect. But with the growth of data comes the natural growth of disorder and chaos, and local directories (as we discussed in Chapter 9) are a great example. At the time of this writing, there continue to be countless local directories for search and reviews with no clear-cut winner. You can argue that Google+Local does a good job of grabbing primary search activity. However, everyone knows Yelp; it has high mobile use and doesn't have the same usability barriers, such as personal Gmail accounts or Google+ accounts do, just to leave a review (at the time of this writing, Google+Local still requires web users to have a Google+ or Gmail account to leave business reviews).

All the local directories seem to battle it out for what location data to use and display for a business. This is why you can see WhitePages.com, Yelp, Foursquare,

Google+, and Yahoo!Local, and they can all potentially have slightly different location info. We should expect strides to clean up these listings problems in the future, or at least fiercer battles among the channels for who's right and who's wrong—who gets to businesses first and gets their correct info from the source, and so on. Sound like fun? Get involved! Start your own local directory or reviews channel!

How else does "infinite niche" present opportunities going forward in content marketing? I've already mentioned the advancing NFC and geo-location channels and their advertising. Even Facebook continues to downgrade business pages in EdgeRank, so you see less and less of their posts in your organic wall (unless the brand in question pays for native listings on your Facebook wall. Interestingly, LinkedIn within the recent year or two has turned on business postings to business pages—pages which used to be entirely static with basically "About Us" copy to show.). So native advertising, content and sponsorship opportunities, I predict, will continue to grow, blurring the lines between organic and paid. Location-targeting—even for eCommerce—will have an abundance of opportunities and usage going forward.

Going Google

Perhaps you've noticed the growth in recent years of universal login capabilities. An easy example we've discussed in this book is Google. When in Google Chrome, on any computer, you log in one time to access your email, your Google Calendar, Google+, Google Drive, GoogleDocs, and so on and so forth. Within WordPress, logging in one time can allow you access to all of your and your client's WordPress sites and blogs, as well as commenting capabilities on others' WordPress blogs. Mobile apps on our own devices allow us immediate access to our own Facebook, Twitter, and any accounts on our own apps, so why shouldn't this work on the desktop web similarly?

An important question here is how do you break down the SERP? In the past it has been almost exclusively composed of text listings. Then Google advanced sophistication with local and maps results, increased the SERP real estate devoted to these, and pushed them to the top of the SERP—in some cases consuming almost the entire visible listings above the fold (see Figure 12.9). Then it increased results showing images within the primary text-based search results (see Figure 12.10), and video.

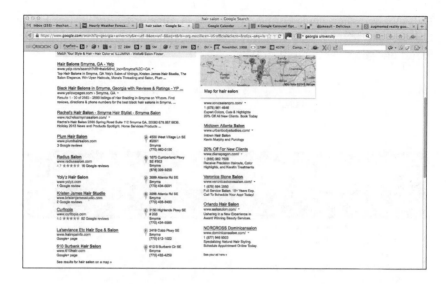

Figure 12.9   Google+Local/Maps in the SERP.

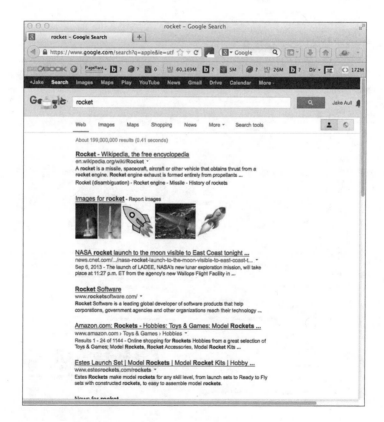

Figure 12.10   Images in the SERP.

Today we have the Google Carousel of images in some search results (see Figure 12.11) and a variety of rich snippet results (as we discussed in Chapter 5, "Real-World Blogging;" see Figure 12.12).

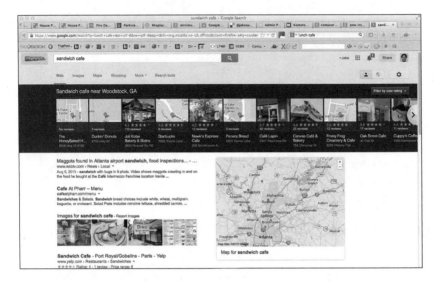

Figure 12.11   The Google Carousel.

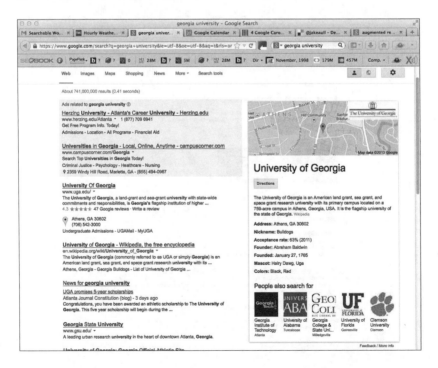

Figure 12.12   A version of the Google SERP.

With all these considerations, it is important to ask which portion of the SERP is most effective (see Figure 12.13). One video result can be large proportionally and jump out at the searcher, but it is only one result among many text-content results. And does it appear in your mobile search results as well as desktop? (Because mobile results are different, and served with different priorities than desktop; see images in the SERP in Figure 12.14.) And what if the searcher wants to read reviews or a reputable article with industry statistics on your product segment's growth? I know of an SEO firm that focuses exclusively on video SEO. At the end of the day you have to answer questions for yourself on what drives consumers to your goal and the issues of qualitative and quantitative results (as we discussed in Chapter 7, "Analytics for WordPress").

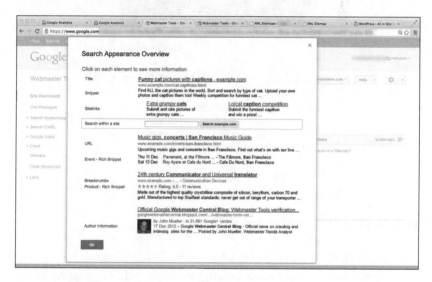

Figure 12.13   Google's breakdown of the SERP.

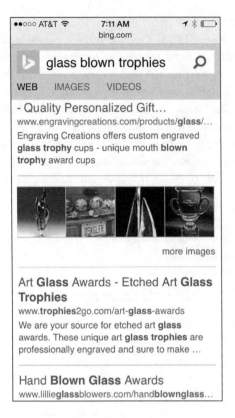

Figure 12.14 Images in the mobile SERP.

Google has been the search industry leader for years and shows no signs of slouching off the research (and experimentation) behind that title. Google Glass aside, other examples of this include its satellite technology for mapping and Google Earth. And most people are aware that Google has its own Google Street cars, which have allowed it to create Google Street View. There have been suggestions across the blogosphere that Google, who has been more recently investing in drone technology, might replace the Google Street View cars (which shoot streets, public places, and neighborhoods to display online in Google Street View) with drones. You may have even seen in the news and on YouTube how some have adapted Google Glass to pilot drones for video filming. Although at the time of this writing Google denies any such plans, we might image drone-enhanced versions of something like a Google Sky View. I just hope I'm not tanning in the backyard the day the drones fly over. For your sake, if viewing this sky view over my neighborhood, you should also hope I'm not tanning that day.

Augment Your Reality

The future is definitely "mobile," and just not the way we currently think about it. That is, up until now we've tended to think about technology as something tied to, and dependent upon, hardware devices. Hence society has progressed from mainframe computers and servers to desktop computers to laptops to handheld and mobile devices to smartphones versus modern tablets. With cloud-computing for device independence, and technology progressions such as Google Glass, the technology we want exists beyond our platforms and begins to become "part of our being." Google Glass allows us to see, through a device-enhanced pair of glasses, more information about the world around us. From combining personal activity data when engaged in sports with history data or statistics, such as with cycling or golf, to viewing recipes while cooking—we have the ability to view both the physical and online world simultaneously (and how is that for the future of search? For more see http://www.google.com/glass/start/what-it-does/).

Augmented reality continues to grow and adds another "layer" of mobile usage to our everyday practice, such as with Google Glass. Traditional virtual reality, however, seems to be stagnant in all areas except video games, as in MMOs. (Massive multiplayer online activities such as MMORPGs, or massive multiplayer online role-playing games—and image advertising options do exist within MMORPGs, such as World of Warcraft; *aw come on—check out WOW and let out your inner geek!*)

Google Glass is an example of augmented reality, which gets buzz as it continues in development and we can expect it to rise in interest. The technical, visual identification of reality around us, and with the digital space, will grow in value. For example, on a more common and basic level, code scanning has become regular practice for many—retail store shoppers who use mobile devices to scan product bar codes and/or printed QR codes to obtain product detail or competitor costs and locations. Adding more data in combinations such as these or with Google Glass can have a lot of consumer value.

The Mobile Tomorrow

Is your smartphone just too big? We've seen the development of smartphone technologies for wrist watches. Similarly, our cars will soon all have layers of pertinent data to display on our windshields as part of our driving and navigation experience. And public touch-screen kiosks are nothing new, but when they can integrate our personal logins and full cloud identities, data, files, options, and the like—well, all this helps define what is the future of true "mobility"; we become one with the technology.

When we can visually "project" our desired usability interfaces and data access upon the tables and walls around us, this is true mobility. And graphic interface can be hardly necessary, thanks to voice-activated search and audio results. All these technologies exist now in some form or fashion and are easily accessible to us. Expecting an increase and blending of these technologies is only natural.

We've seen the power and growth of voice-activated technologies, such as with Apple's Siri and Google Voice Search. And we should expect that technology and voice-activated search to grow. One of the characteristics of this is longer keyword strings in contrast to short-tail keywords. In spite of the complexity and inconsistent patterns of voice search instead of typed keywords, deeper, long-tail keyword phrases will be ripe for the SEO's picking.

The search engines themselves are heavily vested in mobile technology overall. Google has its brand of Android mobile devices, and Microsoft Windows has its own mobile devices (remember that Microsoft MSN shares the technology behind Bing with Yahoo!). These efforts represent not only an interest in mobile, but digital share overall. That is, who will be the king of the digital world? Facebook has definitely been feeling this, especially with its mobile app not having all the functionality of its desktop website. Consequently, Facebook has bought up native mobile apps such as Instagram, WhatsApp, and has incorporated NFC technology, and even virtual reality, into its mobile deliverables.

 Note

Which Mobile Is "Mobile"?

Up until now, marketers have still been largely thinking of the "mobile" category as both smartphone and tablet. But now that mobile is taking over desktop/laptop use, and that newer devices such as Microsoft's Windows Surface and competing Samsung products allow both tablet and laptop functionality, we will have to expand our thinking, especially because smartphones represent "in-transit" or "on-the-go" use for consumers today, and tablets have more use for reading e-books and vacation substitution for the full laptop. Even Google Analytics separates "mobile (smartphone)" device data from "tablet" (see in Figure 12.15). The difference in use and consumer behavior should indicate a difference in marketing approach, particularly because web browser "sniffers" can detect the technology behind the user's platform. Use your mobile device data, research, and industry mobile/social channels to drive your digital marketing strategies.

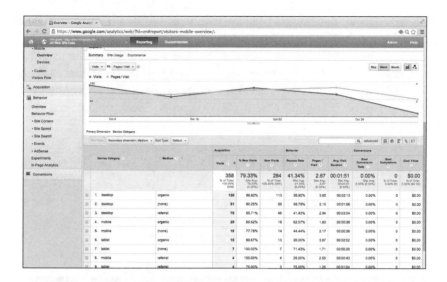

Figure 12.15   Google Analytics report of mobile access for websites.

One of the progressions over time in this "mobile revolution" has been device independence. The combination of technologies previously discussed, such as universal login, cloud software, bandwidth access, and technology and mobile devices and use have given us device independence. We no longer need our own computer or even our own software to do what we want to do online and with technologies. These factors should continue to contribute to our device independence. And technologies such as thinner, smaller smartphones and Google Glass continue to minimize the size of the device itself—pushing us to make more of ourselves and our wishes, commands, our voice, our physical locations, and even our thoughts to become more important than the technological device.

The Future of WordPress

WordPress itself is growing in use, as we've discussed in this book; approximately 23% of new websites are the WordPress platform. Yet the WordPress back-end interface has always been very poor and not at all WYSIWIG (what-you-see-is-what-you-get). I love WordPress, but I am the first to admit it has been saddled with poor usability by its editor. After all these years of use, I still have to pause sometimes to remember where I find that one thingy to do that one thing on the website thing (that's several thingies removed). In fact, over time, WordPress has offered more alternate ways to more easily edit portions of your WordPress site than the traditional WordPress back-end content display allows (one example is shown in Figure 12.16). Original WordPress theme designers have also offered customized login back-end dashboard user interface alternatives for their own themes to compensate for the "messy" UI of the traditional WordPress dashboard. (One example is the StudioPress back-end shown in Figure 12.17. Another example, a plug-in called MP6, has been created to cure this very challenge with its own redesigned dashboard.) If you're seeking front-end WYSIWYG options, there is TinyMCE plug-in. Another WYSIWYG WordPress plug-in is Barley. And there is Visual Composer Page Builder for WYSIWYG pages. Check 'em out.

Figure 12.16   An alternative display of WordPress back-end content editing.

Figure 12.17   Alternative WordPress dashboard customized per themes.

Another aspect of WordPress admin issues is the widget controls. Although the current drag-and-drop widget control is simple, it is again not WYSIWIG and doesn't help control above-the-fold design. Accordingly, a Widget Area Chooser is in the works to help. Perhaps you've had issues trying to find (within the WordPress back-end) which tools or plug-ins on what aspect of your site you are using or want to use. OmniSearch is a new plug-in being developed to give global admin search capabilities to solve and search all. And finally, yes—a new dashboard UI is in the works overall for WordPress with the WP-Dash plug-in. Just by nature of these issues (and the progresses described here) the WordPress IA must continue to be enhanced over time for usability. (For more on these and other future works for WordPress, see www.elegantthemes.com/blog/general-news/what-you-can-expect-from-future-versions-of-wordpress.)

Another issue for WordPress designers is the desire to customize plug-in features. Don't like the field restrictions on your WordPress contact form? Want more control over the image placement in your WordPress art gallery? You don't want to have to build your own plug-in from scratch, so there are WordPress plug-in platforms being developed to allow us all to achieve greater customization for the plug-in functionality we want. This kind of design flexibility and convenience for WordPress's 23% chunk of the web's sites only makes sense. (For more on plug-in platforms, see http://chrislema.com/future-wordpress-plugin-development/).

Also consider progressions like WordPress automatic updates and more frequent minor updates (in contrast to those flags within your WordPress dashboard you've seen in the past asking you to update your WordPress version). And perhaps you've noticed the mess of code written within WordPress site themes by the myriad theme developers out there? The lack of consistency, certain CSS style elements appearing here or there and with mixed up tags, and so on? WordPress is working on inline documentation coding standards to help! Because we should have guidelines to follow on how the code should be written and placed—issues to help us all. Or perhaps you're waiting on the next WordPress default theme? We've seen Twenty-Ten, Twenty-Eleven themes, and more—up to Twenty-Fourteen—a responsive, magazine-style media showcase theme. I've talked about efforts to improve the WordPress UI and make it more WYSIWIG; more specifically, WordPress is building secure, inline editing from the front face of your blog. (For more info on these enhancements, see http://thewebatom.net/blog/wordpress-future/.)

If you're not aware of WordPress multi-sites, it's a growing possibility. This WordPress asset allows many WordPress sites to be architected and tied to same admin platforms. This has allowed some website providers to target similar users or clients within a specific market with like WordPress website themes and architecture. For example, in the restaurant industry, there are two such providers: happytables.com and restaurantengine.com. Although such models built and targeted for specific markets are not a new concept, advances with WordPress multi-sites empower more and more of these for the future. And if it's not multi-site specifically that offers the advanced functionality you want, there is a growing trend of developers building off of WordPress's available application framework to develop whatever application functionality they can dream up.

Perhaps a little less all-encompassing, I also see opportunities regarding support for future WordPress desires. Right now there are certain theme developers who are noted for being focused and reliable on the ongoing support side—those such as Genesis Themes by StudioPress and WooCommerce Themes. I see opportunities here for more support systems to keep all from crashing, as well as opportunities that are more focused on mobile WP sites and their functionality. With the current and future growth of mobile web overtaking desktop, it only makes sense. And because content continues to be "king" for the search engines and social media practice, ways to facilitate promoting immediate and ubiquitous content should only be enhanced. For example, I have read of different approaches to make it easier to push text and images from email directly to WordPress, more cleanly than in past. And whatever new hot social channel is on the horizon? Expect that to soon have integrations with WordPress as well, particularly with mobile.

With the high value and desire for content and easier ways to push it into WordPress, there comes the need to best serve that within your own site to visitors. We've already discussed the challenges and needs for good IA and UI for your site and blog. Those challenges and needs will grow as content grows on your own site. We've all stumbled upon older sites that have grown over the years with endless pages and content, spun out of control like rooms in a house on one of those hoarding reality TV shows. Don't let this happen to you! Reevaluate your own content and the user-friendly means for readers to get to it, which also means onsite search. Yes—the options and design for searching your own site or blog for content. Sounds simple enough, but do you want to have separate search fields for your regular website content versus your blog? What if you have a forum on your site; do you want different search field and results there as well? Identify what makes the most sense from the user's perspective. It may not *sound* smart to have different search fields, but it might make the most sense to the reader. From websites to blogs to forums to an eCommerce site. These are the scenarios showing why user testing is a good idea, even if it's with friends and industry peers instead of actual customers. It's also a great idea to find a similar site you like and identify how they solved the problem.

We can also naturally also expect web-, blog-, and digital-UI-design trends to affect WordPress sites. There are design trends toward overall distillation: flat design; sidebar reduction or elimination; fewer sliders; and long, scrolling pages as opposed to numerous pages of less content (like a Tumblr layout). We can expect to see more WordPress themes in such styles. However, referring back to SEO principles, we must be careful here: With all that content concentrated on one page, page load times can suffer—and consequently, so can search rank. Also, top-ranked pages tend to be under 2,500 words. And what about duplicate content? Without certain common info (such as "Contact" or "About Us") consistently visible in a sidebar or footer, one might feel the temptation to duplicate this content within the page—exposing it to search rank venerability. And don't forget that more than one or two outbound links within page text can dilute your page rank.

But what are your challenges with WordPress? Chances are someone else has the same, and with the WordPress community growing and growing, there's a lot of potential as more and more such specific challenges develop. Therefore, become a theme or plug-in developer yourself! Many WordPress designers/developers out there use this approach to promote their own business of generating WordPress sites and blogs for their own client base! Or write a book like this one (just not better than mine).

As I have mentioned before, there is a line of thinking that mobile apps have existed solely as substitute for the poor usability of mobile websites thus far. But I've seen great growth in mobile website usability, particularly for WordPress mobile sites, and there is no reason to expect this trend to stop. This aside, there are questions about the growth of mobile app capabilities in the short term. For example, mobile app-based search (from within Apple's app store, for example) works nothing like, or doesn't sync with, web-based search engines, leaving a lot of opportunity in this arena.

There are some changes in every update of WordPress, and there is a lot of buzz at the time of this writing as to what will and won't be in WordPress 4.0. Keep your eyes open. There has also been some buzz on Ghost, the new blogging platform originated by a former WordPress staffer. Ghost's interface looks inherited from WordPress, but its claim of differentiation is that it's simply an easy-to-use, wide-open blogging platform, nothing more (while WordPress is increasingly a CMS, or content management system). It claims not to compete with the advancement of WordPress. Personally I wonder why Ghost prospects wouldn't first choose Tumblr or WordPress, and I don't see concern for usage loss for the WordPress market.

Finally...

Just as with SEO, WordPress technological capabilities continue to be offered and continue to progress. On the one hand, these tools make it easier. But the more tools there are, the more detailed and divergent the audience desires. All this technological growth makes someone who best knows how to use it all very valuable. Instead of "programming us out of a job," the technology means that the ability to manage it all becomes high in demand.

Content marketing is on the rise. WordPress is on the rise. It makes sense that these will continue to grow and that more targeted SEO channels will be built for consumer usage. Find your best contributions. So you may call it SEO, inbound content marketing, digital advertising, or web facelifting. Just do it with strategy, do it in WordPress, and do it with class (as classy as this book and its jokes have been).

This wouldn't be a good book on digital marketing issues without inviting you to check out my additional digital resources via my own WordPress site. Please do so at www.zenfires.com/wordpress-seo-success.

Appendix A

WordPress Plug-ins

I've discussed a lot of WordPress plug-ins throughout this book. The following is the list of the names and the chapters where I have discussed them. This is not my endorsement of these, especially because some of these I flat out don't like! Want more? I'll continue to add to this list on my site at http://zenfires.com/wordpress-seo-success.

Simple 301 redirects Chapter 6

ShareThis Chapter 8

Sliding YouTube Gallery Chapters 5 and 6

SocialShare Chapter 8

Sociable Chapter 8

Social Media Auto Publish Chapter 8

Social Media Monitoring Chapter 8

The BuddyPress Plug-in Chapter 8

The Social Marketing Plug-in Chapter 8

Tai.ki Embeddable Forums Chapter 8

Useful Banner Manager Chapter 10

uTube Gallery Chapter 5 and 6

WP125 Chapter 10

W3 Total Cache Chapter 6

Widget Area Chooser Chapter 12

WordAds Chapter 10

WordPress Mobile Pack Chapter 9

WordPress.com Stats migrated into JetPack Chapter 7

WP-Ad-Manager Chapter 10

WP-Dash plug-in Chapter 12

WPDB SpringClean plug-in Chapter 6

WPTouch Chapter 9

Yoast Sitemaps for YouTube Chapters 5 and 6

Appendix B

Support and Education: Forums, Accreditations, Associations, Seminars, and Tech Resources

For more technical education, software such as HootSuite, HubSpot, and Google AdWords all offer a lot. I respect all three of these, and there would probably be some good things learned from their offerings. But be careful here, as it is definitely in the best interest of these suppliers to educate you on their technologies. How objective will such education be? If you want to be the expert on these technologies, by all means look into it. But to be an objective search marketer requires a broader learning approach. Don't forget that you can do a lot of experimentation easily and cheaply; much of this book shows you how.

Digital marketers Google the answers they want on the latest tools and search engine technology issues. And for good reason. I do the same, even for specific issues in this book. Books (hopefully, such as this one) are valuable for a holistic approach, strategic vision, and connecting the dots beyond disparate inputs from random blog post bursts.

There is still great value in searching and reading blogs for staying current with SEO research. When you do this, however, be sure that the sources you read are trustworthy. I put a lot of trust in large industry blogs such as SearchEngineLand.com, SearchEngineWatch.com, and SocialMediaToday.com. Of course, I also trust what Google says about itself. There are SEO tools that have blogs and great info, such as HubSpot.com and RavenTools.com. Just consider that their content may be skewed toward their own products and services. Also, SEO organizations and their online communities are definitely worth participating in, such as SEMPO.

Regional organizations are good for gathering digital marketing and WordPress knowledge; there's always someone there who knows something you don't. But at the same time—particularly with seminars—note that "expert speakers" are not always the experts; often they are salespersons for specific digital tools.

With all of that in mind, here are blogs, sites, associations, and other resources I referenced to write this book:

- http://en.support.wordpress.com/lexicon/ (glossary for WordPress terms)
- SEOMoz.org/blog
- www.wpbeginner.com
- Lynda.com
- W3schools
- SearchEngineLand
- SMX
- SEMPO
- SXSW
- SES conference
- www.liveintent.com
- Mashable.com
- www.internetretailer.com
- http://techcrunch.com
- www.comscoredatamine.com
- Moz.org
- SearchEngineWatch
- SearchEngineLand
- WordPress Codex
- Pew Internet Research
- NetLingo.com
- Ready.mobi
- MoxieMobile.com
- SEOBook.com
- www.wpbeginner.com
- www.kaushik.net/avinash

And finally, if the sites and tools you reference confuse you, don't forget to look for the "?"s and "i"s in those digital tools. Want more? I'll put this list and add to it on my site at www.zenfires.com/wordpress-seo-success.

Thank you so much for reading!

—Jacob J. Aull

Glossary

I have always had trouble finding a good dictionary of digital marketing terms. Here's my attempt to rectify that by citing the words I have used throughout this book. Want more? I'll continue to add to this list on my site at http://zenfires.com/wordpress-seo-success.

API Application Programming Interface, or the means for connecting different technology components.

augmented reality The "added digital layer" of data or image to otherwise normal human perception; as with Google Glasses.

authorship In search engine personal accounts, such as your Google+ account, you can flesh out your whole profile, add your photo, bio, and so on to sync with your website, assign yourself as the author of your site blog posts, and appear this way in the SERP.

avatars Web user profiles (also see *gravatars*).

bots Robots, crawlers, or spiders.

bounces If web searchers land and stay on a site for a while, they are displaying a quality of content, an evaluation, whereas those who land on a site and immediately "bounce" back to the search engine represent a poor quality of content on the site's behalf and a poor resulting search engine ranking.

cached page Previously indexed web content available for viewing as alternative to the live site.

canonicalization The identification of true, singular content, without duplication errors or multiple URLs.

CLV or LTV Customer lifetime value, or averaged long-term spending by your customer on your products or services.

CMS Content management system (such as WordPress).

cookies User- and/or browser-specific info stored by the browser for serving customized content and reuse.

CPA Cost per action; in contrast to PPC advertising, sometimes one has the option to pay only for a specified action, such as an eCommerce sale, or clicking through to a Contact Us form.

CPC Cost per click (for online advertising).

CPM Cost per thousand (for advertising "impressions" or "eyeballs").

CRM Customer resource management—databases for managing customer contact data.

daily deals Sites and apps such as Groupon and LivingSocial that provide targeted mobile and web-based coupons based on mass participation.

DART DoubleClick's Dynamic Advertising, Reporting, and Targeting (from DoubleClick online advertising platform).

day parting The divisions of the day where web traffic occurs.

DB Database.

direct and click-through traffic Two primary ways a visitor can access your site; Direct means the visitor typed your URL into the browser instead of searching or clicking.

DM or DR Direct marketing or direct response ads.

drip marketing An email marketing approach based on serving specific messaging to an audience at recurring time intervals; also often automated and termed "marketing automation."

editorial results For certain, more educational or informational keyword searches, Google will serve primarily editorial results, meaning news and educational content instead of corporate or product promotional content.

forking Splitting and duplicating software platform content for testing and additional building.

freemium A web sales model that has levels for free services as well as those for advanced, paid levels.

Google DFP Double-Click for Publishers; Google's platform to allow bloggers and website owners to have advertising onsite.

gravatar A service for providing unique, referenced avatars or user profiles across different sites.

HTML5 The next level of HTML, featuring rich media and animation capabilities fully responsive to mobile devices and modern browsers.

IA Information architecture, or architect, for sites.

IMC Integrated marketing campaign.

impressions These are basically "eyeballs." An impression is exposure—a consumer's theoretical view of a URL, an ad, a brand, and so on. Impressions on the SERP means that the search engine served your listing to a web searcher. It does not mean that there was a click-through.

index The capability of the search engine to crawl and retain info from a page or site.

link bait Social writing inviting engagement; if you're a great writer/blogger, you can entice others to share or repost your blog links.

link juice Link "value" passed from one link or site to another.

long-tail Niche digital strategies and keyword phrases.

marketing automation See *drip marketing*.

MySQL The database format for WordPress sites; every WordPress site requires a MySQL database and requires a web hosting server that is PHP and MySQL ready.

NAP Name, address, and phone number; the fundamentals that local search engines look for on websites.

NFC Near field communications; technology involved with location identification and surrounding technologies.

NoFollow A command telling search engines not to follow and give link juice to a specific link(s) from a web page.

NoIndex A command telling search engines not to "index" specific site content.

OAO Online Audience Optimization, progressive content strategy for overall organic and SEO.

OS Operating system, as in Apple's iOS for mobile.

page views What we used to call "hits," but page views are better; a page view represents a visit to the total page.

PHP The language platform for WordPress (in contrast to other languages, such as .NET or Java).

pingbacks and trackbacks WordPress text references; duplicated lines of text that are trackable and used to "ping" the originating site.

popover or overlay ads Unlike traditional pop-up ads, these don't trigger a new browser window, but float on top of your other page content.

PPC Pay-per-click advertising; Google AdWords.

referrals The digital source for clicks; leading from one place to another.

remarketing or retargeting Advertising to consistently reappear in front of the same parties who showed some initial interest in your market, such as by searching and visiting your site or a related industry site.

responsive The idea is of websites that "respond" to their environment; software and hardware by platform (smartphone, tablet, or desktop), browser, and the like.

rich snippets Results on the SERP that include more depth and media, such as blog post author information and local data results.

ROAS Return on advertising spending.

ROI Return on investment.

ROMI Return on marketing investment.

RSS Really Simple Syndication (really); content syndication, fed to sites via channels such as Feedler or Feedburner.

SAAS Software-as-a-service, where software is no longer a box and one-time desktop install, but instead monthly payments for cloud-based web services; many SEO tools are SAAS models.

SEM Search engine marketing; typically, this has the connotation of PPC advertising focus.

SEO Search engine optimization or search engine optimizers.

SERP Search engine results page, the list page resulting from a search in a search engine.

sitelinks If you've searched for something such as a specific university or hospital, it can come up number one in Google, and below its link and description you see additional subpage links of the site listed in organized columns; these are sitelinks.

slug The page- or post-level URL (meant to contain SEO descriptions); for example, www.example.com/slug-goes-here.

SMO Social media optimization; very important with WordPress in mind.

SMS and MMS Single-message-send and multi-message-send; these are texting and modern texting options with video and to multiple recipients, and so on.

spiders Crawlers, robots, bots.

subdomain A web page or microsite distinguished by an added sectional "period" within the domain name; for example, http://newevent.example.com.

TLD Top-level domain; the primary extension on which domain names are purchased: .com, .net, .edu, .biz, .tv, .co; and country codes, such as .cc, .us, .uk, .au.

UI/UX Digital user interface and user experience strategy and design.

unique visitors These are first-time website visitors. This can't be known 100%; instead, it's based on cookies. This measurement assumes the web visitor has visited from only one, primary web browser, which has retained cookies on that visitor's history. If your website has never been in her browser history, she is a "unique visitor."

user-agent technology Technology that helps search engines and mobile web browsers identify and serve your mobile website to mobile device users as needed.

USP Unique Sales Proposition.

visits The total visits to your website within the given period.

WP Abbreviation for WordPress; often you'll see it in front of plug-ins, such as WP Image Header.

WYSIWYG What you see is what you get.

XML Extreme markup language as opposed to HTML, hyper-text markup language

Index

WordPress SEO Success
Search Engine Optimization for Your WordPress Website or Blog

Safari
Books Online

FREE
Online Edition

Your purchase of **WordPress SEO Success** includes access to a free online edition for 45 days through the **Safari Books Online** subscription service. Nearly every Que book is available online through **Safari Books Online**, along with thousands of books and videos from publishers such as Addison-Wesley Professional, Cisco Press, Exam Cram, IBM Press, O'Reilly Media, Prentice Hal

Safari Books On   to thousands of technology, digi   leading publishers. With   ss to learning tools and informa   ips and tricks on using your favo   d much more.

STEP 1

STEP 2   rm.

Addison Wesley   AdobePr   Peachpit Press   PRENTICE HALL

O'REILLY   LEY   wrox